Write a Great Novel
The Wonderful Writing Secrets of Oz

by
G. R. Sixbury

Write a Great Novel:
The Wonderful Writing Secrets of Oz

Names: Sixbury, Glenn R..

Title: Write a great novel / by G. R. Sixbury.

Other titles: The wonderful writing secrets of Oz.

Description: Wamego, KS : Kansix Books, Inc [2017] | Summary: A comprehensive writing reference book that leads you through the steps to become a successful author.

Identifiers: LCCN 2017914692 (print) | ISBN 9781947317000

Subjects: LCSH: Fiction--Authorship. | Fiction--Technique. | Creative writing--Fiction. | BISAC: REFERENCE / Writing skills.

About the Author

When I was young and naïve, I thought the best way to launch my writing career was to get my Master's degree in Creative Writing. I dutifully enrolled in a Master of Fine Arts program at a university and took my first class under a long-tenured and well respected professor. On the first day of class, like many good instructors, this professor outlined what would be required in the course.

"If you complete a well-structured short story by the end of the semester and submit it for publication," he said, "you'll receive a C. If you complete a well-structured short story, submit it for publication, and it gets rejected, but you receive personal comments from the editor, you'll get a B. If you complete your story and sell it, you'll get an A."

Listening to the professor, I thought, *Wow, this is going to be easy.* I'd had a couple short stories published already and I was writing a new short story every month. Plus I had several finished drafts that would be ready to send out with just a bit of polishing. More important, I had an editor who always provided personal comments when she rejected one of my short stories. Getting a B was a no-brainer. Getting an A wouldn't be much harder, unless....

After class, I asked the professor, "So all you need to do is sell a short story and you'll receive an A?"

"That's right," he agreed.

"What's the minimum payment?"

His eyes widened. 'Minimum? There's no minimum. You can sell your story to any market at all, even if the payment is just copies." Immediately I started a happy dance inside my head. I knew plenty of on-line publications that paid ¼ cent per word that would gladly accept the dregs languishing at the bottom of my "Don't Ever Try To Publish This" drawer. I was guaranteed an A.

He packed up his leather briefcase, headed for the door, then turned back and added, quite Columbo-like, "Just one other thing. Any market will do for this sale. Any market at all, provided that market is a respected literary journal."

I dropped the class the next day and abandoned my pursuit of an MFA in Creative Writing. While I'm not criticizing literary journals—they have their place—that's not what I wanted to write. If this instructor's idea of success was to teach me how to write for literary journals, I'd rather restrict my publishing pursuits to the local church bulletin.

And so began my independent pursuit of knowledge, the result of which is contained in this book. You'll find out plenty more about me as you read on, but for those who can't wait, here's the typical summary you find in most "About the Author" sections:

G. R. Sixbury has been writing and selling fiction and non-fiction since 1986. His credits include science fiction, fantasy, horror, comedy, westerns, and children's stories published in magazines and international hardcover and paperback anthologies as well as multiple nonfiction publications. An estimated half million copies of his stories exist in print, including international versions in French, German, and Italian. His first novel, *Legacy*, was released in hardback and trade paperback by Tor Publishing. His second novel, *High Plains Moon*, was released in trade paperback, Kindle, and audio versions in 2013. He has been a writing instructor since 1996 and has been involved in numerous writing workshops and other writing-related educational activities since 1988.

Dedications

Thanks to all of my students.
Hopefully I managed to teach you as much as you taught me.

For Gary, creator and friend:
Thanks for your encouragement and unfailing support.

For Selina, who gives so much to so many.

With special thanks to Marie, Leonard, Charlie,
Lynn, Bill, Pat, David, and UFM.

Table of Contents

Preface

Thousands of books about writing have been published. What makes this one different from all the rest?

Quite simply: Me. The Wise and Powerful Oz. Why do I call myself The Wise and Powerful Oz? Like Baum's wizard from his original Oz novel, I'm not actually all that wise or powerful in real life, but I am for the purposes of this book. What you're getting in these pages is pure me. I won't claim to know the best way to write. I won't even claim I'm the most qualified person to create a book on writing. What I will claim is that this book is different from anything else you've ever read before. Why? Because it contains a distillation of my personal experiences and several decades of wisdom gained from learning about writing from many different sources.

Every writer on the planet who's been writing for more than a few years has their own unique style and their own opinions about what makes writing work. Put a hundred professional writers in a room and you'll get ninety-four different opinions about what you should do to be a successful writer. Before I taught my own class, I spent a decade in professional classes taught by a variety of instructors. I read dozens of books about writing that ranged in topics from how to write poetry to humor to pornography to nonfiction. The indisputable fact is that none of them agreed. Rather than ask you to wade through that same morass, I've taken the best of the best from all those sources and brought it together in one place.

In an imaginary sense, what I've done is put those hundred writers in a room, kept them there against their wills for a decade or two for my own amusement, then pared down what they've uttered during their best moments until those pearls of wisdom would fit into this book. At the same time, I've added my own perspective to the mix based on my personal experiences.

Through it all, I've had only one goal. To help you write what you want to write as well as it can be written.

But first...

I have a few tidbits to offer about how this book is put together. My temptation is to skip them, but people always seem to have questions about why I've done what I've done, so I'll attempt to answer them briefly before we get started.

This book is geared mainly toward writing fiction. In particular, it's geared toward writing stand-alone novels. Many of the techniques mentioned apply in whole or in part to writing short stories, novelettes, and novellas. In addition, I've added a section that covers writing novel series.

What's not covered: Writing poetry. Writing memoirs. Writing journals. Writing graffiti. Writing nonfiction. Well, you get the point.

The world, it is a-changin'!

I spend most of this book talking about how to get published the traditional way. Submit your manuscript to an agent or an editor at a large publishing house, get a contract that includes an advance, and have your novel released as a physical book by that publishing house with that release probably including an electronic version. If we're charging toward most new books being available electronically and if publishing your own work is becoming as respected and profitable as going the traditional route, why bother spending so much time on what may someday be a dying marketing model?

No one knows what the future holds, but early indicators are that large publishing houses will continue to exist. Even if they're replaced by some nimbler publishing model, it's likely that successful submission requirements will be similar. It's still true that if you want to become the next *billionaire* writer, going the traditional publishing route is your best bet. But even if you don't win that particular lottery, if your novel is good enough that a traditional publishing house will buy it, it's good enough to publish on your own. The opposite is not true. If you write an amazing novel that has the potential to sell millions of copies, there's a good chance the large publishing houses will reject it. They will claim otherwise, but the examples of their doing exactly that are too numerous to mention. It's a fact that high quality does not guarantee publication. However, low quality is a much better predictor of rejection.

If you want to give your first completed novel the best chance for success, write it as if you were going to sell it through traditional channels. The exception would be if writing it for those channels prevents you from writing the novel you want to write. For example, if you're fairly certain none of the big publishing houses are going to want a werewolf-western-mystery featuring an accountant as your main character, but you believe there's a strong market among hairy six-gun-toting accountants that would allow you to sell several thousand copies of the book, go straight for self-publication. But do not discount the advantages of a traditional model. If the big house that buys your novel is convinced that it's going to be the next bestseller, they almost certainly have a lot more marketing dollars and expertise to throw at it than you do. In these cases, money and experience make a difference. In addition, they will take care of typesetting, copy editing, and cover generation. As an added bonus, they will most likely get your novel on the brick and mortar bookstore shelf. Self-publication is unlikely to do so.

No one said I was right

As you'll discover in the next section, I have only one hard and fast rule for writing. However, as I explain my thoughts on writing, you'll see the words "should" and "must." You'll notice sentences that start with phrases like, "If you want to be successful...." **I do this because it's simpler language-wise to tell you what should be done as if there's only one way to do it.** Even so, *at no time do I believe there is only one right way.* If you have experience or advice that suggests a technique will work that's different from what I've stated in this book, by all means, use that technique. If it feels right to you, it probably is. More important, if it feels wrong to you, your chances of pulling it off correctly go way down.

What I've tried to do in this book is give advice that applies to the broadest number of people across the broadest number of situations. This advice is designed to give most people the best chance to be published, but it's not an end-all, and it's not a book of absolutes—even if it seems that way at times.

Internet Advice

Many starting writers get their info on how to write from the internet. And why not? Just type a few phrases into a search engine and up pops hundreds of thousands of sites, at least two or three of which have something tangentially related to your topic. While the internet's great for getting a particular question answered—such as when to use colons and semicolons—it does suffer from a few shortcomings.

One of the internet's greatest strengths is that the on-line information is always getting updated. Unfortunately that's also one of its greatest weaknesses. That awesome grammar site you discovered last week might be replaced next week by a porn site. The web page that covered synopses in such detail now charges for viewing their pages and sells your email address to spammers if you're foolish enough to sign up.

Another problem with the internet is its ability to waste your time. Searching for that grammar site might take you five or ten minutes, if you don't become distracted while you're checking out all those sites the search engine claimed were relevant. If you flip open this book and look in the index, you can locate the same answer in only seconds.

Even when you do find information on the internet, it can sometimes lead you astray. One of my students based his sf novel length on the numbers provided by the Science Fiction Writers of America (SFWA—via Wikipedia). What he didn't realize was that those numbers were finalized in 1965, when novels were much shorter, and that they hadn't changed because they applied to SFWA's Nebula awards. The information was there in black and white, but he interpreted it wrong because he didn't have the context. Too late, he realized he needed to add 30,000 words to his novel after he'd written THE END.

The internet also suffers from a lack of quality control. Some information is reliable, some is questionable, and some is flat-out wrong. In many cases, you get what you pay for. The internet has its place, but with this book, I've already sifted through the advice and discarded the junk. Your writing time is more precious than gold.

Don't waste it reading about colon polyps when all you want to know is the proper way to connect two independent but related clauses.

...and just a few last details

I have a few housekeeping items to mention before we dig into the meat of this book.

First, the English language has at least one major failing. There is no acceptable pronoun that isn't gender specific. Granted, one can say that one looked upon the beauty of the landscape and that one marveled at one's newfound appreciation of the natural and rugged terrain. But compare that to: He looked upon the beauty of the landscape. OR She marveled at her newfound appreciation of the natural and rugged terrain. Clearly the latter examples are less awkward and more personal than the first, even though they imply a gender specific situation. I detest the use of coverall phrases like "he or she" and "his or her" unless you're talking about bathroom towels. Sentences such as, "He or she looked upon the beauty of the landscape," give me the willies. Bah! So in this book, I will mix it up. Sometimes I'll use "he" or "his." Sometimes I'll use "she" or "hers." And to really anger the grammar purists, I'll even use the singular "they." In all cases, unless I'm quoting a specific example I either made up or pulled from an existing publication, **I'm not being gender-specific**. I ask that you don't take it as such. A futile request, I know, but at least I've asked.

Second, I don't mean to be offensive: it just comes naturally. If you have delicate sensibilities, I question your ability to carve out a professional writing career. More than that, I'm guaranteed to offend you at multiple points in this book as I do my best to state facts and opinions honestly without concern for your delicate nature. Also, I have a distinctive sense of humor. I try to be funny whenever I can because most people find it more entertaining, but there's a fine line between being funny and being offensive. I'm sure I'll cross it once or twice.

Third, you'll notice few if any quotations from other writing instructors, from books on writing, or links to sites on the internet within these pages. Most often, writers who stick in quotes from other writers every other page are simply letting you know that someone else agrees with them. It's not that they read something and said, "Wow, I've got to get that quote in my book because it'll infinitely help the reader." While that surely happens, many times they're putting in the quote so that you, the reader, can take some comfort in knowing there's another writer who agrees with what they *planned to say anyway*. I look at it a different way. As I said a few paragraphs ago, I'm not trying to tell you the one right way. I'm telling you what I believe works best for the greatest number of wanna-be writers. If you don't believe me and want verification that what I'm saying is correct, then test it yourself or go read other books on writing and see if they agree with what you find here. Almost everything in these pages is entirely mine or represents my unique twist on a combination of material from many sources. If you're looking for quotes, I recommend *The Quote Verifier: Who Said What, Where, and When* by Ralph Keyes. Otherwise, trust what I've said or don't. It's your choice. As for links to internet sites, not only do they change, but they just plain go away. A wonderful video that tells you all you need to know may be out there right now, but it probably won't be there tomorrow. I'd rather give you all the information I can in one place rather than have you scrambling around the internet trying to find something that no longer exists.

Fourth, for the examples in this novel, I usually reference novels and movies (mostly movies) that have been widely read or widely watched. No opinion is implied about the quality of these works. Regardless whether you hate them or love them, they are the works that most people know. Examples lose most of their punch if the people for whom they're intended aren't familiar with them. At the same time, if you're unfamiliar with most of the examples I use, I can only say: Get out more. As a writer of popular fiction, it's part of your responsibility to be familiar with today's popular culture. That doesn't mean you need to watch every episode of *The Big Bang Theory* or every episode of *NCIS* (or whatever's popular by the time you read this), but if you want to be read by the masses, you should watch at least one or two episodes of most popular television shows, watch a broad range of popular movies, and read a broad range of popular books. Even if your writing never drifts into popular culture, the goal of every professional writer is to be read, and by definition, a typical audience will have seen or read the examples I reference. For the writers who claim book and movies are different, I agree with you wholeheartedly, but I also encourage you to come down off your high horse long enough to realize that while it's best to be a well-read person before you begin to write, not all writers are now or have been throughout history. In today's attention-deprived world, being interesting is more important than being cultured. While you may not think the works mentioned have any merit and are popular only because they had superior marketing, it's still true that more of your readers are familiar with those works than they are with that gem of a novel from your favorite but relatively unknown author.

Finally, as you read this book, you'll discover a fair number of "rah-rah" passages. These sections justify a particular technique or provide affirmation that what you're attempting will work. The truly gung-ho writers among you will scoff at such fluff. Filled with confidence, you're the ones who are already cranking out ten pages per day and have five finished novels sitting on your shelf. But I have yet to meet a writer with a career of any length who hasn't struggled at some point to get words on paper. I'm not talking about the movie version of writer's block. The writers I'm thinking of are all professional level writers. They don't sit motionless staring at a blank computer screen, rousing only long enough to repeatedly reword the same first sentence. These writers aren't sitting there at all because life and circumstance have combined to grind down their resolve. Very few people *have* time to write. Writers *make* time to write. That requires energy and commitment, and sometimes it just isn't there. If you're lucky enough now that you don't need my words of encouragement or justification, just wait a while. Eventually you will.

At the opposite end of the spectrum, some folks claim I'm all doom and gloom and mention the dreadful "w" word (work) way too often. To that, I will plead "Guilty as charged." Trying to become a writer is a bit like trying to become a successful actor or pop star. It's certainly not impossible, but if I have the audacity to tell you that the road could be difficult and require some effort, take solace from the advice I'm giving you about the best paths to follow. I will do my best to help you make it to where you want to go, but it isn't free. Nothing in life ever is.

Chapter One:
First, a Word...

Passionate Pounding

Most books about writing start with advice on how to begin. That's a logical place to start, and we'll get to that in the next chapter. But before we discuss what happens inside your book, I'd like to cover what needs to happen inside you.

Some people are born writers. When they sit down to write, liquid gold flows from their fingertips and spreads across the pages in nearly pristine form. They don't struggle to get started every day. They don't understand why others have problems writing as much as they do.

That's because they have one thing most wanna-be writers haven't got.

Passion.

I'm not talking about romantic passion. I'm talking about passion for writing. This kind of passion allows you to keep working on a project when you don't feel like working. It drives you to revise until it's right. It allows you to send the finished manuscript out after each bitter rejection letter. This kind of passion gives you the boost you need to market the finished product. It keeps your interest level high from inception to finished novel to memorable accomplishment.

Even short-fiction writers need passion for their creations as a group. I have a cousin who's always loved the ladies. He told me once that he's been with nearly 2,000 different women. Ignoring the moral implications and the amazing fact that he hasn't died from some STD, he couldn't have seduced so many women without passion. Again, not romantic passion, but something akin to it: Passion for the conquest, for the act of pursuit, for the singular experience that each tryst produced.

If you're going to be a successful writer, you need to be passionate about your writing.

The One and Only Rule

It's one thing to profess your undying love for your craft. It's another to do something about it.

When I talk about having passion for writing, I'm not talking about declaring your passion for writing. Claim what you want to your friends and family. Lie to yourself while lying in your bed at night. But if you have passion for writing, it translates into one definite result.

You will write. And write often.

Which brings us to my one and only rule of writing. ***Everything else I say in this book is opinion.*** Everything else is what I've found to work best for me and to work best for others, which means it's open to debate. But there is one rule that is absolute. No arguments. Do it or else.

This one and only rule has two parts. Both are absolutely necessary if you want to be a professional writer. And both, at least on the surface, are surprisingly simple:

- Write.
- Try to sell what you write.

I told you they were simple. At first glance anyway. In reality, they're simple to understand, but not simple to do. To make the doing a bit simpler, let's take them apart and see what's inside.

So Simple... and Yet So Hard

The first rule sounds like the simplest and most obvious rule in the world, but the ugly truth tells a far different story:

> Most wanna-be writers fail to become writers
> because they fail to write.

Tragic, but true. If it's so simple, why is it so hard to do? If we throw out the facts that the world is constantly pulling you away from writing and that writing well is itself hard work, what we're usually left with is a giant gaping emptiness more hollow than the Tin Woodman's chest. If you're like most writers trapped in wanna-be writer land, you need to visit the Great Oz in search of the one thing you lack: Confidence.

I used to say one of the best natural traits a writer can possess is arrogance. I offended too many people by using that term, but it's true. Get to know a lot of successful writers, and you'll see what

I mean. They're arrogant to the point where many turn into dull-ish boors, and you walk away from them wondering how they ever got published. But don't underestimate that arrogance—or as we'll politely call it, that **confidence**. And if I play my part as the great Oz, I can give you a contract for a short story sale and you'd start spouting your own praises.

But that's not how it works in the real world. Actually, maybe it is, but only *after* you make that first sale. It sounds silly, but if you need to sit before your keyboard every day, eyes closed, and repeat, "I'm a great writer! I'm a great writer! I'm a great writer!" before you can begin writing, then do it! You can even wear silver shoes and clap your heels together—what you do in your own time is up to you—but the important point is that you must believe in yourself to be a successful writer, because almost no one else will.

Write On

I've never heard any professional writers argue with me about my first rule: Write. Professional writers know that it's impossible to be a professional writer if you don't write or don't write often. But what does that rule actually mean? How much do you need to write before you're writing? How often? Do you need a system? How many pages must be produced per day before you're writing?

There are no absolute answers to any of those questions, but over time, I've found some helpful guidelines.

Develop a system that works

If you want to be writer, you need to write. Obvious enough. If you're not writing, whatever you're doing isn't working. So *change* it. Remember, the only part of the rule we're addressing here is that you write. If the system you're using doesn't allow you to produce manuscript pages, change your system until it does. It's cliché, but if at first you don't succeed, try, try again.

But how much should you write? Well, that's up to you. I've known writers who produce 15 pages every day of the year and writers who only write one day a week. Both types can be successful. The key is to write regularly. Write as much as you can.

For different people, writing as much as they can translates into different amounts. Only you can decide how much is right. Once you've decided, however, you need to hold yourself to that amount or you need to change your decision. For example, most writers in the beginning are enthusiastic about writing. For the first few days or weeks, they might write for three hours every day. So they set three hours per day as their goal. Then life rears its ugly head, and they have a day where they can't get in their three hours. It simply isn't possible. Maybe they write for two hours. That's no big deal. It's only one day. It's only one hour. Then they have another day like that. And another. Soon they're starting to short-circuit themselves before they even get started.

"I can only write for an hour today, so it's not worth the effort," they think, staring at the computer screen. "I should go wash the dishes or mow the lawn instead, and I'll make up the time lost tomorrow." And off they go, life intruding upon their perfect writing world. Soon, they're not writing at all, because they have a goal that's impossible to meet.

If that happens to you, change your goal.

I know it sounds simple. I know it seems obvious. But I encounter writers all the time who set unreasonable goals for themselves and then get caught up in the depression of not meeting those unreasonable goals. If they were truly born to be writers, they reason, they'd be able to meet those goals. And suddenly we hear that hollow sound inside their chests. No confidence. Listen, you can always change a more modest goal back to a more aggressive goal later. In the short term, feel free to exceed your goals and pat yourself on the back for doing so. But if you fail to meet your goal once, it becomes easier to fail the next time. And the next. Don't get caught in that trap. Set goals you can meet and then *always* do your absolute best to meet them.

When a system is not a system

But do you need to have a goal at all? That's a question people often ask. And like everything else I will tell you in this book, it depends. For a few rare individuals, developing a system that works means developing no system at all. If they're required to produce three pages every day, they produce none. On the other hand, if they write only when they feel like it, they produce a novel every year. Which means they're right. Setting a page goal doesn't work for them. Writing when they feel like it does.

A word of warning, however. Many new writers complain about setting goals or developing a system because it's artificial, because it's not artistic, or *because it's work*. They've never tried writing to a goal or working within a system, because they believe it will stifle their creativity. So they disdain all references to a system and avoid setting any goals for themselves. After a year, most have finished two chapters, both of which need significant rewriting. If you don't set a goal for writing, and after three months, you've only produced eighteen manuscript pages, guess what? Failing to set a goal doesn't work for you. Either set a goal or quit writing. That may seem harsh, but it's not nearly as harsh as the publishing world you're trying to enter.

In all cases, if you want to be a writer, you must write. Simple, but true.

<u>A nudge in the right direction</u>

Most people at this point will ask: "What do you recommend? All wise and powerful Oz, how many pages should I write per day? I know you said to do what works for me, but what is that? Give me some guidelines. What has worked for other people?"

Ah. Now that you mention it, I did promise to distill down my personal experiences. So here's what I've learned over the years.

If you want to be a professional writer and you have a full-time job, aim for a page per day. Does that mean each and every day? Not necessarily. Especially not if you're a person who doesn't deal well with interruptions. Because there will *always* be interruptions. So how many interruptions are too many? How many days can you fail to write before your system isn't working? For some writers, the answer is none. They write when they're on vacation with their families, they write when they're sick, and they write when they're in the middle of their second divorce. Nothing stops them. And they're usually successful. But not all writers are these iron-men (or women) of dedication. Not all writers need to be. For those write-every-day writers, many have discovered that if they take even one day off, the temptation to do life is too great and they lose their flow. One day turns into many. But for most folks, they can miss a day, especially if it's a planned miss. For those writers, it's more useful to attempt to write six days per week. And to produce at least one page of manuscript on each of those six days. In other words, build in interruption time. You know you're going to have them. So allow yourself to have them without beating yourself up. At the same time, have goals that you must meet. If you miss a day you didn't plan to miss, make up the time the next day. If you finish only five pages one week, write seven the next.

Here's the good news: If you finish one page of manuscript six days a week for fifty weeks a year, you'll produce 300 pages. Granted, three hundred pages do not a novel make. But after two years and one hundred weeks, you've produced 600 pages. That's more than enough for a typical first novel in most genres. Those extra pages translate into the extra time you need for rewriting, which we'll cover in a later chapter. The point is: If you aim to produce one page of manuscript per day, it's possible to finish a novel every two years. That isn't nearly as much as most full-time writers produce, but remember, you're not a full-time writer yet. When that first novel sells, you'll probably want to up the amount you produce per day. At that point, you'll have results. You'll have that contract and it'll be easier to hear that beating inside your chest. You might be able to stick with two pages per day or even three. You might even have contractual deadlines for your next book that give you no choice! But even without a deadline, it should still be easier to convince family and friends to leave you alone so you can work. The typical spouse will more often leave you alone to write if she's already seen some indications that you might be producing the next bestseller. If you can quit your day job to write, then set a goal of ten to fifteen pages per day if it works for you. Many professional writers are able to produce fifty pages or more each and every week. The point is: Start with what you can manage and move up from there.

One page a day six days a week, huh? Sounds to me, Oz, as if you're producing another rule. Not at all, dear friends, not at all.

Feel free to adjust the above guidelines to suit yourself. If you know you're busy during the week, but you're willing and able to spend all day Saturday writing (like a second part-time job), by all means, do so. I know one writer who's excelled doing exactly this (writing mainly on Saturdays). He concentrates on his day job all week and then concentrates completely on writing every Saturday. He takes time off to be with his family after work during the week and all day on Sunday. He's successful at work, he's successful at home, and he's a successful writer. It works for him.

If a similar method works for you, use it. If not, try something different.

<u>If at first you don't succeed...</u>

If you're paying attention, you might have noticed that I keep repeating the idea of changing what you do if it doesn't work. It's not merely because I'm a bit dim and can't remember what I've written. It's because most beginning writers fail to succeed because they fail to do what works ***for them***. They've been told by some know-it-all Oz-type person to write a page a day. They try and they fail. They keep trying (and keep failing) because they don't' try something else or they don't try something else quickly enough. While it's true that they may try a hundred ways to write and never succeed because deep down they lack passion for writing, at least they tried. If you follow the yellow brick road because some ditzy broad claiming to be good and helpful told you that was the way you needed to go, but it repeatedly leads you to the witch's castle, then ignore ditz lady and cut 'cross country.

At the opposite end of the spectrum, I know writers who give up on a particular technique before they've given it a fair shot. Making your living as a writer isn't easy. If it were, everyone would do it. Well, maybe not *everyone*. There'd still be singers and actors and plumbers. The world always needs plumbers. But judging by the number of people I meet on the street who claim they have a novel started or who've got a couple stories in a box in their closet, the number of wanna-be writers outweighs the number of professional writers by at least ten thousand to one. So of course it's not easy. Don't expect it to be. When you try a new technique or set a new writing goal, give it a reasonable amount of time to succeed and give it your best effort. That means not giving up after the first attempt. Only you can decide when to pay attention to that little dog and pull aside another screen to reveal a different solution. In the end, all this advice distills down to the simplest of simple:

If it works, do it. If it doesn't work, do something else.

Pages or time?

You'll notice that I mix and match pages and time in my examples above. For myself, I set time goals rather than page goals. That's because I can budget time. I can't budget pages, because I never know how long it will take me to produce a page. This works for me because I'm disciplined when I'm writing. I only count time if it's productive time. This doesn't always translate into pages. Sometimes I'm doing interviews or research, but I always remain honest with myself. If my son calls me on the phone while I'm trying to write and I talk to him for fifteen minutes, I don't count that time. Good intentions mean nothing. Using time goals instead of page goals also requires a way to track your time, which translates into additional overhead (also not counted as writing time). Page goals are much easier. If your goal is to write 10 pages per week, all you have to do at the end of the week is count your pages. Again, do what works for you.

Summary

In order to be a successful writer, you need to write. In order to write enough, I recommend you do the following:

- Write as much and as often as you can.
- Develop a system that works for you.
- If your current system doesn't work, try other solutions until you find one that does.
- If you have a full-time job, your goal should be at least one finished page per day and 300 finished pages per year. If your results are better by setting time goals instead of page goals, do so.

Regardless of how you go about getting words on paper, if you're not producing at least 300 finished manuscript pages per year, consider trying something else. Nothing is absolute, but if you want to be a professional fiction writer, 300 finished manuscript pages per year is a reasonable minimum goal. For some folks, that's not an easy goal, but it's hard to claim it's not reasonable.

Sacrifice: It does a writer good!

When someone tells me they want to be a professional writer, one of the first questions I ask is: What are you willing to give up? Deep down we all know that nothing is free. Yet I can't count the number of people who want to become professional writers but who fail to realize this simple fact. As I delve into their personality, I find they have an extended family, tons of friends, an active social life, fourteen hobbies, and dozens of shows they can't wait to binge-watch. When I ask what they're willing to give up to become a writer, they stare at me with a blank expression as if I've asked them to run naked down a city street. Come to mention it, asking them to run naked down a city street usually receives a more favorable reaction.

Here's what most non-writers fail to understand: If you want to be a professional writer, you're not taking on a new hobby. You're not filling your time with pleasant imaginings of what might be. You're accepting a new *job*. That's right. It's not an adventure, it's a job. If you want an adventure, go join the U.S. Marines. With writing, it's just plain work. Lots and lots of work. It may be work of your choosing, but no matter which writing curtain you pull aside, there's almost always work hiding behind it. If you're successful, the job may eventually become an adventure, but in the beginning, you won't even be paid for your services. If you ever want to reach the point where people are willing to surrender their hard-earned cash for the imaginings that bubble up out of your brain, you need to become a professional in heart and soul so that you can become a professional in fact.

One of the first decisions to make in this process of becoming a writer is to decide what you're going to give up. It's tempting to believe you can simply scale back a bit in several different areas but still do everything you did before. While possible, this lack of sacrifice keeps your writing from becoming part of who you are and instead limits it to being an intrusion. Being successful under those conditions is a much harder road to travel.

If you want to take the most reliable path, you must allow writing to become part of your life. More than that, you'll allow writing to become part of who you are. When people ask you what you do, you'll answer: "I'm a writer." And you'll believe it.

It's precisely this attitude that allows you to avoid the hundreds of time suckers that life hurls at you from every direction. Friends and family want a piece of your time. Cleaning, fixing, sleeping, eating, shopping, relaxing, and other assorted verbs all call out your name. If, at your very soul, you believe and behave as if you're a writer, then it's a lot easier to become a writer. This is the reason so many writers are overweight, in ill health, and a bit psychologically unstable. This is why they often seem egotistical and curmudgeonly. It's why they tend to be selfish friends, inattentive spouses, and non-productive members of society (outside of their contributions to publishing).

Does it have to be this way? Not at all. I know writers who are incredibly successful and who live life just as well as anyone else. But those are usually the ones who treat their writing as a job and behave the same way professionals in any other field would behave. They work when it's time to work and they live life when their work is done for the day. Ernest Hemingway is a well-known example of this. That man was an infamous party animal, but almost every day he rose before sunrise and headed for his office to write.

If you're willing to focus your passion, you really can do it all.

One of the most frequent questions I get from wanna-be writers is: "How do you find time to write?" The real answer, which I rarely give, is: You find time to write the same way you find time to go to the bathroom. You do it because you have to. The most prolific writers I know are the ones who have that constant urge to write. If you want to be a writer, you will write. And don't ever quit trying. I have a friend who wanted to write for decades. There were always reasons why she couldn't write. Then, by sheer force of effort (and perhaps a realization of her own mortality), she decided she was going to write. A year later, she finished her first novel. When your passion for writing becomes strong enough, you will write.

There is too much. Let me sum up

To be a successful writer, you should:

- Be passionate about writing.
- Write.
- Try to sell what you write.
- Find your confidence.
- Write as much as you can as often as you can.
- If you're not writing enough, try a different system.
- Be willing to sacrifice.

Chapter Two:
Begin at the Beginning

The Second Most Important Thing

I'm not fond of beginnings. They're my self-proclaimed Achilles' heel. I labor over them until blood oozes from every pore of my body (an unpleasant and messy process). The good news is that I've paid more attention to beginnings than nearly every other area of writing. My difficulties translate into hard-earned nuggets that you can use to make your manuscript more marketable.

This chapter concerns the importance of starting your novel off correctly. The old saying about never getting a second chance to make a first impression holds perfectly true for writing. The only thing more important than a great beginning is a great ending.

When I was attempting (and failing) to sell my first novel, I grew curious about why my novel couldn't make it out of the slush pile. I'd read hundreds of novels in my life. Being as objective as possible, the overall quality of my novel was certainly not at the top of the heap compared to those published novels, but it wasn't dragging the murky bottom either. Why didn't editors send me a contract?

To solve the problem, I started reading first-novels. While it's always unclear whether the first novel an author sold is the first novel that author wrote, it's hard to argue that a relatively unknown author sold a manuscript. Why did the sale happen? By reading first-novels, I tried to determine if they shared any qualities in common.

That's when I discovered the crap sandwich.

The Crap Sandwich

For those with delicate sensibilities, you might be offended by the word *crap*. If so, take your ball point, scratch out crap, and write poo. Mike Rowe would be proud.

Getting back to my experiment, what I found was that most first-novels had great beginnings and great endings but were laden with crap in the middle. While I would never encourage any writer to be satisfied with a less than stellar middle to his novel, I do claim that it's nearly impossible to sell a first-novel in today's marketplace without having a great beginning and a great ending unless you're famous or have some kind of personal and intimate connection to the editor, and even then, it's unlikely. Without putting your body on the market, especially if your body isn't trading so well against the yen, you have to have a great beginning and ending. You can (and most first-time novelists do) make mistakes in the middle. But the beginning and the ending of your novel must stand above and beyond the competition or your novel will probably fail.

What does that mean?

Funny you should ask. I'm so heavy on Beginning and Ending advice in this book that I could have called it, "Creating the Perfect Crap Sandwich". But having Crap in my title wasn't nearly as appealing as a title that invoked images of singing and dancing little people in colorful costumes and pretty blond witches who commute to work in bubbles. Even so, the number of pages I devote to advice on how to begin your novel may seem a bit excessive. My message in this section is that the time you spend on your beginning is well worth the effort. Craft it. Hone it. Make it the best it can possibly be. It will probably be the greatest deciding factor in whether your novel gets published. If you want to sell your novel, write a great beginning.

In the following chapters, I'll explain how you can do just that.

Ideas-R-Us

I've been attending conventions and panels and teaching classes long enough that it's easy for me to identify the question I get asked more than any other: "Where do you get your ideas?" And my glib answer is always the same: "Ideas-R-Us. I usually wait for a sale and then stock up."

Attack of the ideas

In truth, I don't know any successful writers who struggle to find ideas. They struggle to find *good* ideas. There's a difference. Most writers are constantly bombarded by ideas. They fall like giant hail stones, occasionally bonking us on the head at inopportune times, like when we're trying to sleep or make love or wash that hard to reach spot in the shower. Believe me, it's not always possible to keep a pen and pad of paper everywhere it's useful to have one. So, for most of us, it's not so much about finding an idea and more about whittling the plethora of ideas down to a manageable number.

Since you're reading this book, chances are that you're not a successful writer. Not yet. Maybe the concept of ideas falling like giant hail stones is as foreign to you as putting caviar on pork rinds. (Yes, there's a story there, but now's not the time.) You cry out to the wise and powerful Oz and ask: "What should I write about?"

I have to tell you: most of the professional writers I know dismiss students who ask this question as being obvious amateurs and therefore lost causes, but I disagree. I'm sure an Olympic swimmer would have problems answering the question, "How do you swim?" But like a person standing on shore and wondering at the mystery of the breast stroke, it's often difficult for someone who's never written before to sit down at that keyboard and start clacking her way to immortality.

When students ask me, "What should I write about?" I always answer them with a question. Answering with a question tends to drive them crazy, but that's part of the fun. More important, it's the only answer I can give. "What do you care about the most?"

Passion to begin with

Yes, I used the P word again. What can I say? I'm a passionate guy. Having passion for writing helps you sit down and write every day, but no matter how passionately you feel about becoming a successful writer, if you're trying to write about something that means nothing to you—or worse, if you're trying to write about something you think you *ought* to write about but don't care about much—you're likely to fail. So if you're one of those folks who really is standing in the middle of Munchkinland, ready to start at the very beginning, and you're asking the question: "What do I write about?" you need to decide what you care about the most.

By the most, I mean exactly that. The most. Don't sell yourself short by using your second-best idea because you believe it'll be a good learning experience and then, after that throw-away novel is done, you can write the novel you've always wanted to write. Instead, write the most important novel first. Why? Two reasons: 1) What you care about the most will change over time and 2) Writing a book is hard work. You need all the help you can get, and caring deeply about your topic is the best way to get that help.

So how do you decide what you care about the most? Start by asking yourself: "What moves me? What topic can I never leave alone? If I'm flicking through channels on the TV, what five second clip always catches my eye? What types of books do I love to read the most?" When you know the answers to those questions, you're on your way toward figuring out what your novel will be about.

What if your answer is: "I love American Idol and reruns of Gilligan's Island"? Does that mean you should write a novel where a voluptuous redhead with a lousy voice tries to win a singing contest? You could throw in a love interest involving a skinny kid in a funny hat and have an overly critical professor who says things like: "You've just invented a new form of torture," and "We don't want to hear any more of that, but probably will."

Perhaps such a novel would make the bestseller list. No one really knows. But when I say write about what you care about the most, it goes deeper than mimicking what someone else has done. It means you should examine what you care about the most and figure out why. Granted, if it's 1974 and what you care about the most is a story involving a couple of 'droids, a Wookie, and a scruffy nerf herder, then go for it. After you've made your first 100 million, you can go buy a house in the Redwood forest north of San Francisco and live sequelly ever after. But if your passion seems to have few obvious story elements, it's time to find some. And that leads us directly into where to begin your novel.

The Light and the Way

For most novels, there are two great pillars on which the novel is built: **story and characters** (the Light and the Way). These two elements combined form the reason most people read. Ask someone what she liked most about a book and she's likely to explain how much she related to the main character or how much she appreciated how the main character was better and more interesting than other main characters she's encountered. Or ask a person what he liked most about a novel and he might mention the clever plot twists.

What!? I hope you were paying attention, because that seems a little confusing. First I say story and characters are the most important and then I mention plot. Am I just a little senile or is there something more interesting afoot?

For about a century, various high muckety-mucks have labored intensively to define plot versus story. In my opinion, the definitions in the approved literature are still a little fuzzy. Even the dictionary definitions aren't suitable to our purposes. So like any good fiction writer, I've made up some new ones:

plot   the sequence of events in a story; also called a storyline
story   the dramatic cause and effect relationship that makes a
           series of events interesting by adding meaningful emo-
           tional perspective to those events

The best thing about these definitions is that they're simpler than a lot of the definitions you'll find out there.

For the rest of this book, when I mention "plot", you'll know what I'm talking about. When I mention "story", it might still get a little fuzzy, not only because the definition of "story" is more complicated, but also because "story" is a catch-all term. Worse, "story" is a form of literature, the same as novel, or novella, or short-short. So "story" may try to pull the chameleon act once in a while, but I'll attempt to make it clear from the context.

Here's the fun part. *By definition*, the story is what makes your novel interesting. The plot is the structure that allows the story to be told in an interesting way. It's a bit like looking at a beautiful face. We appreciate the face's overall shape, the person's eyes and nose, and the shape and symmetry of the flesh we see. But without the bones beneath that flesh, support for the entire face fails and it's no longer beautiful. For us, the plot supports the face of our story. Everything works together to create a beautiful whole.

But plot doesn't rank as high as story because the most cleverly plotted storyline in the world won't save a dull story. Plot rarely stands on its own because plot only becomes interesting when *we care* about what happens. That caring is provided by the story and the characters. Granted, an offensive or unsympathetic main character will often keep people from reading a novel, but if the story is good enough, they still read. The same is true with characters. If the readers care enough about the characters, they'll read a novel with the flimsiest of stories.

With all of these concepts, there are no absolutes and there are plenty of exceptions found in captivity at one of the few remaining brick and mortar bookstores, roaming the wilds of the internet, or even meditating peacefully at your local library. Even so, the safest and most well-traveled road to publication is to create a great story and have it told by interesting and sympathetic characters.

I thought we were talking about beginnings

That's my biggest problem with beginnings. I have an irresistible need to tell the reader everything at once. I know better, but sometimes I can't resist. In this case, my little info dump to start this chapter really was necessary for my purposes. That's because:

- Story and characters are why most readers read
- The sooner you establish your story and your characters, the more likely readers will keep reading once they've started

Like most elements of successful writing, these are two simple concepts that are hard to implement for many beginning writers. To ease the path to publication a bit, let's establish what we're talking about.

I've told you what a story is, but how do you create a story that starts on page one? Doesn't the reader have to know all this background information so they can understand and appreciate the dramatic cause and effect relationship of the events you're about to relate?

No.

Don't they need information about the characters' backgrounds so they can understand and appreciate the characters goals and motivations?

No.

Don't they need details about the world they're in? You at least have to have a detailed setting, right?

No.

This is one of those areas where other writers will disagree with me, *ad nauseam*, but that doesn't mean the other writers are right. (There goes that arrogance again.) Granted, background information seems to be necessary because so many big-name writers begin slowly. There are exceptions to this. (Big-name writers, you know who you are.) But in general, long-published writers can get away with what you can't. That is, they can be boring to start with. Readers will happily put up with it. Why? Because they know and trust the writer. Or a friend of theirs knows and trusts the writer and has convinced them that this is a book worth reading. The point is that those famous writers get the benefit of the doubt. More than that, the readers don't even find the slow starts to be boring. They recognize those starts for what they are: Groundwork that will allow the later story to be richer and move more quickly. They expect their favorite writer's novel to have an interesting beginning, and so it does.

If you compare this favorable expectation saved for proven writers to the dread typically reserved for your first manuscript as it sits in an editor's slush pile, you start to understand the difference. The editor's looking for a reason to **reject** your manuscript. The last thing they're doing is reading on faith that it will get better, unless by chance you're friends with, related to, married to, or sleeping with the editor. (Even one of those connections doesn't guarantee your manuscript will get accepted, but it certainly gives the editor a reason to keep reading when he'd normally be reaching for the big rejection stamp.) But if you're a stranger, forget it. If you start off slowly, you're gone.

So how do you start off quickly? Think about it. You're standing at the beginning of the yellow brick road. You've got your basket and your little dog. You're surrounded by singing munchkins. How do you start? Kick some munchkins out of the way? Well, at least that would be interesting.

And that's the key. Start with something interesting. What's interesting? Well, that's why you became a writer: to decide these things. But as the wise and powerful Oz, I'll give you some help.

Relationships and conflicts

Wait. A page ago, I said story and characters. Now I say relationships and conflicts? What's going on?

I'm simply looking at the equipment behind the curtain. Relationships are the reflections *characters* cast in your story. Conflicts provide the fuel that drives your *story* forward. They're more about the how than the what, and the how is what we need at the moment.

So let's ask that question again. How do you begin your novel in an interesting way?

Have your *main character* doing something *active* that's related to the *story*. If you're writing a murder mystery, have your protagonist discover a body. If you're writing a science-fiction novel, have the moon Praxis blow up and a captain on the bridge yelling, "Shields!" If you're writing a fantasy, have your main character's uncle disappear at his eleventy-first birthday party. Want to write a romance? Have your main character meet the man of her dreams who she instantly despises or idolizes. Westerns? Start with a gun fight. Action adventure? A big battle's always nice. Horror? Come on, something horrific, of course.

But if you have a writer's imagination, you can think of a hundred interesting scenes. At the opposite end, perhaps the idea of beginning your novel gives you brain-freeze. What you probably want to know is where to begin *exactly*. No more abstract concepts. Just reveal how to get this journey started.

Okay. I can do that.

The Big Bang Theory

If Jack Dawson (played by Leonardo DeCaprio) hadn't won the poker hand, he wouldn't boarded the Titanic and met Rose DeWitt Bukater (Kate Winslet) and subsequently frozen to death—bad luck for him! If Princess Leia's shuttle hadn't been captured by Darth Vader, her father on Alderaan would have gotten the needed plans days before the Death Star's arrival and some other enterprising pilot would have been given the chance to shoot a couple torpedoes down an exhaust vent no bigger than a womp rat.

With every story, there's one event, without which, the story would never have taken place.

I call this event the Big Bang. Yes, I know some astronomical types stole it from me and applied it to the beginning of the universe[1], but that's okay. The two concepts relate fairly closely.

Without the Big Bang, the universe doesn't exist. And neither does your novel.

To create a great beginning, find your novel's Big Bang. Then start your novel as close to the Big Bang as you can without losing the reader entirely.

Are there other ways to start a great novel? Of course. But the Big Bang Theory works. If you're having problems writing page one, use it.

So what if there's more than one Big Bang in your novel's universe? Which one do you choose? After all, Bilbo would have never disappeared on his eleventy-first birthday if he hadn't gone off on his adventures and found the one ring. Shouldn't the *Lord of the Rings* have started at that point? And what if Bilbo had never been born? Or to give another example, what if the White Star Line shipping company didn't exist? What if the idea to build the Titanic had failed at its first budget meeting? Aren't those all viable places to start?

No, they aren't.

---

1. For all you anal retentive legal types, this is a joke. Wikipedia credits Fred Hoyle with creating the term Big Bang during a 1949 radio broadcast.

The key behind the Big Bang is that the story—*your main character's particular story*—wouldn't have happened if the Big Bang had never taken place. If the Titanic were never built, a million stories change. If Bilbo never found the one ring to rule them all, Bilbo's story changes as much or more than Frodo's.

To simplify this, you're looking for an event with the following qualities:

- The Big Bang affects your character in a personal and immediate way.
- Chronologically, the Big Bang takes place as close to page one as possible.

Once you determine what your Big Bang is, your job is to make it interesting. Often, this is where beginning writers fail. They look at the event that starts their main character down that inexorable path toward their novel's conclusion and all they see is boredom. They have a main character who's uninteresting or a slow start to their story. What this means is that they should fix that slow start by making their character interesting and by getting their story moving more quickly. Instead, they often turn to that holy grail of so many beginning writers: The Prologue.

For beginning writers, my advice concerning prologues is simple: "Avoid them. They're inherently evil." That seems abrupt and suspiciously rule-like, but it's important for you to understand that many editors reject manuscripts out of hand if they start with a prologue. It's a signal that screams, "Amateur!" Not because prologues are bad, but because so many beginning writers lean on them for all the wrong reasons. This doesn't mean you can't start your novel with a prologue, but it's another stone that you'll have to lug up the hill.

Which means we probably should spend a moment talking about what you face when you try to get published through traditional channels. For you indie writers out there who think that the opinions of big house editors are irrelevant to you, you're partly right. They won't stop you from getting published, but any of the triggers that cause a big name editor to reject your novel just might drive away your readers as well.

The Slush Party

Close your eyes. No, wait, don't close your eyes. Then you couldn't read this. Okay, imagine that you've closed your eyes. And then imagine the flood of unsolicited manuscripts that form massive slow-moving, ever-growing glaciers in most editorial offices. For most editors, these horrific piles of paper represent a necessary evil called the slush pile[2]. This slush pile must be dealt with before its gradual growth consumes everything in sight. A small handful of editors have claimed they enjoy reading manuscripts from the slush pile. The fact they've since been taken away by men in white coats so they can get some much needed rest is a clear indication of their insanity. Most normal editors, if you get a few drinks in them and they're sure they aren't being recorded, will admit that they dread diving into the slush pile. It's a task they delegate to underlings whenever possible. Like anyone else, they relish the anticipation that accompanies picking up a book they want to read. It's almost impossible to get that anticipation with a slush pile manuscript.

Going back to your imagination and those manuscript glaciers, let's pretend you're the editor. What's to be done? You hate the idea of reading them, but you and your team of assistant editors need to reach the copier and the piles of manuscripts are blocking your way. What now?

Slush party!

A slush party is a gathering of editors, assistant editors, and first readers who thresh their way through the slush pile and get rid of the chaff. Slush parties are often held on Friday nights. Pizza and drinks might be involved. The exact setup varies, but the goal remains the same:

> Legitimately reject as many manuscripts as possible in the shortest time possible.

This may seem harsh, but imagine you're one of these editors. You're

---

2. Granted, many editors are switching to electronic submissions. But a growing mountainous glacier of electrons isn't nearly as picturesque as that growing mass of paper.

underpaid. You're tired. You've been working hard all week, and your attendance at this slush party is a sacrifice of your personal time. Your grass hasn't been mowed, your spouse hasn't been kissed, you barely know your kids, and your dog growls and attacks whenever you come home because you're less familiar than the pizza delivery guy (and you're not carrying pizza). You have better things to do than attend a slush party.

Keeping you in check is the knowledge that you're not allowed to reject manuscripts without a reason. No one wants the job insecurity that comes from rejecting the next *Harry Potter* series. At the same time, as soon as you find a legitimate reason to reject a manuscript (the CYA principle applies here), your work on that item is done. Reach for the rejection letter, add their name to the email rejection list, or send up smoke signals. Regardless of how you get the word out, or whether you bother to inform the writer at all, that writer's time in the inner circle is done and you can move on.

I've heard that sometimes prizes are offered to the assistant who gets through the most manuscripts for the evening. Only the people at the parties know what really goes on. It should also be pointed out that each publishing house works differently and that this entire slush party concept is just in our imaginations. But one fact is irrefutable. Editors receive more manuscripts than they can buy. For big houses, they reject thousands of manuscripts every month. I've had editors claim they carefully read 10,000 short-story manuscripts per month. Sure. And I can fly provided no one's looking. What's certain is that some places reject 10,000 manuscripts per month, and those decisions have to happen somehow.

Wow, Oz, that's depressing.

It's not meant to be. On the contrary, when that many manuscripts are rejected in such a short time and with such a small amount of consideration, you know several facts that should brighten your outlook: 1) When a novel you've sent into one of the big houses get's rejected, they aren't rejecting you or even any part of you, and 2) In most cases, they aren't even rejecting your manuscript, but rather are rejecting a small part of it that might have no bearing on your eventual readers. I'm not faulting the editors and first readers here. You try painting the *Mona Lisa* in six minutes flat and see how well you do. That's why most editors and first readers have developed handy flags and shortcuts that are reasonably reliable in predicting whether a manuscript will be publishable.

Regardless how the rejections get passed out, it's important to understand that your manuscript faces an uphill battle to reach publication and it's wise to give it the best chance you possibly can.

Editors Have Big Stones

Your chance of getting published is like an empty red wagon. You know, it's like those Radio Flyer® wagons kids used to pull around before the invention of handheld devices and the internet. Imagine you're a kid and you have one of those red wagons. You need to pull that wagon up a steep hill. Unlike Sisyphus from Greek mythology, it may be hard to get your wagon to the top of the hill, but it's not impossible. If you conquer the hill, you get published. Now picture that little red wagon filled with heavy stones to the point the axles are about to break. Suddenly the myth of Sisyphus is looking like a better analogy. You have no chance to ever get up and over that hill. Wouldn't it be nice to have that empty wagon back?

The nature of your book and how it's written determines the number and size of stones that get placed in that wagon. For the particular novel you're writing, you might have to put in a few stones because it wouldn't be your novel if you left them out. Even so, your goal as a beginning writer should be to keep that wagon as empty as possible. To that end, let's take a look at some of the obstacles that stand between you and publication.

Every editor (and every reader) is different. As writers, this makes our jobs more difficult. Even worse, both editors and professional writers often spout publishing absolutes. Do this; don't do that; always begin your novel, "It was a dark and stormy night...." Never begin your novel, "It was a dark and stormy night...." Sometimes they even have the audacity to suggest you should avoid prologues completely.

As a writer, it's futile to guess what a particular editor may or may not like. Even so, if you recognize the stones that you're placing in your wagon, you can make an informed decision about whether the power of your story and your characters is strong enough to get your Radio Flyer® up that hill. I give this advice knowing many writers will reject it. For the ones who willingly overload their wagons, this advice will seem more plausible after they've made seventeen failed attempts to lug those stones up the publishing hill. It might convince them to throw a few stones out during a rewrite or at least help them avoid stacking so many stones in their wagon when they write their next novel.

To carry this analogy entirely too far, I've divided the possible stones you might add to your wagon into boulders and rocks. Stick a boulder in your wagon and you better strap a rocket to its belly if you want to get it up the hill. Rocks are easier to move, but too many together will almost always cause you to fail.

Boulders	Rocks
Bad manuscript formatting	Novel is mismatched for the house or the editor
Language mistakes	Prologues
Unsympathetic characters	Present tense
Irrelevant story	Not enough dialog in first few pages
Clichéd story	Not enough action in first few pages

Let's go through each of these briefly.

Boulders

As a general rule, boulders really are impossible to haul up the hill. Avoid them whenever possible.

Bad manuscript formatting

For proper manuscript formatting, visit the publisher's web site and look for their Submission Guidelines. If you're sending your manuscript to an agent rather than a publishing house, they have submission guidelines, too. Write, call, email, check web sites; do whatever it takes to find out the proper format for your manuscript and use it. Almost all editors and agents consider bad manuscript formatting to be one of those unforgiveable curses. Fail to format your manuscript properly and it'll never be read.

Language Mistakes

This is one of those catch-alls to say that if you want to be a writer, know how to write correctly and well. You should study multiple books on grammar, style, and punctuation until you become an English language expert. Keep language reference materials handy when you rewrite. Also, understand that to be a successful writer, you need to be more than just a grammarian. You need proper syntax (putting together words in the proper order), correct semantics (using words that express the meaning you're trying to convey), and excellent diction (choice of words or style). An editor once told me that all problems with a novel are fixable if the story's good enough, *except* poor diction. Diction forms the underlying molecules from which a novel is constructed. Get that chemistry wrong and nothing can be done beyond rewriting the novel from scratch. Bad diction turns your novel into toxic waste.

Unsympathetic Characters

The sympathy here is on the part of the reader, not the characters. If you have unsympathetic characters, it means the reader doesn't care what happens to them. Usually characters are sympathetic when the reader can easily identify with them. This means it's easy for the reader to understand the characters' goals, problems, and feelings. It's why most fifty-year-olds have such difficulty reading teen angst fiction, why most guys avoid classic romance novels, and why most civilian women have no interest in military fiction. These are generalizations, but if you plan to write fiction, you need to understand the types of characters your audience expects and likes. If your novel's populated with unsympathetic characters, you've just heaved a huge stone into your wagon.

Irrelevant Story

Some story topics are naturally relevant: the entire world in peril, the love interest in a romance novel, the paranormal dangers in a horror novel, the murder in a mystery novel, etc. Once we go beyond the naturally relevant stories, it's impossible to define what's relevant and what isn't just by the topic. Instead, irrelevant stories are most easily identified by their irrelevance to the main character. If the story isn't all-encompassing for the main character, it's going to be difficult to create a relevant story for your readers. Starting off your novel with a Big Bang usually keeps this boulder out of your wagon, but as a test, examine your main character. If you can replace him with another, significantly different character and the resulting story's the same, you've probably got an irrelevant story. That, or you've just written a 1950's science-fiction novel.

Clichéd Story

Clichéd stories are absolutely impossible to define, because it's always in the eye of the beholder. (In this case, the eye of the agent or editor.) A student of mine who we'll call Jake (because that was his name) once wrote a short story where a paleontologist discovered dinosaur bones on page one. The discovery was vital to Jake's story, but beyond that discovery, nothing relating to dinosaurs appeared again. Jake received a rejection letter that explained the editor was sick of dinosaur stories. What this proves is that editors see clichés where they don't exist, and Jake shouldn't have started his story at the dinosaur dig. Since Jake had no way to know that, the only valid way to avoid creating a clichéd story is to be intensely familiar with your market. If tons of stories or novels share the ideas or topics you express in your first few pages, you've knowingly loaded your wagon with a big stone. However, clichéd stories exist for a reason. Most people like those topics. That's why they're cliché. Vampire romances, anyone? The easiest way to change your boulder into a rock is to put a twist on the cliché. Have your vampires sparkle in sunlight instead of turning to dust, for example. The overall topic's still cliché, and therefore familiar, but it's also different and so becomes interesting. If you write that kind of story well enough, then you could have the next bestseller. Just be aware of the load you're placing in your wagon.

Novel is mismatched for the house or the editor

This one should be obvious. Do your research. Don't send stories or novels to editors or houses where they don't fit. By fit, I mean the market you send your manuscript to should publish the type of material you're sending. Don't submit Christian fiction to Playboy magazine's short story contest (or vice-versa). Don't send mystery novels to Microsoft Press. I'm giving blatant examples to make a point, but this stone is usually placed in the wagon when a genre writer sends out queries en mass to agents or sends short stories to every available market without checking out that market's guidelines. It also occurs quite often when writers ignore specific instructions. If an editor's accepting submissions for an anthology containing time-travel stories, don't send them a story where no one travels in time.

Simply put, understand your markets. Find and read the guidelines. Send your manuscripts to markets where they have a chance to sell.

Rocks

It's common to have a couple rocks in your wagon. The ones listed here are some of the bigger ones. Having said that, if you have a need for one of these rocks, add it to your wagon. But be honest. If you haven't tried to write the novel without a prologue, for example, then you don't know if it can be done. Be most wary of adding any of these rocks to your wagon because you believe they will give you a *better* chance to sell your novel. They may be necessary, but they will almost always *decrease* the odds of selling your work versus having no rocks at all. Don't believe me? Then explain why the first Harry Potter novel was rejected so many times and why the first print run for the novel even after it was purchased was limited to only 500 copies. This is a novel that went on to sell many, many millions of copies in the bookstores. It had problems selling to editors because J. K. Rowling loaded her wagon with rocks, several of which appear in my list below.

Prologues

Some of you may still be seething over my recommendation to avoid prologues. While they're often a flag that signals "Amateur!" they do have a purpose. If the beginning of your book lays a great deal of ground work without being particularly interesting or exciting, especially if there's information that can't be known by the main character in the early pages but must be known by the reader, prologues are sometimes necessary. Unfortunately, a prologue is most often written as an attempt to assure your readers that the book will get better. Beginning writers use this technique so often because they're smart enough to recognize that their beginnings are relatively boring, but not smart enough to realize that those beginnings should be fixed instead of throwing a prologue at the reader and hoping it blinds them long enough to sneak in your first three chapters. It's never a good idea to hold a carrot in front of the reader's nose like he's a donkey and expect him to lumber forward until you get to the good part. You never know when the reader will get tired of your little game and realize that what he's reading at that moment is boring. Editors are the least patient of readers. (See Slush Party.) If you must have a prologue because your novel simply won't work without it, then go ahead add that stone to your wagon. But do so knowing how much it weighs.

Also, using flashbacks in your first couple chapters is nothing more than cutting that carrot into pieces before you offer it to the donkey. It's not fooling anybody. What gets you rejected here is starting your novel in the past when your story doesn't exist in the past. Feeding a reader an exciting, interesting, action-packed prologue (or flashback) and then forcing them to return to a mundane, uninteresting first chapter simply highlights why your book doesn't work. Skip the prologue (or flashback) and fix the real problem. Write an interesting first chapter that people want to read.

Present tense

Most writers dread being ordinary. Some inane editor or writer once told them that originality sells. Anyone who's watched the block-buster movies coming out of Hollywood since the invention of "talkies" (and probably before) knows this isn't the case. Originality of method and originality of story idea aren't what sell. Originality of emotion is. You create originality of emotion by having a great story and great characters. Using cutesy techniques just for the sake of being different will get you rejected almost every time. Present tense is the most common of these "different for the sake of being different" techniques. While there are some novels that demand present tense to be told properly (*One Flew Over the Cuckoo's Nest*, for example), those novels are few. If you're telling your novel using present tense, make sure you have a reason that justifies the additional weight you've just added to your wagon. (Note that as more and more novels are written in present tense, this weight goes down. By the time you read this, this stone may be gone.)

Not enough dialogue in first few pages

To some extent, this stone is about present-day expectations. We live in a TV culture. Despite what many editors claim, if James Michener wrote a first novel today in the same style as *Hawaii* or *Centennial*, he'd probably earn a rejection slip. Modern readers are used to sound bites and videos. They don't want fifty pages of info dumps to start their novels. Even ignoring these expectations, there are good reasons to have dialogue in the first few pages of your novel. Readers want story and characters. That means they want conflicts and relationships. It's hard to reveal relationships without other characters present, and it's hard to have other characters present while trying to reveal those relationships, and yet have no dialogue. The random musings of a solitary character are never as interesting as that same character engaged in a dynamic conversation with another character, because that dynamic conversation reveals a relationship between the characters. If your opening scene is active enough, sometimes dialogue isn't needed, but not having any dialogue is still a stone in your wagon.

Not enough action in first few pages

This item is closely related to the last item. Story and characters means conflicts and relationships. You can describe conflicts without having any action, but it's almost always more interesting to reveal conflicts through character actions rather than laying those conflicts at the readers' feet like a package of rotting fish. Sure, the reader knows they're there, but they're not very appealing. As with most rocks, this one can be avoided by starting your novel with a Big Bang. Have your protagonist actively interacting with other characters on page one of your novel and your wagon will be that much lighter.

And all the rest

Enough stones exist that I could fill this book talking about them. I singled out the ones above because they're the most common, or because they appear so often in published fiction that many beginning writers mistakenly believe the rules are the same for them as they are for established authors.

In truth, every editor has a personalized set of stones they drop in your wagon as soon as they see they'll fit there. For example, including a personalized cover letter with your manuscript causes some editors to drop a stone in your wagon. Failure to include such a cover letter causes other editors to put in a stone. Sometimes the stones stop your wagon in its tracks. REJECT appears on its sides and down the hill it comes. The editors never see your stellar prose in chapter two. They never reach the awesome idea you reveal halfway through your first chapter. Your brilliantly witty dialogue on page five is never read. The instant some editors see you start with a prologue or see you're using present tense, they reach for the form rejection letter. You're not getting published with them. If they decide your viewpoint character is unsympathetic, they stop reading. If they catch three grammar mistakes by the end of page two, they never reach page three. You get the idea, but I can't stress this enough. Most manuscripts are rejected in seconds. You can do everything else perfectly, but if your first page is awful, it's extremely unlikely any editor will ever read your manuscript because they've decided your fate before you get the chance to prove them wrong. Give yourself the best chance to get published by keeping that wagon empty.

The Basics

Most of the information I've included so far is a bit different than what you find in a typical book on writing. In the preface I warned you that this book would be unique. But now it's time to go over the bricks and mortar ideas concerning beginnings. Most books and classes cover these same ideas, because they're important and vital concepts. That's why we call them the basics.

Who, What, When, Where

Everything starts with a single point of knowledge. If we're standing in Munchkin Country and we want to travel to the Imperial Capital of Oz, we have to step on that first yellow brick. In terms of a novel or short story, the most basic of the basics are the ideas most people cover in English Class: Who, What, When, and Where. I've purposefully left off Why and How, which are often included in class or in other discussions of beginnings. I'll explain the reason for these omissions in a moment. For now, know that these four words as questions (Who? What? When? Where?) represent fundamental building blocks of information for your reader when they first start your story. Fail to answer one of these questions by the end of your first page, and your reader may fail to read your second page.

Different novels demand different beginnings, but as a general guideline, when a reader picks up a novel, they want to know very quickly **who** the novel is about. They want to know **where** and **when** the novel is taking place (the setting), and they want to understand **what** is happening. In the best novels, the answers to these questions are usually implied rather than stated.

Who

Novels rarely start out with heavy-handed sentences like, "Call me Ishmael," or have first paragraphs with directly stated lines like "I called myself Pip." Even so, establishing **who** your novel is about (or who your novel seems to be about) as quickly as possible is normally one of your main goals on page one. I added "who your novel seems to be about" because sometimes your novel may in fact be about someone completely different than the viewpoint character who appears on page one. The best novels I've read tend to avoid this misdirection for the plague it often is, but some stories must begin before or beyond your main character's entrance onto the stage you've created.

A much greater offense is hitting the end of that first page without introducing any viewpoint character at all. Who is the reader supposed to care about? You've failed to answer one of the fundamental questions a reader asks when they pick up a book. To make up for it, you're forced to wave your hands, stomp your feet, and march about making as much noise as possible. In literary terms, you need to make the first page so interesting that the reader doesn't notice you have no main character. This is easier said than done. Believing you can do it is a common mistake among beginning writers. Here's the problem. Some of you can. Some of you are so talented that you can start with a description of the weather and the reader will be hooked. But for most folks, the safer road is to introduce the reader to the main character as quickly as possible.

And not just any character will do. The person who appears on page one will almost always be taken as your novel's main character, so that character better be as interesting and as likable as your main character. Starting with a character who isn't likable or interesting, as *Harry Potter and the Philosopher's Stone* did, places one of those stones we talked about into your little red wagon. In the first Harry Potter book, the novel starts with the Dursleys (the title notwithstanding). A couple pages into the book, it seems clear the book is about Mr. Dursley in particular. At least it's told by Mr. Dursley (our viewpoint character). We're given his take of the world, which for most people is an unpleasant viewpoint. It's a bit like sprinkling salt on your tongue and then eating an unsalted french fry. The final result might be okay, but it starts off all wrong. The fact the *Philosopher's Stone* is about Harry Potter and is told from Harry Potter's point-of-view doesn't become clear until many pages later. It's no coincidence that both of my oldest children—when they first tried to read the book—couldn't make it through the first chapter and so put the book down. If it had been a less popular book, they would have never picked it up again. I'm sure Joanne Rowling believed her beginning was interesting. She almost certainly believed that Mr. Dursley was interesting. Millions of loyal and fanatical readers now agree with her, but the dozen or so editors who first rejected her manuscript probably didn't. J. K. Rowling successfully walked a tightrope to get that novel printed. If the book had been just a tad less interesting in some other area, it probably would have never seen the light of day.

If you want to get published, you answer who your novel is about in your first or second paragraph. That person might or might not get a description, but he usually gets a name. It doesn't need to be a full name and the first page is rarely the time to provide significant history or background. Typically the gender of the character is made clear, either implicitly by the character's name or stated directly. Who the novel's about can be answered as simply as "Jeff walked out of the glow of one street light and into the glow of another."

Where and When

I've clumped these together because what we traditionally call setting includes both **where** and **when** (as well as much more). The concepts of *where* and *when* seem obvious, and at the basic level they are. When you answer *where*, the reader knows where the book takes place (or at least where the first chapter takes place). Similarly, when you answer *when*, the reader knows when the events in the first chapter happened.

But now it gets a little tricky.

How you answer these questions is entirely up to you. Whatever technique you use shouldn't be intrusive, meaning the reader shouldn't be paying more attention to your writing technique than to the burgeoning story, and the answers to the questions should be clear, or at least seem to be clear. Sometimes, as writers, we intentionally mislead the readers, but it should never be done by accident. Beyond the guidelines above, you're pretty much on your own. Make the answers as interesting and efficient as possible and get on with the story. In the best case, set the story as you tell it, not as a separate task.

A few provisos: If you don't indicate when a story happens, the reader assumes the story takes place in the present time. If you don't state where the story takes place, the reader assumes the novel is set in the country where the reader lives. If both of those assumptions are true, it gives you, the writer, an advantage. You don't have to spend precious words answering *where* or *when* in any detail. You should still give some indications the assumptions are correct, but the example from above works perfectly well. "Jeff walked out of the glow of one street light and into the glow of another." It's a world that has streets and lights. That fits the U.S.[3] in the current time, so the reader will assume the novel takes place in the here and now. For most stories, you still want to let the reader know the exact place and time, but not always. Plus, you can take your time.

What's important is that you don't mislead the reader.

If the novel doesn't take place in the current place or the current time, you want to get that info in as quickly as possible. If the novel takes place in Beverly Hills and it's important that it takes place in Beverly Hills, you want to have a palm tree or Rodeo Drive show up pretty quickly. If it starts out in Oz, there better be some gorgeous flowers on every hand, a road paved with yellow bricks, and some height-challenged natives lurking about. In the case of the actual Frank Baum classic, he takes the obvious route: "Dorothy lived in the midst of the great Kansas prairies...." He immediately answers the questions *who* and *where*. He doesn't answer *when* because *when* is today, meaning the year the book was written.

It's perfectly alright to start your novel with a date and place inscribed above the first line of the book. At the top of your first page, you might have: "Brooklyn, 1949." But even if you never have a reader skip a line, you still need to provide authenticating details that make it clear the novel is set in a large city in the forties or fifties. The setting of a novel almost always influences the way your characters feel, think, or act. As such, you should always reveal your setting through your prose, but you should especially do so at the beginning.

The answers to *where* and *when*, unlike *who*, sometimes need to

---

3. Not all novels written in the U.S. are read by people living in the U.S. But if you're following the advice in this book, it's assumed you're trying to sell your first novel. The extra words required to clarify your setting probably aren't worth the additional delay in getting your story started. For example, the first couple pages of the Harry Potter novel mentioned above state the address where the characters live and even mentions the name of the firm where Mr. Dursley works, but they say nothing about the country where the story takes place.

be answered by the end of page one and sometimes don't. The more likely it is that the reader will be confused if you don't answer setting-related questions, the more quickly you need to answer them. As a result, stories set in another time or another place are always more difficult to begin because you need to provide more information at the very start.

<u>What</u>

Answering *what* means letting the reader see what's happening to your main character. In our overused example, "Jeff walked out of the glow of one street light and into the glow of another," Jeff is walking. This is not a particularly interesting answer, because a man walking along a street at night is not particularly interesting. But there's no confusion about what's happening. This means the interesting part would probably come in the second line. "The blood dripping from the gaping wound in his stomach looked black in the sodium vapor light." Or maybe, "Halfway down the block, he saw his future lover's nude form silhouetted against the shade of her apartment's bedroom window." Or the classic, "From the alley on his right, a woman suddenly screamed."

In my opinion, *what* is the simplest question to answer. Beginning writers often get into trouble because they choose not to answer the question. The act of creation has left them so fascinated with their own imaginings that they feel impelled to provide background information on their character or additional details concerning their setting or some other equally uninteresting bit of info that they consider of vital importance to the reader. Usually the reader doesn't care about these meaningless details because the reader's still waiting for the answers to the basic questions. This is especially true when it comes to showing what your character's doing. Your story begins when your main character starts doing something. And the sooner your story begins, the sooner you have the chance to draw readers into your world and trap them there.

In the best novels, who, what, when, and where are all answered explicitly or implicitly by the end of the first or second paragraph. If you take longer than that to provide these vital answers, then make sure you have a specific and necessary reason for the delay.

Why No, How No

We answer the four Ws in fiction (Who? What? When? Where?) because supplying that information to the reader is necessary for them to understand the story and the characters. We don't answer Why? or How? because our novel as a whole is the answer to those questions. I wouldn't mention this at all, except that many English classes and other writing classes will include them with the four relevant Ws.

Give Your Reader a Hand

For me, stories are a journey. They're a collaboration between the writer and the reader. But make no mistake. The writer's the one in charge. For you anti-establishment types, I'm not talking about a shouting drill sergeant here. I'm talking about taking your reader by the hand and leading them through your story.

The world of your novel is a thick forest. Every other step, dozens of paths shoot off in all directions. Your job as trail guide is to keep your reader on the path. If they stumble into the brambles, it's your mistake, not theirs. Granted, you never know when the village idiot (or an editor) will pick up your book and be confused by it. But as a popular fiction writer, your job is to get as many folks as you can safely through the forest. Later on, we'll get to the techniques you use to keep your readers focused on the trail you need them to follow while still seeing the myriad of possibilities around them. For now, let's focus on how you keep your reader from taking that fatal mis-step. You know the one. It's the moment your toddler goes chasing after a butterfly when you're late for a doctor's appointment. It's the time the dog drools all over your shoes when you're on your way to a wedding. At other times, these actions wouldn't necessarily ruin your day, but like most parts of life, it's all a question of timing.

When a reader begins your first novel, the world of that novel is fully formed (because it's already been written), but the reader knows nothing about it (or depending on the publicity, nearly nothing). It's up to you, the writer, to introduce them to your world in a way that allows them to be interested in that world rather than confused by it. To do this, you give them a starting point. In most novels, that start-ing point is your viewpoint character. Regardless, you must create a point of focus. In movies, this is done through camera movement. The opening shot might be of Earth as seen from orbit. Quickly, the camera zooms down to a country, to a city in that country, to a neighborhood within that city, and finally to a group of people standing on a busy street corner. Regardless whether the camera then zooms in for a close-up on a character, or a building, or on a plastic bag swirling around a leaf-strewn alley, the reader is given a focus.

Typically, plenty of other objects exist in the scene: The red bricks of the wall behind the swirling bag and the cracked concrete of the alley floor below it, the sky above the building and the grass stretching out before it, and the half dozen other people walking beside our main character. But those are background visuals. When done correctly, they add to the focus rather than detract from it.

Most readers enter a story looking for help. They picked up the book because they wanted to be entertained. Desperately they search for a hand to hold. Contrary to what many beginning writers believe, they're not purposefully being obtuse. They want to understand. They want to get to know your characters and they want to be told a story.

I fully realize that tons of folks out there will be insulted that I've implied readers want to be taken by the hand and led through a story. Both readers and writers will shout at me, their faces growing red as they shake their fists and tell me how I'm all wrong. Readers want to discover a story on their own, they will say. Writers who lead a reader rather than allowing that reader to discover their own path insult the reader's intelligence and create a boring story. Not at all. As writers, we like to fool ourselves, and we especially like to fool non-writers, into believing that a story is some sort of magical entity. It grows and expands until it lives and breathes. You can't create life by mechanically inserting tab A into slot B. Really? Tell that to your Planned Parenthood teacher.

If you want to get your story moving, craft each and every word to achieve a particular effect. Granted, some writers seem to achieve this effortlessly, but that's called talent. If you've got it, use it. But if you're like most of us, you better have a backup plan.

Once a reader starts a novel, everything that reader knows comes from the words on the page. As a writer, we're the reader's eyes, ears, nose, mouth, and fingers. Our readers don't touch anything unless we touch it for them. Our readers don't taste anything unless we put it in their mouths. Without a doubt, as writers we've got the reader's hand tightly trapped in ours and that reader's being dragged wherever we decide to take them. As we travel deeper into the novel and the novel becomes more complex, we have more options at our disposal. Inside jokes become available. Winks and nods have meaning.

A subtle gesture speaks volumes. But in the beginning, all we have is a single point of light. Learning to recognize that light and trimming away everything that doesn't immediately add to that light is one of the hard-learned secrets to crafting great beginnings.

Expanding the light

You want to start your novel with a Big Bang. To do that, set the scene and introduce the main viewpoint character by showing them in action. Anything that doesn't immediately add to the reader's ability to understand the situation, the character, and the impact of the big bang should be carefully removed until you've crafted a firm and comfortable handhold for the reader. There are other ways to begin, but this is the easiest and most reliable.

So how exactly do you do it?

First, immerse yourself completely and totally in your main viewpoint character. If you've covered the basics, your main character is standing on the stage of your novel. You've told the audience when and where the novel takes place. An event of a personal and unique nature is about to take place (or is already taking place) that will cause your character to proceed down a path that would not have been taken without that event. This path is your story.

Given that you've set the stage and you have a Big Bang, that means you're starting your novel with the event or as close as possible to the event. If you're not starting with the event, you have a reason for not starting with the event. That reason dictates the contents of your first few paragraphs. Your beginning should be obvious.

To say that it seems obvious doesn't mean it doesn't involve lots of work, multiple false starts, and eventual deletion during the rewrite. But your setting and the actions of your main character should be constrained by your Big Bang.

To start your novel, become your character. You know where that character is and what actions they must take. See what your character sees and feel what your character feels. Think about what your character thinks about. Then write it down.

Immersing yourself completely in your viewpoint character will keep you from having your main character go out of her way to look in a mirror, or comment on the style of her socks while she's fleeing from a tyrannosaurus rex. It keeps her from thinking about that day when she was five or about her life's goals (unless the triggering event would cause her to ponder those ideas). Concentrate on your character's feelings. Don't recite those feelings to your reader. Instead, allow your viewpoint character to express her views on what she sees and what she experiences.

Make your character interesting. The more interesting the character is, the more interesting her view of the world is likely to be. Don't go overboard. Just don't make them a wet rag with no opinions about anything.

There is too much. Let me sum up

Beginnings are vital to the success of your novel. Now you know what you need to get your novel started:

- Beginnings are the second most important section of your novel or story.
- Write your novel using the idea that you care about the most.
- People read fiction for 1) Story and 2) Characters; introduce both as soon as possible.
- Create story and introduce characters using 1) Conflict and 2) Relationships.
- Start your story with a Big Bang.
- Don't give anyone a reason to reject your novel before they've reached page two.
- Answer who, what, when, and where as soon as possible.
- You're all that stands between your reader and confusion.

Now it's time to write. I've given you the tools you need to get your first couple pages in place, but there's a lot more pages that follow. It's high time we talked about the meat of the novel.

That means story and characters.

Chapter Three:
Story

The Formula

It's interesting that formula has such a derogatory meaning among so many writers. If you're visiting a friend and they let you taste some delightful concoction they've just created in their kitchen, do you ask, "What philosophical perspective can you give me related to this wonderful dish?" Of course not. (Not unless you're my wife!) You ask for the recipe.

A recipe's nothing more than another word for formula. How about some other descriptive words, like:

- Methods
- Procedures
- Principles
- Rules
- Blueprint

In a real sense, this is precisely what teaching is about. It's about passing on acquired knowledge. I can teach you about writing by showing you what works or by telling you what works (or some combination thereof). While it might be interesting to have you all over for a couple years so I can dole out some hands-on training in novel-writing, my house simply doesn't have enough bathrooms for that. Instead, I'm providing some general principles that work extremely well for most genre fiction.

To do this, I resort to talking about rules and methods and so on. I've made it clear that my rules aren't absolute and that if the methods I present don't work, you should continue your search elsewhere. Having said that, here's an excellent formula for producing great genre fiction *that sells:*

> A likable character, through his or her own efforts, overcomes almost impossible odds to achieve a worthwhile goal.[4]

---

4. While I'd love to take credit for thinking this one up all by myself, I can't. This idea comes straight from Marion Zimmer Bradley. Ms. Bradley was a relatively well-known science-fiction and fantasy author who was also a successful editor. By chance, she purchased my first story.

While you can certainly write a popular fiction novel that adheres to very little of this formula, you'll find that most popular fiction fits perfectly well (just as most genre plots fall into man vs. man or man vs. nature). Referencing the above formula then becomes a tool that you can use to diagnose what's wrong with your own fiction. If you deviate from this pattern, you should have a reason for doing so and a passionate conviction that the intended deviation is the best way to tell your story.

With that in mind, let's break this sentence down a bit.

A likable character

I'm tempted to skip this part since the next section focuses exclusively on characters, but I'll point out the one change I was tempted to make to the original tenet:[4] An *interesting or* likable character. Not all likable characters are interesting. Not all interesting characters are likable. But most are. If your main character is either interesting or likable (or both!), people will almost certainly enjoy reading about them. The next section of this book will give details about what makes a character both likable and interesting.

Through his or her own efforts

This requirement is simple enough. Don't have your hero's problems solved by someone else. My first novel was rejected because my agent claimed I'd used a *deus ex machina,* which is Latin for "god out of the machine." It's a fancy editor/agent way of saying your heroine didn't solve her own problems. I disagreed, mainly because there was no outside force involved in my ending, but it highlights the fact that people generally like to read about heroes who overcome obstacles without outside help. In classic terms, this means you can't have the cavalry come charging over the hill at the critical moment. Even though that's often what happens in real life and is also what happens in a great deal of popular fiction, it's always better when the hero is a do-it-yourselfer.

But like my example above, we as writers sometimes believe our heroine is acting on her own but agents and editors see it differently. What does the phrase mean: Through his or her own efforts?

It means that—in the climactic scene of the story or the novel— we can't pull out anything that hasn't existed before. If we haven't prepared the reader for our hero's actions by showing the hero take similar actions before or by talking about the objects or ideas the hero uses in the scene, then it comes back to the idea of *deus ex machina*. The hero can't suddenly acquire new skills, new objects, or new knowledge. Everything the hero needs is already there or carried with him when he walks on stage for that final triumph.

In scenes before the climactic scene, that's obviously not the case or there would be no novel. As our heroine travels through her story, she can receive help, acquire new skills, find new tools to use in her quest, and learn facts she didn't know before. But these gains should come through her own efforts, meaning no one is handing her anything unearned. That's why the people who help heroes in stories usually speak in riddles or give false or misleading information. Nothing is free, which brings us to the next part of the formula.

Overcomes almost impossible odds

Imagine the thrilling tale where our lone hero (backed up by dozens of trained SWAT team members) storms into a petty larcenist's home. The thief's asleep on the couch. Our hero (with those dozens of trained SWAT team members, who are now pointing their guns at the sleeping larcenist) rolls the guy over and snaps on the cuffs. Problem solved! No one wants to read about that. It's too easy. The harder the problem, the more interesting the solution becomes.

As to what makes the odds almost impossible, that's easy. If most of your experienced readers, especially potential agents and editors, are fairly certain your hero can't reasonably succeed because there are too many forces stacked against him, then the odds are almost impossible. But there's more to it than that.

Notice that this part of the formula says *almost* impossible. That *almost* is important. When you turn it around, it means that your hero needs to overcome obstacles that are possible to overcome. If you examine the idea a bit further, it means that your hero needs to *just barely* have or acquire the skills, knowledge, and tools needed to overcome the obstacles in his path. That's what makes the odds of success *almost* impossible.

It also means the odds are determined by the hero. If your hero is an aging boxer who had a great deal of potential and natural talent in his youth, the odds are long but not impossible for him to train hard with a championship-caliber trainer and then go toe-to-toe with the extremely overconfident current boxing champion. If that hero who's trying to go fifteen rounds with the champion isn't an aging boxer but instead is Bill Nye the Science Guy, the odds go from *almost* impossible to are-you-out-of-your-mind?

This means that your hero typically possesses some skills that relate to what he's trying to accomplish. Housewives typically don't become ax-wielding orc-killers overnight. Soft-spoken, non-aggressive sales managers from Long Island rarely join the army and get awarded the Medal of Honor the first time they see combat. Hard-nosed cops with twenty years on the force don't often open their own ballet company. Non-typical characters can be interesting, but be wary about going too far. It's typically not believable that a group of children from London can walk through an old wardrobe and immediately become skilled fighters who can hold their own against soldiers with a lifetime of experience.

And here's where it gets a bit tricky. The obstacles your hero can overcome are determined by the genre. For example, most children are more willing than most adults to suspend disbelief. If a person learns how to fly with nothing more than happy thoughts and a bit of fairy dust in a children's story, most children will accept it with even the flimsiest of explanations. In a classical romance, if a relatively normal woman happens to meet a gorgeous, driven, millionaire, there's a good chance he will inexplicably fall madly in love with the woman, even if she treats him like the arrogant ass he often is. She possesses no unique skills or attributes that would make her unusually attractive to said millionaire in real life, but the accepted tropes of the genre inherently give her the skills she needs to overcome this obstacle.

In fiction, what's possible or impossible is always determined by the readers. Know your readers and tailor your obstacles to both your hero and the novel's genre.

To achieve a worthwhile goal

The example above concerning the arrest of a petty larcenist is indeed a worthwhile goal. Worthwhile goals in popular fiction tend to be bigger, but they don't have to be earth-shattering (or more accurately, earth-protecting). In *Ordinary People*, Timothy Hutton won an Oscar for realizing that he didn't need to kill himself just because he survived a boating accident but his bigger, stronger, better brother didn't. As long as the goal is appropriate to the genre, even what some people would consider mundane goals can be good. In an old after school special from the 70's, a teenager built a boat to sail around a lake in Central Park. In most romances, the girl and guy end up together (and supposedly live happily ever after). For James Bond, he really has just saved the world. What's important is that your hero's goal must be large enough and important enough that the reader cares whether the goal is achieved. How much the reader cares is set not only by the goal itself but also by the way the writer presents the goal to the reader. If done well, good writers can give even mundane goals deeper meaning.

No Thanks to Meat Loaf

Contrary to the Jim Steinman lyrics so aptly sung by Meat Loaf, two out of three can be downright awful—or in this case—three out of four is indeed bad. In writing, almost good enough usually means rejection and more than good enough only sometimes translates to an acceptance letter and a check (or loads of readers and a six figure income on Amazon). If any piece of the formula's omitted, the entire formula falls apart. It becomes complicated because everything is relative. For example, a more-than-likable character can sometimes overcome a mediocre goal without the novel becoming tiresome. And if the hero relies only on his own skills and intelligence, maybe the odds can simply be long instead of nearly impossible. But if you're looking for a challenge, try to convince the average reader to enjoy a story that features a run-of-the-mill, despicable character. Or try to sell a dramatic story where the hero overcomes nothing but easy obstacles. Anything's possible, but there are much more reliable ways to make a living.

That means that to use this formula, you need to use all of it. More than that, you need to do your best at each part. Have your main character be as likable as you can make her, have her rely mainly on her own actions to overcome her problems, have her overcome obstacles that are as large as you can make them, and have her goal be the most worthwhile goal she can possibly achieve. If you succeed in creating a novel that does all that, your chances of selling the manuscript are fantastic compared to a similar novel where any piece of the formula is missing.

A Formula That Worked

Like most writers, I started out believing writing to a formula was a bad idea. It would sap my creativity. It would make my stories flat and predictable. So I wrote several dozen stories without any formula in mind. I wrote them the best way I could using all the knowledge I had gained through a couple decades of reading.

None of them sold.

Then I received the guidelines for *Four Moons of Darkover,* an anthology edited by Marion Zimmer Bradley. The guidelines were in a newsletter that also contained an article by Ann Sharp where she presented a formula for writing a short story. The formula was simple enough. In the opening scene, the hero's presented with a problem. The hero attempts to solve the problem three times. The first attempt is, well, a first attempt. The second attempt is a serious attempt where the hero takes a great risk in an effort to succeed—and instead makes his situation much, much worse. All looks lost until the final moment, when the hero has a "Eureka!" realization and manages to pull off an unexpected solution.

Since my methods obviously weren't working, I decided I'd give this formula one chance to succeed. Very big of me, I know.

As you've probably guessed, the story sold. My first one. And to my surprise, the formula's not recognizable unless you're looking for it. Even better, that short story's gone on to make well over $2,000 since its first publication. Not bad for a formula-driven story, eh?

While I wouldn't recommend this formula for a novel—it's a bit too simple for that—it does prove that using a formula is a nothing more than a tool that allows you to write a story most people will want to read. And isn't writing a great story what we're all trying to achieve?

Creating Story

Earlier I claimed that story and characters are the Light and the Way when it comes to creating a successful novel. This entire section is devoted to story, so it's about time we figured out how to create a story.

I defined *story* earlier as the dramatic cause and effect relationship that makes a series of events interesting by adding meaningful emotional perspective to those events. This definition is useful for distinguishing literary terms, but it's not particularly helpful when we're trying to create a story from scratch. We could break this definition down and examine how each part of the definition relates to the tasks we have to accomplish to create a great story—but that sounds remarkably boring. Instead we'll just focus on one part of the definition. ***A story is an interesting series of events.*** What makes a series of events interesting? Put another way, how do you create a great story?

Unfortunately it's not possible to separate our story from our characters, our plot, our theme, our setting, or any of the other components that go into our novel. Creating a great story means doing everything well. Screw up any part and the entire creation fails. In this sense, writers are much like master chefs. We transform quality ingredients using all the skills we can muster to create a homogenous and pleasing whole. While skilled samplers can detect the various ingredients and guess at the techniques we used, the end result depends on the entirety of our particular preparation. In the next several pages I'll attempt to give a bit of separation to most of the major components that go into a great story, but remember that none of these components works without the others.

Conflict → Story

At the heart of any great story is conflict. The status quo leads nowhere, but conflict leads directly to story. Newton's First Law tells us that an object at rest stays at rest unless acted on by an outside force. That means when your butt's parked on the couch in front of the TV, you tend to stay there until you remember that you have a novel you were planning to write.

Stories are about movement. Not uniform, consistent movement, but chaotic, unpredictable movement. The best way to get your characters moving and keep them moving is by throwing a bit of conflict at them.

In this context, conflict does not mean war. A character fighting in a battle can certainly represent conflict in the sense it's an obstacle to overcome, but conflict is any force or obstacle that interferes with a character reaching his or her goals.

Oops. There's that formula raising its ugly head already. In order to create conflict, we need to create obstacles for our characters to overcome. And in order to have obstacles, our characters must have desires or needs. If a character doesn't need or want for anything, then how can any obstacles exist? Even if your character desires nothing more than to be a classic example of Newton's First Law by being an object at rest that stays at rest, they still have a desire. So we provide a goal for our character. Preferably a worthwhile goal. To do that, we poke her with a sharp stick, or we cause the floor to fall out from under her. That provides the desire to move, which in turn allows for conflict because of all those obstacles we've cleverly laid down.

Once we stir our novel pot with a bit of conflict, story naturally develops. But like any great concoction, the quality of our end result depends on our selection of raw ingredients. To create a great story, you need to add in some great conflicts.

Failure is not an option

If you want a great conflict, you must have a character who cares. I suspect that the English roots of the words character and care are not far apart. That's because a character who doesn't care is usually worthless. If your hero can walk away from the goal you've given him rather than confront the obstacle you've placed in his path, then you haven't chosen the right character or you haven't given him a sufficient goal. As Hindu Prince Gautama Siddhartha (the recognized founder of Buddhism) said, "Desire is the root of evil." For fiction writers, desire is also the root of all conflict, because without desire it's impossible to have conflict. Which was ol' Prince Gautama's point, I think.

That means your viewpoint character should be a person with deep feelings. He doesn't need to wear his emotions on his sleeve, but he must have feelings and desires he just can't ignore. When the Big Bang happens, your hero doesn't have any options—not really. As writers, we often like to have our viewpoint character entertain the notion of skipping the conflict. Typically this happens not during the Big Bang but in the lull that often comes afterwards (and just before the world completely falls apart.) Our reluctant hero may even make an attempt to escape his fate, but such an attempt must fail, not because circumstances force him to act, but because he cares so much that he can't abandon his goal regardless how large the obstacles are that block his path or how hopeless his mission seems.

The simplest way to cause our hero to care so much about his goal is to make the result a matter of life and death. The death can be our hero's, family or friends of the hero, or even society at large. If our hero fails, someone dies. Often the intended goal at the beginning of the novel is not one of life and death but develops into that kind of struggle before the novel's finished. For example, many good mystery novels have a hero who starts out just trying to solve the case but who ends up in a life and death situation by the last chapter.

But thousands of novels don't involve a main goal that involves life and death. At least not in the physical sense. There's more to life than just staying alive. Sometimes it's a person's happiness that's at stake. Sometimes it's just a realization that allows future happiness. For example, by the end of *Gone with the Wind*, Scarlett O'Hara is no longer fighting just to survive. Instead, she succeeds when she realizes that the happiness she's been pursuing her entire life has just walked out her door. The insubstantial fantasy of Ashley Wilkes vanishes and the strength that makes her a great character comes to the surface. She can now succeed because she finally knows what she wants out of life. Granted, it helps that what she wants is to spend the rest of her life with a great-looking millionaire who's loved her more than any other man could ever love her. Better late than never, which brings up an interesting point.

Obvious Goals versus Implied Goals

Whether you hate it or love it, *Gone with the Wind* contains twists and complexities missing from many typical popular fiction stories. The heroine shares many traits with a classic villain and is a reluctant heroine even in the best light. At the end of the story, she fails to achieve the goal she's pursued through most of the story. Instead she reaches an unintended goal that's much more satisfying than reaching her intended goal could ever be. So how does a story like *Gone with the Wind* work when it seems not to fit with the formula I outlined a couple pages ago?

In the beginning, Scarlett's very much pursuing an obvious goal. She wants to marry Ashley, but he plans to marry someone else. The problems she encounters early in the story are of her own making and they result from her pursuit of a goal that's not a worthwhile goal. It works because Scarlett accomplishes almost everything she achieves through her own efforts while overcoming almost impossible odds. Additionally, she makes sacrifices that benefit others. While this doesn't necessarily make Scarlett a likable character, the strength she displays through her struggles definitely makes her interesting.

The goals in the story are complex because Scarlett believes her pursuit of Ashley is a worthwhile goal. Since Scarlett shapes our view of her world, we as readers accept her goal as worthwhile *to her* and therefore worthy of pursuit. In reality, her apparent goal is an illusion and her real goal forms slowly throughout the novel. Part of the power of the story comes from the reader's subconscious realization of this goal before it's ever stated. Only at the end, when Scarlett proclaims that she could get Rhett back does the reader fully appreciate that not only does Scarlett have a different goal but that she's already achieved that goal. This is a classic bait and switch technique that we'll cover in a moment, but for now, this example demonstrates the difference between obvious goals and implied goals.

Obvious goals are exactly what their name implies: these are goals that the characters or the writer reveals in relatively clear and concrete terms. That doesn't mean the goal has to be stated explicitly in prose or dialogue. It means that 99% of your readers know what the goal is by reading the passage where the goal is stated. For example, if a group of bandits surprise a post-holocaust traveler and he flees into the brambles while they shoot at him, it's obvious that his immediate goal is to try to escape.

Implied Goals are never stated or never stated clearly. Only by progressing through the story does the reader come to understand what the hero wants to achieve. Often, this realization is shared by both the reader and the hero.

Most good novels contain both obvious goals and implied goals. Obvious goals are easier to understand and use, which is why they work well to get a story started. They take minimal space and they provide an immediate benefit. Implied goals tend to be more powerful but by definition take more time to reveal. Because they're not stated they seem more natural. Often, implied goals are only clear in retrospect.

Bait and Switch

This concept is simple to understand but can be difficult to execute well. If you have an end goal that the main character isn't ready to accept or tackle at the beginning of your novel, you provide a temporary goal (or a series of increasing difficult temporary goals) that the main character fervently strives for. As with *Gone with the Wind*, only in striving and longing for those initial goals do they realize what their main goal should have been all along. Unlike *Gone with the Wind*, it's perfectly acceptable and effective to have your main character achieve her ultimate goal by the end of the novel.

The keys to making the Bait and Switch method work are 1) Keeping the con hidden, 2) Increase the complexity and the intensity of the goals as the main character switches from goal to goal, and 3) Make sure the ultimate goal makes sense as the ultimate goal. When I say you need to keep the con hidden, I mean that the normal reader should not be able to see the goal-switching coming. Each goal you present will seem like the most important goal at the time because of current circumstances. Arranging the goals such that they build provides a force driving the reader toward the end of the novel, and the ultimate goal, when viewed in hindsight, should appear as the obvious ultimate goal. For example, destruction of the Death Star in the original *Star Wars* movie did not become Luke's ultimate goal until about three fourths of the way through the film, and yet, when it does become the goal, it seems obvious that it should have been the goal all along. Granted, in this case, destroying the Death Star was the ultimate goal from the beginning for pretty much everyone on the rebel side except for Luke, Han, Obi-Wan, and Chewbacca. Obi-Wan didn't live long enough to share in the ultimate goal and Han and Obi-Wan only joined the ultimate goal bandwagon with minutes to spare before the credits rolled. But for the purposes of the Bait and Switch technique, what matters most are the goals of the main viewpoint character. Often the ultimate goal is considered worthwhile by nearly everyone (including the reader) long before the main character commits to it. You keep the main character from being an idiot for not recognizing or accepting this obvious ultimate goal by giving them so much other immediate trouble to contend with that the reader forgives their lack of looking past this immediate trouble.

Organic Story

The best stories are based on conflicts that unfold naturally. For Luke Skywalker in Star Wars, his first stated goal is simple. He wants to get the new droids installed and then submit his application to the academy. He wants to leave Tatooine in search of adventure. Then he discovers one of the droids is missing. His immediate goal is then to find the droid. His search leads him directly to the house of Ben Kenobi who tells him about Jedi Knights and his father. Ben then plays the message brought to him by the droid. It's a request for help from Princess Leia. Ben invites Luke to join him in this new quest. When Luke refuses, Ben secretly has Luke's Aunt and Uncle killed by assassins who make it look like the work of the Empire.

Okay. So that last part wasn't explicitly revealed in the movie. But does any Star Wars fan really doubt Ben was behind the killings when he makes inane comments like, "And these blast points—too accurate for Sand People. Only Imperial Storm Troopers are so precise." These are the same Storm Troopers who can't hit the broad side of a space station for the rest of the movie.

The point is that Luke's adventure grows organically. He tackles one problem only to have a bigger problem thrown in his lap. When he solves that problem, it leads to a bigger problem. This process continues until the movie's climactic scene, when he uses the Force and a couple proton torpedoes to blow up the Death Star.

In terms of writing craft, this example demonstrates a protagonist who has an obvious goal and encounters obstacles to reaching that goal. This creates immediate conflict. In the process of completing the first goal, the protagonist obtains a new goal or perhaps a couple new goals. These new goals are more important than the first goal and the obstacles to achieving these goals are also greater. This creates greater conflict and allows the story to build naturally. Rinse and repeat until the final climactic scene. Throw in a love interest and a journey of self-discovery and then start making plans for your royalty checks.

When you grow a story organically, the conflicts the characters encounter, the motivation the characters feel, and the obstacles they must overcome are all based on results from earlier conflicts, motivations, and obstacles. Each new set of conflict, motivation, and obstacle is greater than the one that came before. These building, interlocking conflicts are what create your organic story. Your organic story then becomes an extension of the old idiom, "Out of the frying pan and into the fire." Your main character burns himself on the frying pan. He jumps back and falls into the fire. After leaping to his feet, he runs for the water bucket but on the way steps into an old bear trap. Hand and butt burned, ankle nearly severed, he stumbles back, blinded by pain, and tumbles over a cliff. After bouncing off the rocks and breaking a few bones, he lands in a swift stream. Gasping, barely able to keep his head above water, he realizes he's headed straight for the waterfall.

Our clumsy camper isn't a story many people would want to read (lack of a worthwhile goal, possible lack of a likable character), but it demonstrates the building nature needed in an organic story.

All Together Now

Great stories are driven by great conflicts. Great conflicts result when characters have life and death goals—or goals that the characters feel as strongly about as life and death. A combination of obvious and implied goals give your main characters the motivations they need to overcome the overwhelming obstacles you place in their paths. To make the story seem natural, these motivations, conflicts, and obstacles are grown organically from the events that have already taken place.

I'll admit that writers exist who can create great stories like the one described above in their heads. For such a talented writer, stories flow from their subconscious the way sap flows from a maple tree in the spring. Granted, the writer still needs to distill the result through editing and polishing, but the basic building nature of a great story described above is already there.

I am not one of those writers. Fortunately for me, most writers aren't any better at bleeding great stories than I am. So how do you create a great story? The simple answer is work. Lots and lots of work. The form of this work is usually expressed as your novel's plot.

Plot

Several writers I know have compared the plot of the novel to the foundation of a house. Without a great foundation (plot), a house (novel) can't stand. Personally, I disagree with this. I agree that a great novel usually has a clever and interesting plot, but I don't agree with the house foundation metaphor. For me, *a plot is nothing more than a structure imposed on the story* already present in your novel. It's the plot that allows the story to unfold organically. It's the plot that keeps the story logical and orderly. To return to the house metaphor, our plot forms the framework of struts and joists that keep our house upright.

To plot or not to plot

I know multiple writers who never create a plot—at least not one they write down in any recognizable form. They believe plotting robs them of their creativity. It never ceases to amaze me how many activities rob writers of their creativity. It's a wonder we ever get anything done.

Like everything else I tell you in this book, learning to create a plot is a technique meant to help you write. If you're one of those lucky writers who bleeds story or one of those committed writers who doesn't mind rewriting your novel twenty-two times, you probably don't need to plot. Feel free to skip this section. But if you're a normal writer who can't keep the whole novel in your head, creating a plot allows you to write your novel faster and reduces the amount of rewriting needed. It also allows you to be more creative. That may sound counterintuitive, but once you've learned to work with a plot in place, you're free to explore and invent additional story elements that will fit within that plot framework.

Carpet, Wallboard, and Paint

Like the struts and joists in most houses, your plot should never be visible to the reader. Plots start to show through their coverings when the reader is able to recognize what the outcome of each event is going to be before it happens. While you can sometimes guess the immediate future quite accurately in real life, predictability is rarely interesting in fiction. That doesn't mean that what happens should necessarily come as a surprise. Readers should know when a storm's coming, but they shouldn't be able to predict how much rain will fall. Instead, just as in real life, an event should be able to produce many results.

But having your plot be visible isn't nearly as bad as having it collapse on top of the reader's head, which is what happens when the events in your story lose their credibility. This is especially problematic when your characters—for the sake of your plot—act in ways they wouldn't act. (We cover this in detail in the "The Center of the Universe" section.) You lose credibility whenever your reader doesn't believe that what they're reading would really happen. There are exceptions to this. For example, dialogue in fiction is rarely like dialogue in real life, and when it is, it's usually boring and wordy. The same is true with the selection of events. In fiction, we typically see only the interesting events. "George got up. He yawned. He scratched himself. He yawned again. Bleery-eyed, he looked around the room. He scratched himself again." This kind of tripe rarely appears in real fiction but happens all the time in everyday life. At least it does in my house. At least when George comes to visit.

Don't confuse the lack of credibility with "willing suspension of disbelief," which simply means your audience isn't completely stupid. For example, your audience knows they're reading a story. As such, they know the characters aren't real, the actions described didn't actually happen, and the book eventually ends. Even if you're creating a nonfiction novel where the events are based on reality, the reader still recognizes that the events have been fictionalized and that the book has an ending. No matter whether your audience is reading your story in traditional print form or via e-book, they can tell how much of the book is left with just a quick glance.

The Perfect Plot

What you should be striving for is that organic story mentioned a couple pages ago. Your plot should have events that happen in the proper way and at the proper time so your story unfolds at a steadily growing level of intensity until the final climactic scene. If you've searched the internet for topics related to plot (or maybe taken a poorly taught English class), they've presented you with a plot that looks something like this:

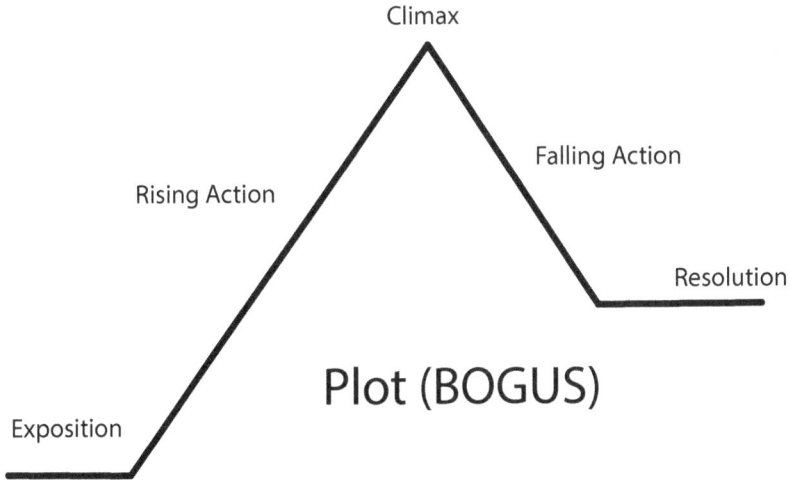

I understand the intention of such a graph. It's to demonstrate an idea in the simplest form possible. But this graph is misleading unless you're talking to a class of third graders—and even then it may be misleading. In a novel or even a short story, the plot does not rise at some sort of smooth and steady pace. Also, if the graph is drawn to scale, the exposition, falling action, and resolution are ridiculously long while the climax is completely misrepresented as a point. I could also nitpick at dozens of other aspects of this graph. Instead, I'll just say that this is *not* what I'm talking about when I say you need a steadily growing level of intensity. What I mean is that each conflict should be larger than the last conflict. Each obstacle should be greater. As the novel unfolds, the motivation of your characters should increase. If we attempted to use the graph above, we'd start by inserting jagged peaks and valleys into the rising action line. But even that is too literal.

An organic story is natural. While the dramatic nature of our overall story should increase, nothing is absolute. Characters are allowed to have breaks in the intensity. Giving your character a break means giving your reader a break. Some writers will claim this should never be done, but I disagree. Especially in our attention deprived world, people simply aren't used to non-stop action. Later, when they think back your story, they should describe it as having non-stop action, but in reality, there should be moments of seeming calm. This calm may be an illusion in the sense the villain may be galloping toward the hero's location or a tsunami may be cruising in toward the beach. But it's perfectly alright to give your character some successes along the way. Returning to the Star Wars example we used earlier, after Luke, Han, Chewbacca, and Ben escape Tatooine, they believe they've got it made. We know better, especially when Ben swoons and complains about a great disturbance in the force. (We know what all that swooning is about. The planet of Alderaan has just been destroyed.) But even after Ben's Excedrin headache #24, Han and Luke debate religion and Ben shows off his teaching skills. Relatively speaking, this is a much calmer moment than the blaster-filled fight scene from a few minutes before.

Even during these moments of calm, it must be perfectly clear that the end goal has not been achieved. The exception might be the climactic scene. If you're trying to pull a James Cameron style ending, where it seems the characters have escaped only to have Mama Alien step from beneath the ship and void the warranty on your android, then allowing the reader to believe all has ended well becomes a technique to increase the shock value and intensity of your real ending.

You Use the Plot: The Plot Does Not Use You

Quite a few writers get hung up on plotting. They dredge up memories of English class and outlines. Trying to create a plot stifles their creativity, not because they can't plot but because they can't write the plot down. Remember, your plot is nothing more than a tool. If it's not useful to you, it's not useful. The form it takes is irrelevant as long as it helps you write.

When you think about creating a plot for your novel, think about what technique you might use to write down an idea in the middle of the night. Your goal isn't to record that idea using some particular format. Unless you're a complete insomniac, you don't worry about spelling or grammar. You're simply trying to get the idea down before it slips away.

Plotting is a slower process than recording an idea because a plot typically contains more detailed information. But you still shouldn't worry about formatting, spelling, or grammar. Record your plot in as much detail as you need and in whatever form you find most useful.

The goal of your plot is to move your story forward in a logical and believable way. Clever plotting also allows you to make the events in your story more interesting by helping you present those events and the information surrounding those events in a more interesting way.

Theme

Many writers talk about theme as if it's the only reason for writing the novel. And it may well be the reason they wrote that particular novel. But most genre readers don't read for theme. They read for story. So how does theme relate to story?

Theme forms the universe that contains your story. Theme therefore governs the physical laws that control your story. In classical terms, ***the theme of your novel is the message you're trying to convey.*** True love triumphs over all, for example. To combat evil one must become evil. Setting a theme both gives your novel direction and also establishes boundaries. Typically, your theme shows up most directly for your main character. If true love triumphs over all, that true love is triumphing for your main character, not the ditzy blond your main character's love interest just dumped. If one must become evil to combat evil, your main character's usually the one who sacrifices a bit of his morals or his sanity in order to bring down the bad guy.

Theme is your opinion. You can state that opinion openly and risk having people throw rotten fruit in your direction—or worse, ignoring you completely—or you can dramatize your opinion. You tell an interesting story and get to slip in your point when they're not looking.

Test Question #4:

As with almost every other topic in this book, theme is a tool to be used. If you start on a novel but struggle to find a direction, imposing a theme on your story can sometimes get you back on track. If you feel passionately about a topic, often the theme (your message concerning that topic) is what drives you to write about it. For most genre writers, that's not usually the case, at least not consciously. Most often you write about what you care about and the theme of your novel evolves naturally from the story you tell.

To put this another way, theme is usually an idea imposed on your writing by others. It's the fourth question on the test in literature class: 4) What is the theme of *The Grapes of Wrath?* Typically we see such a question, scratch our heads, and try to remember what the teacher said the theme was. That's because she read somewhere what someone else thought the theme of the story was and the myth successfully propagated. We end up writing down phrases like, "The Individual in Society" or "Man's Inhumanity to Man." These phrases really don't mean much, but they do give literature teachers something to put on tests.

It's always fascinating to me to watch writers as they're told what the theme of their work is. Most of the time, the writers scoff and say, "That's not right." Well, usually what they say is a little more colorful and definitely not G-rated. But they shouldn't be so harsh. Sometimes the teachers are right. The writers scoff because they didn't realize that they had subconsciously imposed a theme on their work. Sometimes the teachers are full of it. They're imposing their own theme on the story because they're seeing what they want to see.

For you, the writer, theme can be a powerful tool but it doesn't need to be. Tell a great enough story and chances are that your theme will end up as question number four on a test someday. Then you can find out what you were really writing about.

Moments

People say that when you're about to die, your life flashes before your eyes. But not your *whole* life. No matter how hard you press the flash-forward button, it's not your entire life you see. Rather it's the important *moments* in your life. These moments are important because they're tied inseparably to the emotions we experienced during those moments. Think back to your own life. Your clearest memories are almost certainly tied to moments where you experienced strong emotions.

These moments are like pearls on a necklace. The line of our life runs through them and ties them together, but when we look at the necklace, all we see are the pearls. Not that all of life's remembered moments are pleasant or pretty. But they all share that strong emotional component.

Life is experienced and remembered as a series of emotional moments. So, too, is a novel.

Wait! Was that a moment?

Most books on writing talk about scenes or segments, incidents or sequels. At first glance, moments might appear to be the same sort of creature. They're not. Moments don't take place on the page; they take place in the mind of the reader. Usually they can't be mechanically created (although we often try). They work best when they grow out of our story organically and are simply recognized and enhanced.

So what is a moment exactly? It's a period of heightened emotion experienced by your reader. When readers say they enjoyed a novel, what they usually mean is that their emotional needs were satisfied often and well. Moments are a reader's reward, the reason a reader reads. Learning to recognize these moments and take advantage of them is one of the secrets to writing a great novel.

People often talk about talent. For me, a writer's ability to recognize moments in their own writing is the one true talent that great writers universally possess. While I can give you general guidelines about what a moment is, what can be done to create a moment, and what can be done to enhance a moment once it's recognized, your innate ability to recognize a potential moment is a talent that is uniquely yours. By definition, moments can't exist until a novel's read, but good writers can identify moments because they can correctly interpret how their readers will react to a given passage.

In many ways, reading a novel is an intimate experience. It's like a whispered conversation in a quiet corner. The difference is that you, as the writer, are the one doing all the talking. Even so, if the conversation is effective, you must correctly understand why your reader's bothering to listen.

Learn to recognize and enhance the moments you've created and your chances of creating happy readers will be much higher.

Who Was That Masked Moment?

Moments are the times when—if you interrupt someone while they're reading—they get grumpy and tell you to leave them alone. I've experienced this many times myself when I've interrupted my wife. As she likes to say, she was just "getting to the good part." So the big question is: How do we recognize these moments? What are "the good parts?"

The good parts are the payoff. If you're looking for a handy example, grab your best-loved novel and locate its biggest moment. It should be easy to find. Chances are the biggest, boldest, and best-loved moment in any given novel is hiding right there in plain sight, just before the end of the book. That's right. The climax.

The end of a book typically contains the biggest moment because writers discovered long ago that big moments make readers happy, and if you want a reader to buy your next book, make them happiest just before they close the back cover. So how do we create that biggest and best moment that our readers love so well?

What makes a moment work is more art than science. However, most moments share several properties in common:

- Great Risk/Reward combination
- Established setting, characters, and conflict
- Appropriate level of tension

Great Risk/Reward combination:

The greater the risk to the main character, the easier it is to create a moment. If a character sits down to balance his checkbook, the risk seems fairly low. If that same character sits down to balance his checkbook while a highly trained assassin is carefully sneaking around the house with a silencer-tipped pistol in his hand, suddenly the risk of balancing that checkbook goes way up. Granted, balancing that checkbook isn't much of a reward. Compare that situation to the same hero sitting down beside an armed nuclear weapon so he can disarm it. If he fails to disarm it in time, obviously he will die, but the city where he's at will also be destroyed. His girlfriend, his mother, his house, and his favorite motorcycle will all be blasted to nuclear vapor. The entire world where your reader now lives will be destroyed. Now have that same assassin creeping around the corner, pistol in hand. Think you're going to put that book down? No way. And for you spoilsports who claim you don't give a hoot whether the guy disarms the bomb or not, you don't count because you would never encounter this scene in isolation. Remember, by this point in the novel, you've been hanging out with this guy for hundreds of pages. You have a sense of where he lives. You have feelings for his girlfriend, his mother, his house, and even his favorite motorcycle. If you hated everything about him and his life—or worse, were indifferent toward it all—then you would have put the book down long before you reached this climactic scene. The reader's proven interest in the novel's situation and characters is part of what allows you to create a high risk/reward moment.

Established setting, characters, and conflict:

The main reason established situations create better moments than new situations is simple enough. Providing information to a reader slows a scene down. If you have all aspects of the scene established before the scene starts, you can concentrate on the action of the scene rather than on its preparation. That's why moments are often thought of as the payoff by both readers and writers. The pages leading up to any given moment are mostly preparation. Without them, the moment isn't possible, but trying to achieve a great moment while also introducing a place, a time, a character, and a conflict is extraordinarily difficult. That's one of the reasons why the biggest climax in a novel typically happens at the end. You've completed all your preparations. Everything in the novel has led to this moment. That's also why beginnings can be so difficult. It's hard to create an emotional moment when the reader knows nothing about your novel's universe. This difficulty is why so many writers start their novels off quickly by relying on a reader's expectations. Utilizing easy-to-recognize settings, characters, and conflicts provides an immediate base for the reader to stand on. For science fiction, an alien ship appears on the scanners or a moon explodes sending out a massive shock wave. For mysteries, a dead body is discovered. For romances, the heroine meets the man of her dreams or meets a man she hates who will later turn out to be the man of her dreams. For horror novels, the monster takes its first victim (although we usually don't see the monster at that point). For spy novels, a dead man washes up on a lonely beach with a locked briefcase handcuffed to his wrist.

Appropriate Level of Tension:

All moments have a level of tension they'll support. Finding the right balance can be tricky, but the longer you can extend the moment without losing any tension, the better the payoff will be. For most beginning writers, they rush through their best moments. Because they lack control, they get used to cutting early scenes that are slowed by gluts of information. Then, when they arrive at a moment, they speed through it, believing that everything needs to happen quickly or the reader will grow bored. The reverse is actually true. Because the moment is the payoff, the longer it lasts without losing tension, the more the reader enjoys it. That's why finding the right level is risky. Push a scene too far, and you risk losing the reader. Don't push the scene far enough and your novel will become one of those easily forgettable novels that inspire no one. Quicky moments are fine, especially if they come fast and furious, but to truly satisfy your reader, you need to have some bigger moments, especially for the final climax.

Fire up the generator! We need another moment!

As I said, moments are typically better when they happen as the natural result from telling a great story, but there are general writing principles you can follow that almost guarantee at least the kindled flicker of a moment now and then.

In character-driven novels, moments usually occur during times when your viewpoint character experiences strong emotions. That's why having a main character the reader identifies with is so important. If the reader cares about the main character, the reader will care what happens to that character. While it's impossible for a reader to experience what the main character feels directly, readers can experience a shadow of what the main character feels. The more intense the emotions experienced by your main character, the more likely those emotions will transmit an emotional moment to your reader.

But moments aren't limited to feelings experienced by your main character. They can be feelings experienced by your reader alone. Imagine a man hiding in the shadowy corner of an inner city alley. He carries an opened switchblade. Sweat runs down his face and he nervously fingers the handle of the knife. From the mouth of our alley, a young groom approaches in his tux. He carries a wedding band destined for his one true love. As he rolls the gold ring between his fingers and thinks about how his life's about to begin, he approaches the dark corner. He has no idea an ambush awaits.

If the reader cares about the young groom, the reader will mentally grip the edge of her seat, leaning forward in fear and anticipation. "No! Don't go that way! Turn around! Go back!" The more the reader likes the young groom, the more intensely she will feel this fear and anticipation. In a similar but related way, if the reader doesn't care about the groom or if she has no interest in what's about to happen to him, then she feels very little. No moment is created. Perhaps the reader becomes dissatisfied and never finishes the book. She may go online and publish a scathing review. She doesn't buy the next book. If enough other readers feel the same way, the book is a failure. The writer's career may be ruined.

While it's possible to create moments without characters that matter to the reader, it's exceptionally difficult. The same difficulty applies when trying to create great moments with characters alone.

If the story is lacking, the reader may care about the characters but they don't care about what the characters are doing. It may sound like a cop-out to claim that you need a great story and great characters to create great moments, but there's a reason why I claim story and characters are the two great pillars on which a novel is built. Having a great story and great characters won't turn your novel into one giant moment. A natural ebb and flow exists. You still need preparation, information, and plot development.

Moments tend to occur at points of motion. Not necessarily physical motion, although for many genres that's true, but rather emotional motion. These moments tend to be marked by immediacy. Not impending danger but immediate danger. Not eventual decision or promised risk, but immediate risk that forces immediate decisions.

So creating moments is rather simple in theory. Have a great story driven by great characters. Look for moments at points of conflict resolution or creation. Once you discover your moments, you'll want to enhance them for greatest effect.

O Moment! My Moment!

Most writers create moments naturally, but rarely do those moments flow off the pen as powerful as they can be with a bit of revision.

Once you've recognized a moment, how do you enhance it? Your first step is to remove everything from the moment that can be removed. The most obvious target is preparatory information. This includes descriptions, background information, and explanations. All these items may be necessary, but if you can move them into earlier sections of your novel, do so. I've already said that moments work best for established settings, characters, and conflicts. Often you recognize a potential moment at a point when some or all of these items are not established. To establish them, sometimes you need to create a new scene (or scenes) earlier in the novel where you introduce these items. You may need to give the reader a reminder when you arrive at the scene with the moment, but the scene can then proceed unencumbered.

Your next step is to remember that emotions, especially powerful emotions, are the fuel that drives a moment deep into your reader's brain. Those emotions can be strong emotions felt by the characters that bathe the reader in their powerful aura, or they can be emotions that are generated in the reader alone. The more powerful and overwhelming the emotions created, the bigger the moment will be. To enhance the moment, jettison anything that doesn't increase the emotions you're creating.

The most common extra baggage writers have during moments is complexity. Complexity creates confusion, which is not moment-inducing under any circumstances. A novel I read recently had its big climactic moment set in the sewers of London. Not only was this a problem because the reader had never seen this setting before, but also the author insisted his characters guess at the names of various streets and locations on the surface above them. I surmise he did this as an attempt to avoid confusion. He wanted the readers to know where the characters were, but what he achieved was the opposite effect. Even for lifelong Londoners who knew those streets better than the back of their hands, that knowledge did not help them imagine the characters trapped below. It forced them to think of the streets above, which distanced them from the characters and from the emotions those characters were feeling. More important, he entirely missed capturing the nature of the moment. This was the climax of the novel. His characters were in the sewers during a thunderstorm. They were trapped. The flood waters were rising and they had just come to an iron grating that they couldn't open. They had no escape. As the waters continued to rise, it became clear that they were all going to drown unless one of them could find a way out. Instead of focusing on that moment, which should have been extremely emotional for both the characters and the readers, the author confused everyone with a setting they couldn't imagine easily. Even though this is an experienced author who's been writing for decades, he made two more mistakes. First, he didn't extend that moment. He didn't hang on to that tension he'd spent dozens of tedious chapters building. Second, he saved them through *deus ex machina*. None of them solved their problem. They were going to die violent, horrible deaths, trapped there in the dark and the muck. Instead, when the wall of water hit them, the locked gate slid aside to release them and the rush of water pushed them into a room with a grate for a floor. Saved! As a reader I certainly felt cheated.

Nuggets

Not every scene can contain a moment, but most scenes can contain nuggets placed there for the reader's enjoyment.

Nuggets are not full blown moments and they're not necessarily driven by emotions. Instead they're delicious morsels of information, insight, or humor that most readers treasure. If you have enough nuggets in your novel, you can get by with hardly any moments at all. Nuggets tend to be what readers share with other readers when they're trying to convince them to read this great book they just finished.

The most common forms of nuggets are bits of humor, witty dialogue, quirky character behaviors or actions, fascinating tidbits of history, and clever plot twists. In simplest terms, nuggets are what make your novel interesting. If someone ever tells you to punch up a scene, generally they want you to add more nuggets.

In practical terms, most writers are either interesting or they're not. Like moments, nuggets tend to be a reflection of talent. But even for writers who can't charm a room just by walking through the door—which is most of us—they can still consciously watch for opportunities to add bits of life to their prose and their scenes. Sometimes, as writers, we're so worried about accuracy, pace, grammar, prose, scene structure, consistency, and all the other techniques related to writing proficiently that we forget to make it interesting.

There is too much. Let me sum up

Stories (and the moments found in great stories) form the reason most readers read. Creating a great story is vital to the success of your novel.

- One way to create a great story is to follow a proven formula:

    A likable character, through his or her own efforts, overcomes almost impossible odds to achieve a worthwhile goal.

- A formula (like the one above) is just a tool you use to improve your story.
- Formulas only work if you use the entire formula, doing your best with each part of the formula.
- To create a great story, use the tensions naturally created when powerful motivations encounter nearly insurmountable obstacles.
- Grow your story organically by having each succeeding conflict arise from an earlier conflict, by increasing the intensity of each new conflict, and by having those conflicts bounded strongly by motivations versus obstacles.
- A good plot is a structure you impose on your story in an effort to remove obstacles to a reader's enjoyment of that story.
- Allow your plot to assume whatever form you find most helpful.
- Write a great story that you care deeply about and your theme will emerge naturally.
- If your story lacks a moral direction, imposing a theme can sometimes help you regain focus.
- Moments produce heightened emotions in your readers. These moments are what most readers would call the good parts of a novel. They are the "good parts" of any given novel and the enjoyment they provide is the main reason readers read.
- Moments work best for established settings, characters, and conflicts.

- Most moments are based on a great risk/reward combination and are powered by the tension of that conflict. Moments should extend only as long as that tension lasts.
- Generate moments by putting likable characters in situations with immediate physical and emotional peril. Increase the intensity of those moments by allowing your reader to experience them through your viewpoint character.
- Raw emotional truths provide fuel for moments that can't be matched by intellectual complexity.
- Readers treasure nuggets, which are bits of humor, witty dialogue, quirky character behaviors or actions, fascinating tidbits of history, and clever plot twists.
- All writers should seek to add more nuggets to everything they write.

Story and characters form the foundation stones upon which nearly all great fiction is built. We've covered story. Now it's time we tackled characters.

Chapter Four:
Characters

The Center of the Universe

There is no single greater concern to a writer than his characters. Of what interest is 221B Baker Street without Sherlock Holmes? What is *Gone with the Wind* without Scarlett O'Hara and Rhett Butler? How mundane would Scout's life be in *To Kill A Mockingbird* without Boo Radley? Fiction is driven by the characters who live it. Take a great story and replace the main characters: You've just created a completely different story. (If that's not the case, you have an anecdote—not a story.)

Long after the last page of a modern novel has been read and the details of the story are forgotten, readers remember the characters. That's why so many genre writers exist who can't plot their way out of a rounded corner, whose prose sounds like it came off the back of a cereal box, and who seem to tell the same story over and over. They have characters we care about. We forgive a lot from writers who create characters that we enjoy.

Theory of Relativity

To start with, all characters in your novel should believe the story is about them. Think Ginger on Gilligan's Island. Without question, she was the most useless castaway of the bunch. Even Mrs. Howell had a trunk or two of goodies, plus she spoke fluent Italian and French. Yet, Ginger thought the world revolved around her, and whenever she discovered she might not be the center of everyone's attention, she found it devastating.

This doesn't mean your characters should all trounce about wearing nothing but an old sail and high heels while singing bad imitations of Marilyn Monroe songs. It means they see events unfold around them from their own unique points-of-view. They act based on their own motivations and they struggle with their own sets of problems.

Paper or Plastic

Telling you that all your characters should believe the story's about them may seem like an odd place to start, but when your characters believe that, it solves a great many problems. For one, it eliminates cardboard characters. If each character believes your novel is about her, how can she not have strong personal concerns and motivations? How can she not be interesting—at least in her own mind? You've written an entire novel about her. If every character in your novel is fighting for the spotlight, they all possess that critical spark of sentience that's so vital to any lifelike character.

Stated another way, all characters should have passion. Each of your characters should care, and care deeply, about what's most important to them. It's this ability to care, this *passion* for what's personally important, that turns a lifeless name into a living, breathing character.

Take Samantha for example. She's a college student at Kansas State University. She's a sophomore. She lives in a dorm. Her birthday is June 1, and she's nineteen.

Samantha is not a person. She's a statistic.

Let's provide a little more information. Samantha wants to be a scientist. Her mother died of cancer when Samantha was fourteen. At her mother's funeral, Samantha swore she would become a research doctor and would do all she could to find a cure for cancer so that other girls would never need to lose their mothers the way she lost hers. But just last month, Samantha met Tom, a philosophy major. On their first date, Samantha revealed her childhood pledge to become a doctor. She thought Tom would be impressed by her commitment to her mother. Instead, Tom told her that she had no right to live her life trying to please someone else, even her diseased mother. Now she's unsure what she should do. In truth, she's always hated life science classes and would rather work with computers. But the idea of switching majors makes her feel as if she's abandoning the memory of her mother.

Caring about her future transforms Samantha from a statistic to a person. She starts to move, breathe, and live.

Take my Pawn, Please!

Having characters believe the novel is about them also prevents them from acting in ways that they wouldn't act just to forward the plot. The characters in our novels aren't there for us and they're not there for the story. (Selfish bastards!) When writers talk about listening to their characters, this is often what they mean. They've tried to turn a living, breathing character into a pawn and the character has rebelled. What's really going on is that the writer's subconscious has picked up on the difference between how the character would act based on that character's morals and motivations and how the writer needs that character to act for the sake of the plot.

As writers, this doesn't mean that we should listen to our characters and let them run off in whatever direction they want. That way lies madness—and multiple rewrites! Instead, we need to maintain control. But how do we get our characters to do what we need them to do without bonking them on the head and dragging them in that direction? We give them a reason to do what we want.

If one of your secondary characters needs to break up with the novel's hero and then drive down a rain-slicked road where she loses control and plunges down a cliff to her death, give her a reason to do exactly that. Since your hero is awesomely perfect and would never do anything to give her a reason to break up with him[5], then change the circumstances. Maybe her vile and jealous friend gave her some photoshopped pictures that led her astray. Maybe your perfect hero got caught hugging a cancer-surviving colleague in public and the girlfriend misunderstood. Perhaps the girlfriend's being noble: Knowing how much the hero wanted children of his own, she broke up with him when she found out her ovaries had long ago shriveled to the size of peanuts.

The key to your invention is that it should serve two purposes. It should cause your characters to act the way you want them to act but it should also reinforce the plot and character motivations you already have in place. Many times these inventions-of-necessity lead to the best-loved and most memorable parts of a novel.

Never be afraid to invent. That's your job.

---

5. Yes. This is sarcasm. Heroes are rarely perfect but their actions have far-reaching implications. For this example, it works better to have the secondary character trigger the event.

Heroes and Villains

All major characters in a novel are either heroes or villains. The only variability is the degree to which they are heroic or villainous, and the timing of the measurement.

This is one of those statements that generates constant argument from other writers—with good reason. Literature is full of heroes who aren't particularly heroic. It also contains plenty of villains who aren't particularly villainous. That's not what I'm talking about here when I say all characters are heroes or villains. If you look up the definitions for hero and villain in the dictionary and then strip away the literary and circular references, you end up with the following meanings:

hero:	someone who's admired
villain:	someone who's not admired

You can't get a better illustration of my meaning, probably because I trimmed the existing definitions to get what I was looking for. That's one of the advantages of making up your own definitions, but the meanings above really are there if you look for them.

The point is that if you want a reader to care about your main characters, the easiest way to make that reader care is to have them take sides. You want them either rooting for your characters or rooting against them, even if they're not conscious they're doing it. This doesn't mean your heroes should be perfect or that your villains must be totally evil. It doesn't mean your heroes can't have moments of doubt or that your villains can't perform acts of kindness. What concerns us here is the way the reader feels about your characters. If that reader's ambivalent about your main character, that's perilously close to not caring whether your character lives or dies. If you force your reader to dance along the tightrope of caring or not caring, you risk having the reader fall—and once your reader's gone, that reader's gone for good. Creating a main character that no one cares about is the best way to write a novel that no one wants to read.

That's why the first step in creating a great character is to decide if that character will be a hero or a villain.

Creating a Great Character

As it turns out, great characters are great characters. Regardless how Yogi Berra that sounds, it's true. Heroes and villains are much more alike than they are different. Many times villains end up being more interesting than heroes, but that usually has more to do with the writer than it does the character. I'll explain that bit of psychobabble later, but for now, let's take a look at what traits most great characters have in common:

1) Passionate
2) Active
3) Capable
4) Interesting
5) Believable

These traits aren't absolute, but if you're looking for the most sure-fire method for creating great characters, they provide a great start.

1) Passionate

The larger the character, the more deeply that character should feel, and the more revealing the writer should be when dealing with those feelings. Passion gives your character life more than any other trait. Nothing is less interesting than a person who doesn't seem to care deeply about anything. Nothing is more mesmerizing than a character who is fully committed to a cause, whether he admits it to himself or not. Passion is the wellspring from which all character life flows. Only characters that care can have motivations and goals. Only characters that care can have desires and hindrances to those desires. Without passion, motivation disappears. Without motivation, goals become irrelevant. Actions stop. Your story withers and dies. But in the presence of deep and energetic passion, stories grow almost out of necessity. Create passionate characters and half the battle of storytelling is won. This doesn't mean characters feel the same way about everything. Typically their passions lie along the same paths as your story, but not always. What's important is that their passions are larger than those around them. That's what makes them main characters.

2) Active

In real life, some people care deeply about their concerns, but they lack the fortitude and ambition to rouse themselves from their comfortable niches and initiate movement in their desired direction. In fiction, these people are known as whiners. They are the most pathetic and uninteresting of characters. While they are quite good at complaining about their lots in life, they take no action to remedy their difficulties. Whiners sometimes work as secondary characters, performing useful services as backdrops to highlight movements of main characters, but they are almost never capable of sustaining a story on their own. To avoid creating whiners, keep your main characters on the move. They should always be striving to reach their goals. More than that, they should be performing *to the best of their abilities.* This doesn't mean your main characters are perfect or that they can't have one or two points in the novel where they knowingly fail to do their best (and suffer the appropriate consequences). It means that when your characters are trying to achieve their goals, they use all the skills and effort they can muster. Nothing is held back. *Nothing is artificial in order to make it easier for your heroes or villains to succeed.* When they go against their nemeses, they go against the best those nemeses can muster.

3) Capable

While all characters fail and few characters are perfect, readers tend to care more about capable characters than they do inept characters. If a character's active but never accomplishes anything, she usually becomes boring fairly quickly. Interesting villains are almost always capable. Interesting heroes are usually capable but their emotions often get in their way. That's part of what makes them heroes. Your main villain and your main hero don't need to be the most capable characters in your story, but they usually rank near the top.

4) Interesting

I've never heard a reader complain that the characters in a novel were just too interesting. Most characters who are passionate, active, and capable are already interesting, but the more interesting you can make your characters, the better. You don't like hanging out with boring people in real life, so why would you ask your readers to hang out with boring characters for a whole novel? To make your characters more interesting, take cues from real life. Just as with people who fascinate the masses, interesting characters are often witty, charming, good-looking, talented, and unusual. Unusual doesn't mean you need to create a side-show freak or an idiot savant, but characters who possess at least one unusual trait are more interesting and memorable than characters who fit the norm across the board. At the very least, you don't want to cast all your characters from the same mold. These unusual traits can be based on appearance, personality, or both. One of the unusual traits that's often taken for granted is a character's looks. With the exception of comic relief characters, most main characters in fiction are more attractive (or much less attractive) than people in real life. I've never personally been drawn to the pretty people, but if you search your favorite works of fiction for attractive main characters, chances are you'll find them. You'll probably also discover that characters are not only more attractive than real people but also more attractive than more minor characters in the novel.

5) Believable

This trait is mentioned last for a reason. If you create a passionate, active, capable, and interesting character, there will always be readers willing to suspend disbelief just because they enjoy reading about that character so much. Conversely if you create a believable character who isn't passionate, active, or capable, you'll face an extreme uphill battle to keep the reader interested. You want characters who give the impression of reality because you don't want to jolt the reader out of your story by having a character suddenly fly or come back from the dead without explanation. Even so, believability for characters is more important for the fictional world in which they exist than it is in the real world. For Luke Skywalker, his ability to move objects with his mind is completely believable because something called the force exists in his world that allows him to do these things. Sure, Luke may be able to blow up a Death Star with a single shot, but if he made a suggestive comment about how Leia's thin white dress clings to her unsupported breasts, the reader would be shocked. That's not what Luke would do. Han could make that comment, at least in the PG-13 version, but never Luke. Your characters should be believable within the reality you've built for them, especially in reference to their morals and their personalities.

Hero vs. Villain

First, I tell you your characters are all either heroes or villains. Then I claim there are five main traits shared by both heroes and villains, which, uh, makes them the same, right? Hey, no sane, intelligent person has ever said great writing was easy. There may not be much difference between your heroes and villains when you break them down into their component traits, but readers don't do that. They either root for or against your characters, and that difference is like night and day. Where do you think the whole white hat/black hat idea came from?

The major trait that differentiates a typical hero from a typical villain is motivation. If a character's motivation stems from a need or desire toward the greater good, which means it stems from a need to help others, then that character's typically a hero. If that motivation stems from a desire to further the personal situation of the character, then that character's typically a villain. In short, heroes are selfless and villains are selfish.

The line separating hero from villain is often quite fine. As the villainous Belloq said to the heroic Indiana Jones in *Raiders of the Lost Ark*, "Our methods have not differed as much as you pretend. I am a shadowy reflection of you. And it would take only a nudge to make you like me, to push you out of the light." While great heroes and great villains are vastly different, the motivations and resulting morals that differentiate the two character types sometimes appear murky if examined too closely. Both Belloq and Indy wanted the Ark. Both were willing to kill to get it. Neither took pleasure from that killing but both felt a grim satisfaction from the resulting triumph. Both would be paid for retrieving the Ark for the people who hired them. If you examine the movie, you'll see that Indiana Jones intentionally killed or injured a ton of folks in self-defense and even threatened to shoot Belloq in cold blood whereas Belloq intentionally murdered no one. So why is Indy the hero and Belloq the villain?

Hitler, who'd hired Belloq to retrieve the Ark, wanted to use its destructive power to murder millions and conquer the world—and Belloq knew this. The U.S. government, who'd hired Indy, wanted to stop Hitler from using the Ark to hurt people and had no desire to use the destructive power of the Ark themselves. While both Indiana Jones and Belloq acted selfishly, the end result of Indy's actions helped others while the end result of Belloq's actions would have hurt many others.

For those writers with a good moral compass, the difference between heroes and villains is even simpler. Heroes do the right thing, no matter how hard. Villains do the wrong thing because they enjoy doing the wrong thing, or because doing the right thing will keep them from getting what they want.

In general, this means a hero will risk his own life to save the life of another. A villain will often sacrifice the life of another—especially a loyal servant—to save his own life or even accomplish his goals. This mortal choice exemplifies more mundane choices. If a hero spills his friend's mocha latte, he'll surrender his own to replace the one that's lost. If a villain spills his mocha latte, he'll steal his best friend's and won't feel bad for doing so. This selfless/selfish nature of heroes and villains isn't absolute, but it works as a general rule: Heroes help others. Villains help themselves.

I should mention one final difference between heroes and villains. All characters will generally have a weakness. This weakness typically doesn't define them, but sometimes it can. Having a weakness isn't so much a trait as it is being realistically human. Real people aren't perfect. Characters shouldn't be perfect either.

The difference between heroes and villains is that heroes overcome their weaknesses. That's part of what makes them heroes. Villains succumb to their weaknesses. That's usually what defeats them in the end. Heroes may or may not know what their weakness is. Villains usually know what their weakness is. When they do, they try their best to conceal that weakness but it typically gets revealed through their actions.

Who Needs a Villain?

Lots of beginning writers believe that villains aren't necessary. Perhaps they were told in English class that there are four types of plots: Man vs. Man, Man vs. Society, Man vs. Nature, or Man vs. himself. Hey, three out of the four have no classical villain. So you don't need a villain, right?

Wrong!

If you want to write a great novel, film script, play, teleplay, or short story, you're going to have the easiest time doing it if you personalize the obstacle the hero must face. I admit, I did the whole "Wrong!" thing above for dramatic effect, because technically, it's more than possible to write a great novel without having a villain. But take a look at the successful novels that have sold like crazy for decades. What would the Harry Potter series be without Voldemort? What would *Lord of the Rings* be without Sauron? What would *The Da Vinci Code* be without Silas? Okay, I admit, that last one is pretty weak. Maybe Dan Brown doesn't do villains so well.

How many of last year's best-selling novels have villains? Most. Not all, though. So maybe you don't *need* a villain. But let me tell you why you want one.

People like reading about entities that are alive. This has been true throughout the entire known history of human storytelling. Why do you think our ancestors personalized the mountains and the trees and the oceans? Because the stories they told were more interesting that way and because, as humans, we tend to see humanity wherever we look. When we talk about our cats, we talk about them as if they have human thoughts and feelings. (Ack! I can hear the unanimous cry of the cat-lovers now wailing at me that cats *do* have human thoughts and feelings.) Hey, I talk to my cat, too. It's a human thing to do. People tend to humanize everything. Not all people, of course. But the more imaginative a person is, the more likely they are to humanize the world around them. And coincidentally, the more likely they are to read lots of fiction.

Whatever conflict you have in your novel, that conflict will be more interesting and appeal to a wider range of people if it's personalized. That's because, for most of us, people are more interesting than things. But it goes well beyond that. Here are just a few of the advantages you get by having a villain in your novel:

- Focuses the conflict
- Villains are more dangerous than nature or society
- Sequels are more likely to feature existing villains than existing nature or society conflicts

Villains can be defeated. Society and nature can't, at least not in their entirety. Because of this, the conflict in any novel can easily be more focused with a villain to personalize that conflict than it ever could be without a villain. Novels featuring a conflict against society or nature typically try to mimic this effect by focusing on a particular, easily definable part of nature or society. That's why "stranded on an island" stories (and now "stranded on Mars" stories) are popular. They allow the author to create a single obstacle. Defeat that obstacle (escape the island, escape Mars) and the conflict is resolved. Man vs. himself novels are unique beasts all to themselves and beyond the scope of this book. They operate under their own rules, but put simply, you can't wholeheartedly cheer for the hero and root against the villain if they're the same person and personality.

Nature and society can't immediately respond to a hero's efforts to solve a problem. They don't react by throwing obstacles in the hero's way the instant she starts to make some progress. Human villains can and often do. That makes villains into much more dangerous foes. That increases conflict. In turn, this allows an author to take luck out of the equation. If your hero's intention is to climb a mountain, the novel is only interesting when the weather and the mountain fail to cooperate. If he's a competent hero, he's brought along climbing gear and he knows how to climb. Conflict arises only from bad luck. A sudden storm appears. A rope breaks. An avalanche comes tumbling down the mountain and buries them all. In contrast, villains by design attempt to thwart the hero. If you have a villain around, problems aren't always based on bad luck. The villain could have hacked into the weather system and created a faulty forecast. He sabotaged the rope. He exploded dynamite causing the avalanche. Fighting the elements is interesting, but fighting the elements and a villain is nearly always more interesting.

What about sequels? The easiest path to success given today's readers is by writing sequels. Nature and society conflicts (without villains) don't lend themselves to sequels. This isn't Gilligan's Island.

When the castaways escape the island, they don't magically go back. In your first novel, if your hero overcomes the natural barrier or manages to change society for the better, that's usually it. Sequels become trite, implausible, or downright ridiculous. But villains can be defeated without being killed. In the Harry Potter series, J. K. Rowling had Harry thwart Voldemort at the end of four of the six novels before his final defeat in novel seven. As the novels progressed, the defeats became less about Voldemort's plans being thwarted and more about Harry escaping certain death. The advantage is that— after the first novel—J. K. Rowling's readers understood the character of Voldemort and the danger he presented. That allows for a deeper, more dramatic, more meaningful story in less pages. That increases reader excitement and tends to allow for much better series of novels that retain their popularity over time.

I admit that you don't absolutely need a villain, but if you have a novel that works if you personalize the conflict with the hero, why not use the advantages a villain provides?

Redeemed Villain, Fallen Hero

A character that has the traits described above might seem like some kind of super hero (or super villain). This isn't the case at all. While I state that heroes generally are selfless and villains are selfish, this is just Character Building 101. Heroes are allowed to be selfish at times, especially when it comes to traits secondary to the main goal. For example, Sherlock Holmes was often a very selfish person. Scarlett O'Hara is the classic example of a selfish heroine. She always thought she was acting for herself, but it was precisely her naïveté concerning how much she helped others that makes her a heroine rather than a villain. While she barely mentioned the many kindnesses she thoughtlessly and instinctively performed for others, she often chastised herself for acting selfishly and constantly rationalized her selfish behavior. This apparent selfishness gives her the appearance of a villain. It's only by reading between the lines and acknowledging that Scarlett was doing the best she could that she becomes a hero.

By altering the subtlety of a character's actions and motivations, you can alter the degree to which a character is obviously a hero or obviously a villain. This provides a great deal of freedom.

What you don't want to do is craft a novel where your readers don't know whether to cheer for or against your main character, even if that confusion exists for just a single chapter. If you insist on writing a first novel with such a character and it gets published, either you're as talented as you think you are or you benefited from a happy accident. If you simply must write such a novel—if the passion for your story is so strong that it overcomes logic and common sense—then by all means write the novel. But don't lie to yourself. If the story's not that powerful—if you're not writing the next *Gone with the Wind*—you should reconsider the mistake you're about to make.

A special instance of creating main characters who are either heroes or villains allows for your heroes to become villains and your villains to become heroes. This is an advanced technique when the converted character's your main protagonist or even your main antagonist. In the *Star Wars* trilogy, for example, Darth Vader is evil for nearly three complete movies. At the end of the third movie, he becomes a redeemed hero. What's worth noting is that he also immediately becomes uninteresting—which is probably the real reason he dies. This is common. The lack of interest—not the dying. Convert your hero to a villain or your villain to a hero and most of the time you've just decreased your reader's interest in that character. You, as the writer, might be completely fascinated with the change, but if this is the only way for you to generate interest in your own story, maybe you need to consider writing a different novel.

Some common guidelines to consider if you simply must have a redeemed villain or a hero who stumbles and falls:

- If the character's not the main protagonist or the main villain, and especially if you don't focus on the change from villain to hero or vice-versa, then have your way with him. Even in *Star Wars*, Darth Vader had fallen from his perch as the main antagonist by the time he made his conversion. Conversions by secondary villains—especially after being betrayed by the primary villain—are quite common.
- Each of your characters is only allowed one conversion per novel. Typically this conversion will come at the beginning of the novel or at the end.

- If the conversion comes at the end of the novel, the character often dies as a result—or lives happily ever after (as with Ebenezer Scrooge). Either way, readers instinctively recognize that such a core change in a main character should lead to broad sweeping results in the character's life. Many times, if a conversion occurs at the beginning of the novel, it forms a major part of the Big Bang.

Like nearly all my rules in this book, these guidelines aren't absolute. If you think of an interesting and effective way to go against these recommendations, do so. Just don't go against them for the sake of going against them.

Too Much Terminology

For those of you who aspire to be English majors, you should note that I've butchered the long held beast of character terminology. We haven't talked about protagonists, antagonists, deuteragonists, tritagonists, focal characters, foil characters, narrators, anti-heroes, or any of the other technical name calling that makes certain literary folks so happy. If you want to know what these terms are, go look them up. Better yet, find me at a convention or other public appearance and ask me. I'll be happy to talk to you about terminology *ad nauseam*. I don't have anything against using exact terminology, but I tend to avoid it when possible.

While knowing the terminology inside and out may be useful to your ability to speak intelligently with other writers (or English teachers), that knowledge won't help you write a great novel. That's why I've twisted the classic meanings of hero and villain. Heroes are characters you want to win. Villains are characters you want to lose. Heroes are typically decent folks. Villains are typically a bit (or very) nasty. If you're writing a novel and you want your readers to love the finished product, you nearly always want them to feel strongly about your main characters, either for or against. That means your main character is usually a determined and likable hero who's going against an equally determined but morally corrupt villain.

Viewpoint Characters

In most good novels, the reader doesn't get to see through the eyes of every character—or even through the eyes of most characters. As a result, our story is shaped as much by the person telling the story as it is by the characters that populate our fictional world and the events that take place there. These viewpoint characters may be heroes or villains. They might be main characters, secondary characters, tertiary characters, or pure narrators who play no part in the story at all. What differentiates a viewpoint character from a non-viewpoint character is that viewpoint characters provide a window through which we see our novel's world. For example:

> Cathy walked into the classroom. Jeff raised his head at the squeak of the door.

Given these two sentences alone, we don't have a viewpoint character because the reader's unable to pinpoint which character is telling the story. But what if we add this?

> He had never seen Cathy look so mad.

Or this?

> She'd expected to find the classroom empty. Now what would she do?

The first example would shift the scene to Jeff's point-of-view, making him the viewpoint character. The second example makes it clear that Cathy's the one telling us the story.

Know Your Viewpoint

Most readers pay little attention to who's telling the story. They're focused on the story and the characters. But they sense when you don't have control. Editors not only notice but also tend to reach for a rejection slip.

If you're going to maintain control of your viewpoint, you first have to know how to recognize a viewpoint. In the above examples, when we see inside Jeff's head, we're in his point-of-view. When we get Cathy's thoughts, we're in her point-of-view. Check out this example, which combines the examples above:

> Cathy walked into the classroom. Jeff raised his head at the squeak of the door. She'd expected to find the classroom empty. Now what would she do? Jeff had never seen Cathy look so mad.

At first we hop into Cathy's head, which means we're telling the story from her point-of-view. Then we reveal something that only Jeff could know, meaning we've jumped to his point-of-view. This is generally called **head-hopping** (or more technically referred to as an unnecessary viewpoint switch).

Did you feel the vertigo as you read the passage? Perhaps not, but to a professional writer, this passage reads like fingernails scraping across a chalkboard. If you didn't notice, it's probably because this is just an example and you're not deeply involved in any story. As readers, we live inside the skin of our viewpoint character. If you forcibly jerk a reader out of one character's skin and shove them roughly into another's, they notice, whether they've ever heard of viewpoint or not.

This is why writers stay in one viewpoint for an entire scene, chapter, or part of a book. They switch viewpoint from one character to another only at the break between these easily identifiable sections. Switching only at these breaks allows readers to take a breath before proceeding. They're expecting something new. If they find themselves living inside a different character's skin, they may not like it, but it doesn't give them that disjointed sense of vertigo.

Keeping viewpoints straight is a basic skill, but failing to keep them straight drops one of those giant boulders in your wagon that will keep you from getting published. That's because editors see this problem daily. To an editor, head-hopping screams, "No control!" It makes rejecting the manuscript easy. So why is it so hard to keep viewpoints straight? Maybe this example will help.

> Cathy walked into the classroom. Jeff raised his head at the squeak of the door. Jeff had never seen Cathy look so mad. She'd

> expected to find the classroom empty. Now
> what would she do?

To some people, especially editors expecting to find head-hopping in a beginner's manuscript, this example screams out as strongly as the other. But to readers who've been in Jeff's point-of-view for half a chapter, this is a problem that's often overlooked. That's because they pull Cathy's thoughts out of her head and drop them into Jeff's. He's their viewpoint character. He's the one telling the story. When he says, "She'd expected to find the classroom empty. Now what would she do?" it means that he read the expression on her face and figured it out. That's a cop-out that editors don't fall for, but it's one of the reasons why writers keep making viewpoint mistakes. These writers either make the same switch as the typical reader or they don't realize head-hopping is bad. Then the rejection letter comes back with no explanation and they wonder why no one recognizes their awesome story for what it is.

To Hop or Not To Hop?

Part of the reason doing viewpoints correctly remains a constant source of trouble for beginning writers is that they don't accept the admonition not to do it. "Why can't you just jump into anybody's head you want?" they ask. Here's the trick. You can. But you need to do so intentionally. Otherwise you've lost control of your writing. Besides the vertigo that often comes with head-hopping or the confusion that results when readers attribute omnipotent powers to your main viewpoint character, you also lose emotional power when you head-hop. In response, readers put your book down (or they don't buy the next one you write). Often, they're not sure why they don't like the book—but they don't.

Why is that? Why do you gain more emotional power from a single viewpoint than you do from multiple viewpoints?

The greatest emotional power a story can have comes from creating a shared experience with your reader. They feel what the viewpoint character feels. If you're feeding them different emotions because those emotions have many different and alternating sources, then you're going to be invoking a rapidly changing set of different emotions—or little emotion because whatever you're trying to generate is lost in the confusing signals.

Every time a writer switches viewpoints, the connection between reader and viewpoint character is lost. Even when done correctly without head-hopping, switching viewpoints requires a disconnect and a reconnect by the reader. This action takes them out of the story. How much it takes them out of the story depends on how deep their connection was to the viewpoint character. That's why having a single viewpoint allows you to invoke greater emotions in your reader; the connection you form between the reader and the viewpoint character can be much deeper. If you try to form a connection that deep between a reader and a viewpoint character, then jerk them out of it and stuff them into another viewpoint, you risk losing the reader to vertigo, confusion, or just plain apathy.

That's why writers of epic novels, sweeping historical novels, hard science-fiction novels, and many other novel genres can get away with more viewpoint switches than writers in other genres. Whenever the story steals the spotlight from the characters and the emotional response in the reader is triggered more by the story's events than by the character who experiences those events, then head-hopping can work. These kinds of novels (epic, sweeping historical, hard sf, etc.) also demonstrate when frequent viewpoint switches are worth the emotional loss. Having many viewpoint characters allows you to have a broader, more flexible stage. Instead of one window on your world, your reader is given many windows. You gain the power of knowledge, but you sacrifice the power of emotion.

So why do beginning writers so often resort to head-hopping? They're trying to recreate the power of knowledge that comes from switching viewpoints properly but they end up dropping into any character's head that can provide a bit of fluff that they want to poke into the reader's brain. It's a beginning technique in part because writers who head-hop rarely get published and because experienced writers know it's not necessary. Take our well-worn example from earlier:

> Cathy walked into the classroom. Jeff raised his head at the squeak of the door.

> Jeff had never seen Cathy look so mad. She'd expected to find the classroom empty. Now what would she do?

This is an easy fix, provided we're in Jeff's point-of-view:

> Jeff raised his head at the squeak of the door. Cathy walked into the classroom. He had never seen her look so mad. What had she expected to find? An empty classroom? Now what would she do?

This doesn't convey the exact same information that head-hopping would convey—remember, we lose knowledge when we stay in one viewpoint—but it keeps the reader where they should be, which is living inside Jeff's skin. If the reader needs to know a fact, generally the viewpoint character needs to know that same fact. Stated more clearly, if the viewpoint character's not allowed to know a fact that you think the reader needs to know, then you're probably wrong. Tons of exceptions disprove this, but not in emotionally-driven stories where the reader's connection to the character is more important than the story. I'm sure you could invent one if you tried, but if you were that inventive, I'm sure you could also invent a viewpoint that would allow the reader to know facts conveyed by the viewpoint character without his conscious knowledge.

In the revised example above, you'll also notice that we use more pronouns. Having only one viewpoint character tends to allow a greater use of pronouns. We use more pronouns because doing so forms a closer emotional connection to your reader. Names are formal. Pronouns are informal. You never want to confuse the reader by using pronouns, but if the scene makes just as much sense with pronouns as it does proper names, use pronouns whenever you're looking for greater emotional punch.

Viewpoint Character Wanted: Apply Within

Viewpoint characters color what we hear, see, taste, touch, and smell. They also define our moral boundaries. If we're writing a story from a hooker's point-of-view, having sex with a john is a tedious chore and part of life's daily routine. If we inhabit the life of an armed bank robber, murder might be an occasional necessity—or it might not. A soldier sees a battle differently than a refugee. As a result, the viewpoint characters you choose give you the power to tell your story but they also limit the story you can tell.

So what qualities should a good viewpoint character possess? In my opinion, every great viewpoint character (who is also a main character in your story)[6] should have the following qualities:

- Can tell the story you want to tell
- Is someone the reader can identify with
- Is a good hero or villain
- Is someone you (the author) can readily identify with

Let's break these down in a bit more detail.

<u>Can tell the story you want to tell</u>

Viewpoint characters are worthless if they have no way to communicate. While they typically focus this communication on their own senses, thoughts, and feelings, this isn't always the case. One of the most famous examples of this is Dr. Watson, who focuses on the actions and struggles of Sherlock Holmes. Regardless of where his focus lies, a good viewpoint character is articulate. If a viewpoint character can't describe what he feels or senses in a clear and interesting way, readers will be unable or unwilling to share in the experiences presented.

A viewpoint character's ability to communicate goes deeper than just being able to put words on the page. Viewpoint characters typically supply the emotional energy that drives your story forward. Many of my beginning writing students employ a viewpoint character who's a cold fish. When I encourage them to employ a viewpoint character that's more emotionally driven, they almost always explain that this particular character isn't an emotional sort. My response: "Then choose a different viewpoint character or fix this one." (Ya, I'm a hard-ass.) Your reader experiences the story through your viewpoint character. If your viewpoint character's never moved by emotion then your reader won't be, either.

---

6. Tertiary characters and pure narrators are not involved in the story. As such, the only quality they must possess is the ability to tell the story.

Because your viewpoint character needs to care about the world he inhabits and the situations he experiences, a reader's perception of the character and the character's world is distinctly shaded by that character's presentation of the scene at hand. While it's usually desirable to slant the reader's view of the world by filtering it through the eyes of your viewpoint character, the perception of the viewpoint character is also altered by that view. The viewpoint character's descriptions and feelings aid the reader in deciphering clues about that character's abilities, beliefs, and charisma. This is why it's often easier to maintain a character's villainy if that character's not a viewpoint character. If we have an articulate villain, his view of the world becomes our view of the world and we risk having the villain become a hero. One way to prevent that is to communicate the villain's thoughts and desires through his actions, his creations, and the thoughts of others about him rather than through his personal viewpoint. Not that there's anything wrong with a viewpoint villain—far from it—but be aware of the villainous charisma you create.

Some stories must be told from a newcomer's view. This is nearly always important with fantasy and science-fiction stories, but it crops up in any story that requires the writer to give a great deal of background information to the reader. Typically this is accomplished by having a newcomer in an otherwise established world. A classic example is Moby Dick. Ishmael has been to sea before, but he's never served aboard a whaling vessel. This allows him to be reasonably fascinated and inquisitive with everything around him. A more modern example is Harry Potter. As a newcomer to the wizarding world, it's expected and reasonable that other characters will explain the reality of this magical world (and as a result, explain that reality to the reader as well). Instead of using a viewpoint character who's a newcomer, you can also explain your world by using a non-viewpoint character who acts as an ignorant foil and requires detailed explanations, but doing so isn't as effective as using a newcomer. The ignorance of such a character will eventually generate feelings of impatience in your viewpoint character. Since the reader's just as ignorant as this character, you risk alienating your reader by having your viewpoint character express impatience with that ignorance. That's why so many stories have an inexperienced or newly arrived viewpoint character. Any confusion or curiosity felt is shared by the reader.

In addition to all the qualities already mentioned, viewpoint characters can only tell stories they're morally capable of living. In *Gone with the Wind*, Margaret Mitchell took a huge risk by using Scarlett O'Hara as her main viewpoint character. Scarlett is not a nice character. She's a character many readers can't identify with naturally. Why use such a character? The answer is relatively simple: Margaret Mitchell had no choice. If she used a more compassionate, traditional southerner (such as Melanie Wilkes), she couldn't describe the Old South in such a pragmatic, realistic way—and she very much wanted to tell the story of the Old South from a true southern aristocrat's point-of-view without being limited by that same point-of-view. Scarlett O-Hara allowed her to do that. Using Scarlett also allowed her viewpoint character to participate in a relationship with a strong, insightful male lead like Rhett Butler from a position of strength rather than simple compliance, which would have been the standard burden of a southern woman at the time.

Is someone the reader can identify with

Typically, it's easy to identify with characters you like, so if you want your readers to identify with your viewpoint character, create a character that's as likable as you can make her. That generally doesn't mean the character's completely noble with no faults. Likable doesn't necessarily mean nice.

This is not as simple as it sounds. For example, I have many writer friends who think Harry Potter is an arrogant, spoiled git, and they have no interest in him whatsoever. It comes as no surprise that most of these folks don't like the series of Harry Potter books. The fact that J. K. Rowling has sold an estimated 400 – 500 million (and climbing) Harry Potter books probably says more about my writer friends and less about how likable Harry is to the general public. Since creating a likable character is so much a matter of taste, what qualities besides likability should your viewpoint character possess?

For a reader to identify with your main character, they first must understand that character's motivations, setting, and problems. For example, a villain who wants to set off a nuclear device in Detroit just in case his Aunt Marge happens to be passing through during detonation is probably not a character most readers could identify with. Readers don't need to agree with the decisions made by your viewpoint character, but they must understand those decisions. When your viewpoint character makes decisions contrary to what most of your readers would like to think they would make in the same circumstances, those decisions should be rationalized, either through dialogue, narration, or previous reader experience within the current novel or series. Your viewpoint character's recognition that his actions aren't normal helps the reader identify with that character because it places the viewpoint character and the reader within the same moral framework.

Is a good hero or villain

Being a good hero or villain means your viewpoint characters will be passionate, active, capable, interesting, and believable. It also means the reader should be hoping for their success or failure. For more details about these traits, see the previous section "Heroes and Villains".

Is someone you (the author) can readily identify with

This may sound like a strange requirement, but all the characters we create must live somewhere within us, even if their stay is only temporary. If you as an author can't readily identify with your main viewpoint character, you'll find it extremely tough to write your story—or worse, you'll end up creating an unbelievable story because you can't fully grasp your viewpoint character but your readers can. In the first case, the writing is extraordinarily difficult because the mindset of a viewpoint character won't come naturally no matter how hard you try.

I once wrote a story from the viewpoint of an elderly woman who was raised Catholic but converted to the Methodist faith as an adult. She was judgmental, irritable, and a lousy cook. I didn't think I'd have a problem slipping on her skin, especially for a short story. After all, I was raised Methodist, I've dated a few Catholics, and I can certainly be judgmental and irritable. Apparently, it was the lousy cook part that I just couldn't grasp because every time I forced myself inside her head, I lost all desire to write. I did eventually write THE END to that particular story—and I even sold it shortly thereafter—but I'd never choose to go down that road again. You can write a story where you can't readily identify with your viewpoint character, but not without much wailing and gnashing of teeth.[7]

The second possibility—that you're not capable of getting inside the head of your viewpoint character but think you can—is much more problematic. A writer friend of mine once suffered this fate. She's one of those truly sweet souls. While she believes she's rough around the edges, in reality she lives in a world filled with incessant optimism and quirky humor. While she knows bad people exist, she either's never been close to one or she's consciously blocked all emotional connection to the event. As a result, when she attempted to get into the head of a truly nasty gang leader, she failed miserably. In her mind, this villain was indeed horrible and evil. She couldn't see that she'd created the fluffy bunny of villains and refused to believe me when I pointed it out. It's just that she's such a good person at heart she can't imagine the true evil she wanted to create.

Of course I might have been wrong. Maybe her fluffy bunny really would have come across as evil to most readers.

Such situations are always tricky. I've often been told that I couldn't write about a character. Not because someone had read a passage from the viewpoint character and told me I got it wrong, but because they'd looked at who I was—a middle-aged white male—and insisted that I couldn't write a story from a female point-of-view, from a Native American point-of-view, from an elderly point-of-view, from a dog's point-of-view (yes, I have such a story!), etc. When people say you can't write from a particular viewpoint for reasons related to natural prejudice or politics, I'd ignore that advice. When another writer who has no such prejudices but who's much closer to your intended viewpoint character than you can ever be gives the same advice, it's at least worth soliciting a few more opinions.

---

7. If you don't have problems, then maybe you just *think* you don't identify with that particular character. None of us likes to admit we can readily identify with a child molester or a serial killer, but identifying with one doesn't mean becoming one or agreeing with one.

Choose your Family

They say you can choose your friends, but you can't choose your family. Obviously *they* weren't writers. Your viewpoint characters not only supply windows through which your readers see your world, but they also decide what you, the writer, can tell about that world and how you can tell it. And you never know. If you write a best-selling novel, you might just create a viewpoint character that you live with for the next fifty years. So choose your viewpoint characters like you'd choose a new member of your family. It can be a life-changing decision.

Viewpoint

I covered what makes a good viewpoint character in the last section, but I barely mentioned viewpoints. I hesitate to talk about viewpoints because it's nearly impossible to talk about point-of-view in general without buying admission to the terminology tent. It should be clear from the last section that viewpoint means the point-of-view from which you tell the story. What may be less clear is that you don't need to get inside anybody's head to tell a story from a particular person's point of view. Most movies are told from a limited set of viewpoints, but rarely do we hear any person's thoughts directly. Viewpoint is instead revealed through dialogue, actions, blocking, direction, and cinematography.

Modern genre fiction is dominated by two viewpoint types: 1) Third Person (He, She) and 2) First Person (I), so we'll spend most of our time talking about them. Regardless which viewpoint type you employ, viewpoint is set not only by the pronouns you use but also by the character's perspective of the world around him. While pronoun choice isn't the deciding factor, if you tell your story using third-person pronouns (he, she, it), then you're typically using a third-person viewpoint.

> Justine pursed her lips, and then frowned. How could Jacob ignore her? She'd taken this stupid class just so she'd have the chance to talk to him, but even though she'd smiled at him twice since the bell rang, he had yet to speak to her. Gathering her courage, she cleared her throat. When he glanced up, she fluttered her eyelashes and forced her face into what she knew was her prettiest smile. "I can't figure out question 17. Do you think you could take a look at it and tell me what I'm doing wrong?"

If you tell your story using a first-person pronoun (I), then you're almost always using a first-person viewpoint. But the story you tell changes in more ways than the pronoun you use, as you'll see by comparing the two examples.

> I frowned. How could Jacob ignore me? I'd taken this stupid class just so I'd have the chance to talk to him, but even though I'd smiled at him twice since the bell rang, he had yet to speak to me. If we were ever going to be a couple, I'd have to make the first move. I cleared my throat. When he glanced up, I smiled as sweetly as I could and said, "I can't figure out question 17. Do you think you could take a look at it and tell me what I'm doing wrong?"

The different pronouns and associated verb conjugations are obvious differences, but why did I alter the prose in other ways?

In real life, if a girl walks up to you and tells you that she's smart, pretty, and has the best fashion sense in her entire high school, you'll probably doubt her claims, at best. At worst, you might decide she's a conceited jerk and quit listening to anything else she has to say. But if your best friend walks up to you and tells you that the new girl is smart, pretty, and has the best fashion sense in the whole school, your reaction would be completely different. This is part of what I mean when I say that viewpoint is set not only by the pronouns you use but also by the character's perspective of the world.

That's why Justine in less conniving in the second example. She frowns rather than pursing her lips and frowning. She smiles as sweetly as she can rather than fluttering her eyelashes and smiling in an obviously practiced way. You can have Justine perform the same actions in the second example as the first, but doing so produces a stronger negative impression of Justine. That's because using first person binds your reader more tightly to your viewpoint character. This tends to exaggerate the emotions the character feels. This is a desirable trait most of the time, but you need to be aware of this effect if you're going to produce the impression you want.

It's this tight binding between reader and viewpoint character that prompts me to reveal more of Justine's thought processes rather than simply saying she gathers her courage. Some authors would argue that we should always see these thought processes (part of the "show, don't tell" philosophy), but one of the advantages of using a third-person viewpoint is these shortcuts. They should be used with care—showing is usually better—but they can be used. In comparison, if Justine says in first person, "I gathered my courage," it comes across as forced and produces a distance between the first-person viewpoint and the reader. That defeats part of the purpose for using a first-person viewpoint. That doesn't keep writers from using these shortcuts in the first person, but that's why it's important to understand why you're using a particular viewpoint.

The differences illustrated by these examples produce a small result individually, but when these small differences are compounded over an entire novel, the overall effect is significant. Each viewpoint type has its advantages and its disadvantages. You can certainly pick a viewpoint just because it feels comfortable, but you should be wary of doing so. It's a bit like wearing shorts, flip-flops, and a T-shirt to prom. You might be extremely comfortable, but you might not achieve the effect you'd like.

Third Person

Knowledge is power. Using a third-person viewpoint typically provides more opportunities to convey factual information to the reader without having that information overshadowed by the character's emotional state. By definition, third-person viewpoint is one person (the writer or narrator) telling us (the reader) about another person. That distance between the person telling the story and the object of the story makes it easier to convey objective information about our characters and our world without becoming unnatural. It also allows us to take shortcuts by logically summarizing emotional states rather than revealing them. These two traits are illustrated in the examples with Justine.

Since a third-person viewpoint is more disconnected than a first-person viewpoint, we can switch between viewpoint characters more easily. The closer the connection a reader has to a character, the greater the chance of losing that reader when you switch viewpoints. Also, if *I* am telling you a story, then it's a bit of a shock when *I* suddenly vanish and get replaced by either a different *I* or by a third-person viewpoint.

Third-person viewpoints are naturally more precise and descriptive than first-person viewpoints. The language-dictated space between narrator and viewpoint character allows for cleaner and more direct prose. It also allows for greater expression of language, which tends to produce more eloquent and fluent prose. While it's feasible than your first-person narrator might say something as flowery as "All our words are but crumbs that fall down from the feast of the mind," it's not considered normal speech for a hard-nosed Chicago police detective or a mask-wearing serial murderer (or many other genre protagonists). Using a third-person viewpoint allows you to go beyond the language your viewpoint character possesses. You might wish to avoid going so far afield because the further your prose deviates from the natural language of your viewpoint character, the greater the emotional distance you create—but at least you have the option.

Close In or Back Off

Part of the power of using a third-person viewpoint comes from its flexibility. As the writer you set the distance between your reader and your viewpoint character. This distance can be great or nearly as small as a first-person viewpoint. The factors that control this distance are summarized below:

- Language: The closer your prose comes to matching the character's natural speech, the closer the connection between reader and viewpoint character.
- Viewpoint switches: As you increase the number of evenly distributed viewpoint characters, you also increase the distance between the reader and any given character. By evenly distributed, I mean that each of your viewpoint characters has significant time on stage. For example, if you start out with one viewpoint character but then spend the rest of the novel with a single viewpoint character, the connection between your long-term character and a single viewpoint character is similar.
- Perspective: The closer the knowledge and opinions of your viewpoint character come to matching the knowledge and

opinions expressed in the prose, the closer the connection between your reader and the viewpoint character.

The connection between reader and viewpoint character isn't necessarily fixed throughout the entire novel. You can gradually close in and back off as the novel progresses. Typically connections are looser at the beginning of a novel than they are at the climactic scene.

<u>Summary</u>

The advantages of using a third-person viewpoint versus using a first-person viewpoint are:

- Convey additional information
- Present information more objectively
- Switch viewpoint characters with less danger of losing the reader
- Employ more complex and articulate language without requiring a matching viewpoint character
- Control the closeness of the connection between your reader and your viewpoint character

First Person

In general, the advantages provided by using a third-person viewpoint are disadvantages when using a first-person viewpoint. Rather than regurgitating those and calling them disadvantages, I'll concentrate here on what's gained by using a first-person viewpoint. Be aware, though, that advantages of one viewpoint type tend to be disadvantages of the other.

Employing a first-person viewpoint character provides an easy and reliable way to bring your reader into your story, provided the reader can identify with your viewpoint character. While it's usually best to have a viewpoint character that your reader identifies with, this need increases when you use a first-person viewpoint. That's because a first-person viewpoint forces the reader into the mind of your viewpoint character. That's much easier to do if the reader goes willingly. However, sometimes using a viewpoint character readers don't identify with is done out of necessity—*Lolita* comes to mind. If Vladimir Nabokov had used a third person to tell the story of pedophile Humbert Humbert, readers would have been better able to maintain their distance, but he didn't want them to be able to maintain that distance. Using an unlikable first-person viewpoint character in this way requires more skill—this is certainly true with *Lolita*—but sometimes it's necessary to tell the story you want to tell.

Using a first-person viewpoint also allows you to naturally limit the information you convey. Because you tie the reader to the viewpoint character's window on the world, you're allowed to state information that isn't accurate or complete but is what the character believes. While you can invent clever ways to get information that you need into your story without leaving your first-person viewpoint, it seems quite natural for your reader to discover facts as your viewpoint character discovers them. This makes it easy to conceal information from the reader until you give your viewpoint character a reason to discover that information. Why would you want to conceal information? Mystery novels come immediately to mind. You, as the author, know who the guilty party is before the reader's finished page one—but your first-person viewpoint character doesn't know. While it's true that your third-person viewpoint character doesn't know either, it's slightly less natural to conceal the information since someone else (who does know) is telling the story. This is one of the reasons why so many mysteries are written in first person.

Another reason many mysteries are written in first person is that most of these stories take place in the here and now. Compare that to historical romances, which by definition involve people who live at some past time. If your dialogue is colored with thee's and thou's or other archaic language, it's unnatural to have a first-person casual narrator—and using a more formal narrator who works with the language of the time makes the novel a much more difficult and typically less appealing read. What this means is that the **language** in first-person novels is typically easier to write. I'm not saying that first-person novels are easier to write, but if you can use a natural voice, the prose is easier. This doesn't mean that a first-person novel is less work, just that you can spend more time figuring out how to get the information into the book and less time figuring out how to say it.

Above all other factors, first person shines best at creating greater emotional impact. This is partly due to the close connection between reader and viewpoint character that we've already mentioned, but mostly the difference comes from the personal nature of first person versus third person.

> I stood mesmerized. I'd read about the Tyrannosaurus rex in books. I'd seen artist renderings. But when I craned my neck and stared at the enormous head forty feet above me, when I saw the saliva glistening on the eight-inch teeth, when the tremor rippled beneath me as the giant beast shifted its weight, only then did I understand. And I don't mind telling you, if I hadn't been so scared I couldn't move, I'd have been running like hell.

Compare that to:

> Jack stood mesmerized. He'd read about the Tyrannosaurus rex in books. He's seen artist renderings. But when he craned his neck and stared at the enormous head forty feet above him, when he saw the saliva glistening on the eight-inch teeth, when the tremor rippled beneath him as the giant beast shifted its weight, only then did he understand. And if he hadn't been so scared he couldn't move, he'd have been running like hell.

The second example is more detached and less immediate. Blame it on the Me generation or on survival of the fittest, but as humans, we're programmed to respond to first person differently than third person.

Summary

The advantages of using a first-person viewpoint versus using a third-person viewpoint are:

- Limit information in a more natural way
- Draw readers into a story more easily
- Create prose more easily
- Produce greater emotional impact

Combining Third and First: Wait a Second

Some enterprising writers have sold novels that feature both third person and first person in the same book. Generally these authors follow the accepted custom for switching viewpoints in these novels, but even then, mixing viewpoint types like this is typically more of a literary trick than a useful technique. It adds a rock to your wagon that's best avoided unless you have a good reason for using it. If you want to change it from a rock to a boulder, combine both first person and third person, and past and present tense.

Generally a story works best if it's first person or third person, but not both. To decide which viewpoint you should use, examine the strengths of each and decide which set of strengths is needed for your story. If you need both, you probably should attempt to tell your story using third person, immediate. All that means is that you tie your third-person viewpoint as tightly to your viewpoint character as you can. When you need to deviate from this close connection, deviate. Most readers will accept that without too much problem. And who knows? By the time you finish the novel, you might realize you don't need most of the parts that fell outside that immediate viewpoint.

Mr. Know-it-all

Beyond first and third person, the most common viewpoint is an omnipotent viewpoint. Many writers call this omniscient, the difference being that they're uncomfortable attributing omnipotence to non-deities, but in my version of Oz, the writer is God for the purposes of writing a novel. Regardless which word you use, the difference between an omnipotent viewpoint and a third-person viewpoint is that **the omnipotent viewpoint has the flexibility to reveal facts that the viewpoint character doesn't know**. These can be facts about the world, events in nature that no one witnesses (such as the birth of a volcano before humanity existed), and facts about a character that even that character doesn't know.

Many writers slip into an omnipotent point-of-view by design or by accident at the end of a chapter in an attempt to create an artificial cliffhanger.

> If only Sally knew then that she would
> never see Billy alive again, she wouldn't have
> flipped him off as he walked away.

Personally I'd recommend avoiding this obvious cheat, but writers have been using it successfully for centuries. Technically this is an example of an omnipotent viewpoint, but novels with a few instances of this aren't thought of as being written with that omnipotent viewpoint.

Use of an omnipotent viewpoint by design tends to show up mostly in epic novels. When a novel spans generations, having an omnipotent viewpoint provides a consistent thread that ties together the various viewpoints that are required to tell such a story. Omnipotent viewpoints are also often used for novels that involve a great deal of technical information (including world-building) or a large number of relatively equally important characters. A famous example of this would be *The Lord of the Rings*.

The main advantage in using an omnipotent viewpoint is that you can convey information without restriction based on viewpoint. This provides a great deal of power. The disadvantage of using an omnipotent viewpoint is that you need to work harder to create a connection between your reader and your viewpoint characters.

Most of the novels produced today that use omnipotent viewpoint have a connection between the reader and the viewpoint character that fluctuates. While entire sections exist with little to no viewpoint, other sections are written in pure third person. Controlling viewpoints to this extent generally requires more experience and control than most first-time writers can muster, but if you're one of those writers and you have a sweeping tale that would be better told through an omnipotent viewpoint, you shouldn't be afraid to use it.

A Different Point-of-view

All viewpoints beyond first, third, and omnipotent are niche viewpoints. Some of these viewpoint types include second person, epistolary, first person plural, and third person plural. You should be able to guess at the first person and third person plural forms: The viewpoint character is actually a group of characters. Many times these plural viewpoints have a shared consciousness and rarely is the entire novel told from this plural viewpoint. For a second person viewpoint, the story is told by revealing what *you* do. Since you know *you* are not actually living the story and since you probably wouldn't make the decisions or take the actions as they're told to you, it becomes a much less believable story. Epistolary novels are told through letters or other written forms of communication. A modern but not particularly well known example of this is Denise Mina's novel *Sanctum* (*Deception* as published in the U.S.) where the novel is supposed to be the main viewpoint character's verbatim electronic journal that he entered on his wife's computer. Judging by the extreme mixed reactions this novel received among many readers, it's clear that not only are epistolary novels harder to write but also they're harder to read. Personally *Sanctum* is one of my favorite novels, as is another famous epistolary novel: *Dracula* by Bram Stoker. If you feel the need to tell your story in this way, I'd strongly recommend reading as many of these novels as you can find before you make the attempt.

Overall these other points of view shouldn't be used unless you have a strong reason for doing so. All are viable but all require an additional degree of skill. If you choose to write your first novel using one of these viewpoint types, you're placing a large rock in your wagon, but if you go into it with open eyes, all are viable viewpoint types.

A Tense Note

For too long to contemplate, works of fiction have been written in past tense. He said, she said, they went, the dog barfed, etc. Lately several authors have made good money writing books in present tense. *The Hunger Games* and *California Fire and Life* come to mind. *One Flew over the Cuckoo's Nest* is a classic example. There's nothing inherently wrong with writing in present tense, but I wouldn't recommend it as a style statement. It's one of those rocks that will make your wagon harder to haul up that traditional publishing hill. Sometimes the need for present tense will be worth the weight it carries. Certainly with *Cuckoo's Nest,* the unusual use of the present tense helped add a surrealism to the tale since it was told by a viewpoint character with mental health issues. I don't know what reasons Suzanne Collins or Don Winslow might have cited for using present tense—maybe they just liked it—but as you can tell, it didn't hurt their sales any.

I include mention of tense here because the tense your viewpoint character uses is meaningful. That's why it should fit your story and your viewpoint character. I recommend using past tense except where present tense is needed, but I'm probably just old-fashioned.

Characters Types

No, we're not talking here about the sultry seductress, the hard-boiled cop, or the absent-minded professor. Those are character stereotypes, not character types. What we're covering here would be more accurately called character levels:

* Main   * Secondary   * Tertiary

Some people call these major characters and minor characters. Or viewpoint characters and non-viewpoint characters. Or Team Edward and Team Jacob. Whatever. Most writers claim these distinctions are made because there are different types of characters, but I contend that's not really true. That's why I introduced this major section on Characters by saying every character should believe the novel's about them. If you follow that edict, the difference between character types isn't based on any fundamental difference in the characters at all but rather on how often and how long you shine the spotlight on those characters. That, in turn, is based on the story that needs to be told.

What's the Difference?

While the difference between a main character and a tertiary character may have little to do with the characters and everything to do with the story you're telling, those characters will be perceived differently by the reader. That difference creates different expectations. If a reader finishes one of your novels without learning any personal facts about your main character, it's unlikely you'll ever sell another novel to that reader. Many times the personalized facts and unique take on the world supplied by your main viewpoint character is what turns a reader into a fan. At the other end of the spectrum, if you always give a full personal background for every tertiary character, the reader will probably be bored silly and never finish the book.

So what's the difference? What makes one character a main character and another character a tertiary character? Are there any handy guidelines that will help you create characters who are effective and appropriate for the character level they occupy?

Main Characters

Main characters believe the novel's about them—and they're right. While you need to pick and choose the times to reveal background information regarding your main characters, most main characters get their wish and steal the spotlight for long periods of time. Readers learn the likes and dislikes for main characters. They know what they look like, including how they walk and talk. They learn about their fears and aspirations. They come to understand those main characters as well as they do many of their friends. They know them so well that they'd probably recognize them in real life if they got trapped on an elevator with them for more than a few minutes. Your main characters are like the recurring characters in a television series. They're the stars of your show. Without your main characters, your novel either wouldn't exist or would be a very different novel. As such, killing off a main character (unless it's the final chapter) is a risky proposition. Viewpoint characters are usually recruited from the ranks of main characters.

Secondary Characters

While your secondary characters should believe your novel's about them, they're wrong. Don't ever let them know, but their purpose is to prop up the main characters. They provide motivation, contrast, and support. Unlike main characters, secondary characters tend to come and go. Killing a secondary character is usually not going to cause a reader to hurl your book against the wall in disgust. Secondary characters have more freedom to be funny, fallible, and less complex than main characters. The way they look is usually defined as much by their quirks as by their base qualities. Although most of them have names, readers sometimes need reminders about who they are if they haven't been on stage for several chapters. Secondary characters sometimes act as narrators but they're rarely true viewpoint characters in novels with limited viewpoints.

Tertiary characters

In movie terms, tertiary characters are bit players. They may have a few lines of dialogue and a scene or two, but they rarely grab the spotlight long enough to become anything more than props or stereotypes. They exist more for a purpose than for who they are. The classic example of a tertiary character is a messenger. He walks onto the stage, delivers his message, and walks off again. Descriptions for tertiary characters are usually limited to one major feature or even just a major item of clothing. Tertiary characters are rarely named. When they are, it's often a name given to them based on their one major feature. Examples: "Mohawk Guy stepped back into the room and I shot him between the eyes." "Long Black Coat sprinted into the dark alley and vanished in the shadows." "Slutty Red Dress paraded her cleavage in front of Jim several times but fled when he didn't even glance in her direction." Tertiary characters typically act as viewpoint characters only when they have information that must be conveyed but that can't be conveyed in any other way.

Less, Less, Less

If you've done a good job creating your characters, they should all want more time on stage. They should always have more to say, more to think, and more to do. Your job as the writer is to restrain them. Sometimes you may feel like you're herding cats, but you can always console yourself with the thought that these particular cats exist only inside your brain. On second thought, maybe that's not consoling.

To succeed at character control, shine your spotlight on a character only so long as necessary to accomplish your goal—no matter how much the character screams for more. In the broadest sense, your goal is to entertain and enlighten the reader (and sell books!). In a more specific sense, your plot might require that certain events take place. Perhaps a character dies. Maybe two characters make love. There could be a murder investigation or a journey to another planet or a three-way love triangle that must be resolved. If you want a book that a reader can't put down, you want to maximize your effect on that reader. To do that, you need to create the greatest emotional impact possible with every scene you write. Since excessive words sap emotion from a scene, don't waste words on any character unless these woods increase the emotional impact that character creates.

This may sound complicated—and doing it well is an art form—but the idea behind it is CIA simple. The reader exists on a need-to-know basis. If you can remove information from a scene without losing emotional impact, then remove it. If you can reuse a character from earlier in your novel in the current scene rather than inventing a new one, then do so. If your reader doesn't need to know a particular character was born in Surrey, England, then don't waste words supplying that information.

Removing information you don't need will automagically divide your characters into the various types. Like so many parts of good writing, the process should be organic rather than artificial. On the other hand, if you find yourself writing a seventeen page scene focused on that messenger mentioned above, you might want to take a second look at the scene to figure out what's going on. Is the messenger more important than you originally thought? Or is the messenger so interesting that he somehow hoodwinked you into keeping him in the spotlight longer than the plot justified?

When in doubt, cut.[8] Writers are almost always more fascinated by their own words and ideas than anyone else on the planet. If you believe you're giving too much spotlight time to a particular character, you're probably right.

More, More, More

While most writers are more fascinated by their own characters than anyone else could ever be, that's a necessary evil. If you find yourself struggling to come up with backgrounds or interesting details about a specific character, you've probably got the wrong character. If you want to create interesting and memorable characters, you have to love the characters you create. If you don't love them, spice them up. No hard and fast rules exist here. If your characters bore you, they're almost guaranteed to bore your readers. Even if you hit that one in a million combination where you hate a character but your readers love him, you're setting yourself up for misery. Imagine writing a series of twenty books featuring a character you can't stand. Now that's hell on Earth.

If your attempts to spice up the character fail, jettison the

---

8. Never cut during the original draft. If you're inclined to put in information, let the words flow. You can always take out information later and you don't want to lose a special scene because your conscious mind had yet to catch up to your subconscious.

character, or your story, or both. If you fire your main character half-way through your novel, you'll probably need to rewrite the novel, but that's better than continuing your relationship with a character you don't love. Just be wary of making this decision quickly. Hitting a rough patch or becoming momentarily disenchanted with a character is not what I'm talking about here. It's a bit like a failed marriage. The first step in divorce is typically marriage counseling. Just because you're having problems, that doesn't mean you don't do what you can to save the relationship.

Stereotype Is Not a Four-letter Word

Most writers I know bad-mouth stereotypes the way high school seniors badmouth freshmen. And like those freshmen, there's nothing wrong with properly used stereotypes that a little time wouldn't solve.

For example, let's pick a stereotype and try this out. To avoid the PC[9] Police, we'll pick on Star Trek nerds. For most folks, this stereotype calls up images filled with bad prosthetic ears and split-fingered hand gestures, but in our version of Oz, stereotypical characters believe the story's about them just as much as main characters do. Does that mean that a typical Star Trek nerd can't tell you what the T in James T. Kirk stands for? Of course not. Even many non-Trekkers know it stands for Tiberius. What it means is that some of those Star Trek nerds are businessmen, some are pastry chefs, and some are supermodels (really!). But at first glance, especially at a Star Trek convention when they're in full makeup, these unique individuals are recognized first by their stereotype and all the baggage that stereotype carries with it. If you ever gave them enough stage time, they'd become real people the same as any individual would who seems to be part of a homogeneous group but who is actually a unique individual. It is this closer examination that allows you to discover facts that distort or even ruin your comfortable stereotype.

In fiction, using stereotypes for your tertiary characters allows you to create an impression in your reader's mind without wasting

---

9. That's PC as in Politically Correct, not as in Personal Computer or the hundred or so other possibilities. And yes, it's still politically incorrect to pick on Star Trek nerds, but their lobby's not as good as other groups.

words on that character's unique traits, which are irrelevant at best and disruptive at worse. Returning to that messenger, if we try to reveal his unique traits, it creates a disturbance in the flow of the story. Instead of being able to dismiss the tertiary character for what he is, the reader now devotes valuable neurons examining why the messenger is not a simple messenger. If the uniqueness of the messenger makes him interesting, the reader wants to know more. Suddenly your reader is stomping off through the brush. Worse, when the reader realizes he's off the trail, he trudges back reluctantly, irritated that you sent him into the wilderness for no reason.

For tertiary characters who only appear once or twice in a novel, stereotypes are a great time-saver, but what about for more important characters? Should they be stereotypes? For main characters, we know they can't be. Stereotypes aren't passionate, active, capable, interesting, and believable. If they were, they wouldn't be stereotypes. But what about secondary characters?

In our version of Oz, secondary characters can't be stereotypical characters any more than main characters can. Since a secondary character has time on stage to reveal those facts that distort or even ruin the stereotype, the only reason you'd end up with a stereotypical secondary character is if you don't know your character well enough or don't bother to reveal the uniqueness of that character. That's why so many writers recommend creating character background sheets. I said earlier that a character might be from Surrey but that you didn't need to reveal that fact to the reader. But if you don't know that fact, you can't reveal it should the need arise.

Creating Great Characters

So far we've learned a great deal about what great characters should be but very little about how to actually create such characters. That's because most of the writers I know (including myself) don't create characters artificially. Our characters grow out of our stories or come to us fully formed and demand to have their story told. That doesn't mean every character detail is in place and unchangeable, but it does mean that character creation isn't a task that can be conquered separately.

Many writers claim that one of the first steps in writing a novel is to create complete character backgrounds. If that works for you, do it. In my experience, most of these artificial character building attempts don't work particularly well, especially for first novels. Since story and characters are so closely linked, it's difficult to create either in a vacuum. Instead of forcing character creation, I recommend recording character details as they come to you. As with most of what I recommend, this produces a more organic result. Your characters grow out of your story and vice-versa. But this organic process doesn't work for everyone. What if you're one of those writers who can't create stories organically? Have no fear. Oz is here to help.

The Frankenstein Approach

Writers tend to exist in three camps: 1) writers who are character-centric, 2) writers who are story-centric, and 3) writers who are both. If you're one of those writers who thinks character first or even if you tend to see stories and characters as inseparable sides of the same coin, your characters generally spring to life quite readily in the same tank that holds your story. If you're one of those story-first minds, your characters tend to just lie there while the story gradually consumes their lifeless corpses. For writers in this group, they must always be wary of creating cardboard characters. Such characters lack depth and are usually devoid of genuine emotions. To avoid cardboard characters who only exist to serve the great story god, you artificially create the characters you want; then you rough them up a bit.

For example, let's say you want to write a police procedural novel. Lying awake at night, you've already concocted a complicated plot involving unexpected turns and interesting twists. You've been inundated with ideas for an interesting murder weapon, a fascinating and complex motive for the killer, and a set of interlocking circumstances that will lead to the final resolution. You see your story pieces clearly, but your sleuth remains a faceless automaton. How do you breathe life into your main character so that he becomes as complex as your story?

One way is to interview yourself concerning the character. This sounds artificial because it is. That's why I call this The Frankenstein Approach. You're creating life from lifelessness. If naturally interesting characters just came to you, then you wouldn't need to force it, but don't take it as any slight. There are tons of best-selling writers who live more on story than on character. They're often the ones who extol the virtues of creating character sheets, and for story-first writers, they're right.

You can create your own interview questions, but these will work for most genres:

1) What positive quality or trait must your main character possess?
2) What weakness plagues your main character?
3) What motivates your main character to overcome the book's main obstacle?
4) What is your main character's profession?
5) Would you describe your main character as clever?
6) Is your main character attractive?
7) How old is your main character?
8) What religion is your main character?
9) How much education does your main character have?
10) What's your main character's favorite pastime?

Now go back through this list and answer "Why?" (or "Why not?") for each question. If your main character needs to be intelligent, why does he need to be intelligent? If his biggest weakness is that he loves to smoke, why does he love to smoke? He knows it's bad for him, doesn't he? Then why do it? To answer questions involving physical details such as age and attractiveness, write a relatively complete description of your character.

When you ask why, look for the deeper answers, even if the first answer seemed obvious. For example, if the character's main motivation for overcoming the book's obstacle is that "He's a good person," then ask why is he a good person? Did he have parents who instilled these values in him? How did they do that? By setting a good example? By setting a bad example that he never wanted to mimic? Tie your answers together whenever possible. Look for links. For example, if he's a good person because his parents were critically flawed, then perhaps his biggest weakness is his constant struggle to do what's right because it always seems easier and more natural to follow in his parent's footsteps and do what's easy.

Watch for possibilities to build a character history. For example, if your character has a Doctorate of Philosophy from Penn State, then how did he end up becoming a twenty year veteran detective on Chicago's police force? Did he teach first for several years? Perhaps he had an affair with one of his students and got fired. Maybe he thought all of his colleagues were arrogant overly educated assholes and he wanted to go where he knew he could be the most overly educated asshole around. Perhaps his father was a cop and he promised the old man on his death bed that he would follow in his footsteps

Don't be afraid to ask yourself the tough questions. Be wary of answers like, "Because it's easier to write the story that way." Answers like, "Because I like him better that way," are perfectly acceptable provided you have some level of confidence that at least some of your readers will like him better that way, too.

As you answer these questions, record any past experiences that seem to fit. For example, when you decide how much education your main character has and then you try to answer why, your answer might include the fact that neither of his parents went to college and they wanted their son to go. So did he rebel against that expectation? Embrace it? Did he pass his SATs with flying colors? Did he pass them even though he got drunk the night before and still had a hangover that morning? Let your imagination run when answering these questions. The more you imagine now, the less you have to imagine later when you're doing the actual writing.

Once you have a basic understanding of your character, go deeper. One way to do this is to create a dream sheet, which tries to capture a bit of the character's imagination. Ask yourself what your character dreams about. Late at night, with the power out and a thunderstorm raging outside the window, what thoughts intrude into the quiet spaces of her mind? What life aspirations does she cling to? What are her ambitions? What are her fears? What does she love? What does she hate? What secrets does she hide from everyone?

Both the basic questions and the dream sheet questions are just a sampling of the questions you should ask. You can think of additional questions as well as I can. Cover topics that help you get to know your character. Get the facts and then go beyond them. Your goal is to understand how the character thinks and feels.

You'll know you're doing your character creation right when you're forced to change your perfectly imagined story to accommodate your character.

Always Passion

Passion rears its head in most sections of this book for a reason. I mention passion so often because passion is a controlling factor in fiction just as in life. Granted, talent, good looks, and great genes are handy, but those are all beyond our control. Society tends to shy away from passionate people. That's because passionate people can be a little scary. But success in life comes from passion more often than any other quality. Passionate people find a way to succeed despite the obstacles that rise up to block them.

Like real life, if you allow your characters to be passionate about their goals and about the world they inhabit, many problems you face in creating believable, memorable, and interesting characters disappear. "The Frankenstein Approach" described by the previous section will allow you to mechanically build a character, but it can only take that character to the edge of life. To truly bring that character to life, you need to infuse that character with all the passion you have to give. Allow your characters to care deeply and in return you and your readers will care about those characters and about what happens to them.

The easiest way to create a passionate character is to give them a reason to feel and then let them do so.

Misery Loves Readers

People say misery loves company. When it comes to fiction, misery loves readers. Or more appropriately, readers love misery, especially when we're talking about misery suffered by the main characters. If you ever want to write a dull-as-death novel, make all your characters happy. It's almost impossible for any completely happy character to be interesting for more than a couple pages. Even then, the character's usually had to go through hell to reach that bit of nirvana.

We don't inflict all this misery on our characters without reason. Making them miserable is nothing more than a brute force approach to get them moving. An unhappy character who's active and capable won't sit still for long. Poke them and they will poke back. At the very least, they'll try to move out of the way.

Readers love miserable main characters because those characters move and by definition, those characters *feel*. This doesn't mean you can force-feed feelings to your readers. Emotional involvement should develop naturally, not come at your readers like a freight train. Do this by creating characters who feel and by placing them in a story that gives them a reason to feel. Emotions are created by story and shared with the reader through viewpoint characters.

This touchy-feely advice may sound esoteric but it's completely practical. Give your main character a worthwhile goal and create almost impossible odds against achieving that goal. View this story through the eyes of a passionate and likable main character. Emotional impact results as your characters live the life you've given them.

More Than Bones

Using these techniques allows you to create a character with a past, a present, and a future, but these are just the bare bones of our creation. Once you have the skeleton or your character in place, you need to flesh it out. Do this by bestowing behaviors, habits, speech patterns, likes, and dislikes that are all unique to the character. Unique doesn't mean only one character per novel can like sushi, but not *all* of them should like sushi.

For example, a certain popular military fiction writer (who shall remain nameless because his lawyers are much more expensive—and numerous—than mine) exhibits this exact problem in several of his novels. All of his heroes drink beer and like to barbecue. All of his villains drink hard liquor. Call me a Carrie Nation hater, but I shouldn't be able to tell how villainous a character is by examining his bar tab. If two of your characters love Guinness, have a third be willing to drink it but only if it's ice cold, which horrifies the first two. If five of your characters go off for a hen weekend in Dublin, all five can love the magnum of champagne that shows up in the room from a secret admirer, but have four handle it well and send one overindulger to the bathroom so she can spend some quality time with the porcelain goddess.

Characters should vary but each new trait should build on what already exists. The hard-nosed cop we mentioned earlier's probably not a ballet fan. If he is, then supply a reason for it. Perhaps his mother was a famous ballet star who was first granted asylum by his father the cop. By allowing your main characters to live, you guarantee that they won't be stereotypes, but you also define those characters because people are shaped by everything that happens to them.

Most cops on the street can handle themselves in a fight. Most firefighters have upper body strength. Nurses typically have a no-nonsense attitude toward illness and even death. This doesn't mean you can't create a weak, sissified ex-cop, ex-firefighter who now works as a nurse and faints at the sight of blood—but you've got your work cut out for you. If you're not writing humor, why make your life difficult by using an ex-cop, ex-firefighter, fainting nurse? You don't avoid stereotypical characters by mechanically going against the grain. You create interesting characters with unique and dramatic past experiences, then allow those experiences to shape who the character is now.

This integration extends in both directions. While it's true that most college professors aren't body builders, plenty exist who are.

You can certainly create a muscle-shirt wearing professor who pumps iron six days a week without losing believability, but creating such a strong devotion to his body will likely influence his other habits. Your buff professor's unlikely to smoke, get drunk every other day, have unprotected sex, or gobble Cheetos™ every morning for breakfast. Yet it's natural for his colleague to do all those things. What's more, these two characters can be the best of friends. Perhaps both are fascinated by string theory and share a common sense of humor.

Once your characters are fleshed out, consider roughing them up a bit. Originally that buff professor would have never dreamed of smoking. Give your health nut some character by having him light up a good cigar after any workout where he sets a new personal best at the bench press. If you personally hate the smell of cigars—or you're from California and characters who smoke tobacco have been outlawed—you can have your professor engage in unprotected sex every time he gets the chance. He knows it's dangerous, but like the cigar, his zest for clean living produces an itch he needs to scratch from time to time.

This roughing up the edges of your character not only makes him more interesting but also helps your reader remember who he is.

Leon's Getting Larger

All main characters should have size. I'm not saying they all shop at Big 'n' Tall, but when they enter a room, they should leave a wake. This isn't typically a physical manifestation, but it can be. A main character influences others. People often describe this ability as being larger-than-life. Create this impression by showing the reactions of other characters. As these other characters focus on your main character, so too does the reader.

For example, people get quiet when a main character enters a room. When they finally react, they experience different reactions. This isn't typically true for minor characters. If a minor character claims the sky is blue, people will react as a homogeneous group. They will ignore the claim, accept it without comment, or view it as obviously incorrect. If a main character makes the same claim, some people will argue against it while others will vehemently defend it. Main characters create waves. Minor characters rarely create even a ripple.

Main characters also remain visible even when they're not on stage. Other characters often talk about them or make plans with them in mind. This guarantees that main characters remain in the minds of our readers.

Only You Know

To create great characters, either become a great character yourself or pay attention to other people who are. Only you can know if you're a naturally interesting person. When you speak, do people stop to listen? If you tell an anecdote, do you dominate a room? I know many writers who are natural born entertainers. If you aren't lucky enough to be such a person, take heart. I know plenty of writers who bore others to tears with their constant and aimless yammering.

If you doubt your inherent ability to enchant others just by being yourself, you're in luck. As a writer, you have hours to think of that witty comeback. Your knowledge about any subject can appear to be as vast as most experts in the field. Even so, never forget that you're an entertainer, both on the page and off. If your novels make the bestseller lists, expect interviews, teaching opportunities, and movie deals. Invent great characters and don't be afraid to become a great character yourself.

Boring Hero, Interesting Villain

Have you noticed that some writers create villains who leap off the page? These villains have charm and charisma. They're attractive and confident. They become fan favorites without flexing a muscle. In comparison, these same writers produce heroes that are mundane and predictable. They struggle to hold the reader's attention, and are only slightly more interesting than the world tic-tac-toe tournament. Why the difference?

Most of us create heroes out of qualities we admire. These heroes often represent what we wish we could be. This tends to cause us to associate too closely with the viewpoint of these idealistic heroes. As a result, we freeze up like a shy debutante at her coming-out party.

We want our hero to be talented and intelligent, attractive and witty. Instead our hero comes across as boring and somewhat simple.

Heroes should be capable, but capable doesn't mean perfect. Perfection is worthy of admiration but it's rarely interesting. If you want to create memorable heroes, allow them to screw up. They may have moral fiber—even more moral fiber than you—but they also have weaknesses. They get tired. They get angry. They feel fear. They may fall in love with people who are terrible for them or they may be germaphobes. Your heroes are not you. They may be morally superior, but they also make mistakes that you would never make, especially when it comes to following their hearts rather than their heads.

Most of all, allow your heroes to feel. Society teaches us that expressing our feelings is inappropriate and dangerous. Feelings can be used against us. But feelings are interesting. They allow our heroes to act in ways that aren't always logical or preferred. Painless success rarely happens in real life. In fiction, such success is just plain boring. To succeed, heroes usually need to compromise their integrity, their relationships, or their health. That's why heroes, like villains, are often rule-breakers.

Character Porridge

All great writers have great characters living within them. Often these characters aren't recognized for what they are. Instead they sneak onto the stage when we're not trying to find them. Other times we force them from the shadowy corners of our mind through brute force. When we're lucky, they scream to be set free in voices we can't ignore. For most writers, creating great characters is a learned skill that requires trial and error, practice, and dedication. Fortunately, characters bring life to our fiction, so the struggle's worth it.

In this section, I've mixed together leftover tidbits of advice that are meant to help you get the most from your characters, with or without their help.

A Rose by any other Name

Our collective consciousness associates names with traits. These associations change over time, so if you happen to have one of the names I disparage in this section, take heart. You can wait for society to move on or you can rise above your name. Who knows? You might be the one responsible for changing the traits associated with the name.

Glancing today at some of the hero names in the best-selling section of the bookstore, I came up with names like: Billy, Laura, Stephanie, Amanda, Nathan, Lisbeth, Sean, Michelle, Ben, Christine, Cotton, Mikael, Harriet, and Josh. This list does a good job demonstrating some general principles about naming your characters:

- Most popular heroes have relatively common names, but not too common
- Just like real people, sometimes heroes spell their name in a less common way (Lisbeth and Mikael), but usually it's the most common form and spelling.
- Popular heroes typically have names that are easy to pronounce

If you create a name your readers can recognize, pronounce, and spell, it's more likely those readers will remember that name and feel comfortable reading a story featuring that character. That means one less rock in your wagon. If you go against these principles, it means you'll be adding a rock. How big the rock is depends on how far off the beaten path you go. For example, Cotton, Mikael, and Lisbeth are all unusual names. Mikael and Lisbeth may be hard to spell correctly on the first attempt, but their spelling is easy enough to learn. All three names are easy to pronounce, so the weight they add to your wagon are nothing more than pebbles.

So what about going further afield? For example, could you create a hero named Groucho? Of course you could, but doing so will carry its own set of problems. For one, Groucho's an extremely unusual name. It's relatively easy to spell and to pronounce, but it carries with it several connotations. One comes from the most famous Groucho of all time (Groucho Marx), who had a distinctive comedy style. Another comes from the root of the name itself (grouch). If you saddle your hero with such a name, you'll have a lot of reader expectations to overcome. That doesn't make it impossible, but it's certainly taking the road less traveled.

The same is true if you're trying to create effective names for your villains. Unless you're going for humor, don't create an archvillain named Myron or Sheldon. I'm not criticizing the Sheldons or tMyrons of the world, but some names just don't inspire fear or respect. If you're creating a tough female lead, you usually stay away from names like Candy, Precious, Bambi, or Mercedes. Going against these social norms can be done intentionally, often for comedic effect (think Joss Whedon's *Buffy the Vampire Slayer*), but you're swimming through treacherous waters if you're trying to be serious and yet you give your main heroine a silly name. It can be done, but it's an advanced technique. Attempt at your own risk.

Your goal as a writer is to communicate. If you give your characters names that don't help your reader recognize and remember those characters, then you're intentionally making it harder for the reader to understand and appreciate your story. The question is why? You may have a personal attachment to a particular name, but if it makes your novel harder to sell, is it worth it? If so, then use it. But don't use a name blindly. In writing and in life, names have power. If you've given your main character an unusual, hard-to-pronounce name, make sure you have a good reason for doing so. If you want to avoid the problem, take a lesson from those best-selling novelists.

Give your characters names that are somewhat common. As long as it fits your character, the exact name usually doesn't matter.

<u>More than one way to name a cat</u>

Two other ideas to keep in mind if you want to avoid confusing your reader:

1) Don't use similar names for different characters
2) Don't use multiple names for the same character

If you have two characters named Bart and Bert, don't be surprised when your readers can't tell them apart. Almost as bad is using names like Ryan and Brian or Karla and Carol. After working so hard to create characters who are unique, why would you want your readers to mix two of them up?

The same goes for referring to your characters in different ways: don't do it without reason. If your viewpoint character calls his mother "Mom" in dialogue, don't have him refer to her in first person prose as Mrs. Langley. The same goes for the use of nicknames. If Bob always refers to Jim as Knucklehead, don't suddenly have him refer to him as Jim unless there's a reason for the change.

This highlights the fact that there are reasons to change what one character calls another character based on the situation. I once had a girlfriend who called me by my first name until the day we broke up. After that, she always called me "Sixbury" until many years later when I told her I was getting married, to which she responded, "Oh, no," and used my first name again. Why the change? She had serious misgivings about marriage. The revelation of my upcoming matrimonial bliss struck her a bit like it would if I told her I had a terminal disease. In fiction, such a change is used to convey information.

Consistency with names applies to you as the writer, too. If you refer to a character as Bob, you shouldn't suddenly refer to that same character as Dr. Skoleton. Most writers typically reveal their character's full name at some point, but they then call that character by a single name in prose.

Give Me Another

When it comes to deciding how many characters should exist in your novel, many factors come into play. Length and intended audience are obvious ones. A novel like *Gone with the Wind* has dozens of named characters and dozens more tertiary characters. A much shorter children's novel like *Charlotte's Web* might only have a dozen or so total characters.

In general, create characters only when you need them. If you later notice that you can combine two characters into a single character, do so. In general, having less characters is preferable to having more provided you don't lose any of the story's emotional power by reducing the number of characters.

There is too much. Let me sum up

Characters provide the energy that drives your story forward. They rule your fiction and your life in ways cardboard characters never could. With the right character at the helm, you have the power to tell almost any story you can imagine.

- All your characters should believe your story's about them.
- Characters care deeply about what's most important to them (not what's most important to you, the writer).
- Invent circumstances that cause your characters to **want** to fulfill your plot objectives.
- Readers care most about characters when they're rooting for or against them.
- Most great characters are: 1) Passionate, 2) Active, 3) Capable, 4) Interesting, and 5) Believable.
- Heroes are typically selfless and villains are typically selfish.
- A great viewpoint character controls the story as much as the story controls him.
- The best viewpoint characters are interesting characters you like who can tell your story.
- For greatest emotional impact, have as few viewpoint characters as possible.
- Always maintain control of your viewpoint and switch viewpoints only when you have reason to do so.
- Third-person viewpoints provide flexibility.
- First-person viewpoints carry emotional impact.
- An omnipotent viewpoint can carry an epic story across many cultures and generations.
- Choose a viewpoint type that matches your story.
- Give your characters an appropriate amount of time in the spotlight.
- Stereotypical characters are useful for purely functional characters.
- Character creation works best when it's organic but you can "Frankenstein" characters if you need to.
- Readers like embattled, complex, believable, passionate characters.

- Heroes must be allowed to make mistakes.
- Choose names that match your characters.
- Avoid character names that confuse your readers.
- Populate your novel with the fewest characters needed to tell your story.
- Creating great characters is an art form, but it's one worth pursuing.

Chapter Five:
Go On Till
You Come to the End

Endings Aren't Crap

Unlike beginnings, I've have no problem with endings. Endings are the reason I write. If I can't see my ending, no matter how good the idea, I don't write the story.

Not everyone works that way. Some people are so good at beginnings, that's all they ever write. Soon they've finished the first several chapters of half a dozen novels or so, but they can't ever seem to get past the crap and get to the ending, even when they know what they want the ending to be.

Other writers stick with a single novel, but they can't resist rewriting and reworking their beginnings until they're just right. While this allows them to sleep at night, this repetitive pounding of the same material tends to produce a dried-up husk of the original beginning. It's often polished to perfection but lacks soul. The juice has been chewed out of the story and the result's less appetizing than day-old gum. And all that rewriting effort isn't free. After spending their precious writing energy to hone and craft their beginning into that shell of perfection, these writers are often so sick of their novel midway through that they find themselves fighting a losing battle. Frequently they point to these lackluster half-finished efforts as justification for starting over. Even if they do finish their novel, they have so little gas left in the tank that despite their best efforts the ending is a shadow of what it could have been if they'd just let go of their beginning a bit sooner.

Here's a secret that you can take to the bank: Endings are more important than beginnings. Granted, they're not a lot more important. If your first few chapters—or first few pages—or first few sentences—are lousy, chances are good that most readers will never see your ending. But if a reader does make it to "THE END," nothing says "Buy my next book now!" like a great ending.

Ending Ho!

The easiest way to write a great ending to your novel is to discover your ending as soon as possible while remaining flexible and open to alternate possibilities. If you're like me, you have the ending in mind before you begin to write the first draft. It doesn't get much earlier than that. But even if you're one of the writers who worships at the "knowing what will happen will kill my creativity" altar, you still want to discover your ending sooner rather than later. With the "Writing Quickly While Writing Well" section of this book, I drop you at one end of the road of yellow brick and recommend you follow it to Oz. Granted, you still might need to battle a wicked witch or two and make your way through an internet-generated field of deadly poppy distractions, but it can be done.

So why is it so important to discover your ending sooner? Because everything in your novel leads to the ending. Knowing your ending allows your mind to dwell on the details of that ending while you write (or rewrite) the book. It gives your subconscious time to identify and work out problems you didn't even know existed. It makes it easier to add foreshadowing, reveal the setting that will be used in the climactic scene, and allow your characters to experience the trials and tribulations that will prepare them to overcome that final obstacle to their success. If you don't know where you're heading, you're trusting that fate will allow you to stumble onto the right path, force you to choose correctly when that path forks in multiple directions, and magically prepare you for what lies ahead. Blindly trusting to fate to lead you to the best ending is an extreme act of faith deeply seated in the "discover what happens next" writing religion. I'm not saying you can't write a great novel without knowing the ending early in the writing process, but you've definitely chosen the harder road. In all likelihood, your journey will be less fate and more trial and error. The problem? Trial and error takes time and energy. With all the dangers on this more difficult road, I recommend you spend as little time on it as possible.

Knowing what your ending will be does not create a perfect first draft—or even a perfect ending. On the contrary, knowing your ending allows you to modify it repeatedly as you near its blessed sanctuary. That's where flexibility comes in. Without question, sticking to a bad ending is much worse than having no idea of the ending at all. More important, the ending should be just that: an idea. Your final scene might happen on a deserted island instead of the office building you originally imagined, or it might happen at 40,000 feet rather than in a cave after the batteries for all the light sources have gone dead. What's important is that your ending must have a satisfying emotional impact on the reader. The exact setting, the exact characters involved, the defining climactic moment where all looks lost but the hero miraculously saves the day are all mutable.

Hold it, Oz! Didn't you just tell us that knowing the ending as soon as possible was important and useful? Now you're saying that you can change anything about the ending you like. Isn't that the same as not knowing your ending?

Granted, I admit it sounds a bit confusing, but being able to change your ending and not knowing your ending aren't the same at all. That's because the examples I gave above are extremes. Typically your endings come off pretty much the way you first imagined them. You need to be able to tweak those endings as your book is written because you will uncover facts, scenes, and even characters as you write your novel that you didn't expect. So maintaining flexibility in your ending is key, but knowing even half your ending is better than not knowing where your novel's headed at all.

On the Other Hand…

All of the above advice applies to most writers and especially beginning writers. But if you're one of those other writers—you know, the ones with dozens of bestsellers to your name who never know the endings to your novels until you write them—then I applaud your talent.

There really are people whose subconsciouses are smarter than they are. When they consciously try to plan and plot, they ruin the excellent story their subconscious has so graciously provided. If you're one of these writers, I give you the same advice I always give: Do what works! My only caution is that if you believe you're one of these subconscious savants but you continue to struggle with your endings, or worse, you keep writing lots of beginnings but few endings, consider trying something else.

Ultimate Satisfaction

What is the end of a novel, anyway? I mean, what is it we're trying to do here? When we speak of great endings, what do we mean?

As a writer, you create an unwritten contract with your readers to entertain them, to make them laugh, to make them cry, to give them what they want. Your job is to satisfy the reader. If we look up satisfaction in the dictionary, we get phrases like "the fulfillment of one's wishes, expectations, or needs, or the pleasure derived from this." Legally we're told satisfaction is the fulfillment of an obligation. As writers, we have an unspoken promise to meet a reader's expectations. But we need to do that throughout the novel. What makes the ending different?

Often, it's the characters.

If you continue to build the story, making it ever more interesting and entertaining, most readers would be content to read forever. But that translates to an unending amount of work for you and a terrible hit to all those royalties you planned to make from the subsequent books in your series. The easiest way to create a satisfying ending for your novel is to satisfy your main characters, particularly your hero.

Your hero has been struggling throughout the novel to achieve a goal that she feels is important, or even vital to her (and possibly everyone else's) survival. When she finally achieves that goal, or possibly an unexpected but related goal, she feels satisfied. And her feeling of satisfaction translates to your reader.

So one possible great ending to a novel is one where the main characters end up at peace. Granted, there can be danger looming somewhere beyond the horizon, but the most important and immediate concerns have been taken care of: The Death Star has been destroyed, Lord Voldemort has been permanently or temporarily vanquished, the kids have made it out of the wardrobe and back to England, the evil has been defeated, the hero and heroine are in love, the mystery's been solved, the monster's been vanquished, the battle's over, and the teen feeling so much angst is now a little less angsty.

On the surface, this seems completely obvious—and it is. As writers, we started as readers. We know what makes a good ending, at least from our own cultural viewpoint. But writers have a dangerous tendency to muck up the works in the name of creativity or originality or some other bit of self-delusional drivel. If you want a great ending to your novel, make sure your main characters (not the villain) are satisfied before you type THE END.

The question now is: How do we do that?

That Bestseller Ending

Before I go into detail about how to construct a great ending to your novel, we should figure out what we mean when we say the ending. What exactly is the ending of the novel? The last sentence? The last few pages? The last chapter? The words THE END?

It's all of those and more.

To explain this, we need to talk a little bit about the life cycle of a novel, which we can roughly approximate with the figure below:

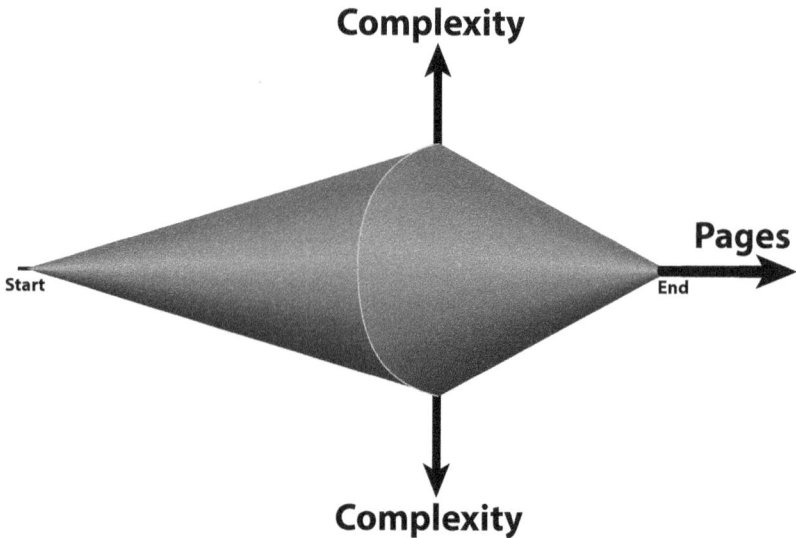

Complexity

Pages

Start   End

Complexity

In a more detailed rendering of this concept, the figure above would be far from smooth, covered with ripples and tentacles as well as bumps and pits. While the general trend would follow the above representation, it would be much more complex. For our discussion of endings, however, simpler is better.

The best novels start from a single point. As they progress forward, they grow in complexity, spawning plot lines, introducing characters, presenting conflicts, revealing settings, and providing background about the world in which the novel exists. Eventually—about $^2/_3$ to $^3/_4$ through—these novels reach their point of greatest expansion. After that, they narrow and tighten around themselves. Minor plot lines are resolved. Characters complete their time in the story and exit, stage left. Conflicts are resolved. Background information and new settings are no longer given. This doesn't happen all at once. It's a careful pruning process that whittles down and focuses the story. The aim is to reduce the novel's focus until all attention is on that final climactic scene where the hero faces her greatest peril. If she fails, all is lost. Instead, she succeeds at the last possible moment, overcoming whatever great obstacle the villain has placed before her.

Some novels have a few trivial loose ends that are tied up in a denouement. These denouements are not necessary to a novel, but are especially useful when readers still have questions that can be easily answered. As long as these denouements don't increase the complexity of a novel's ending to any significant degree and the final great objective of the hero is not dependent upon them, they do not detract from the satisfaction of the ending. In the diagram above, the denouement would occur after the shape is reduced to a point.

Damn the torpedoes, full speed ahead!

Above I mentioned that as you round that corner and change the shape of your novel from one of expansion to one of convergence, you should:

- Eliminate minor characters by killing them off or resolving their contribution to your story.
- Conclude minor plot lines.
- Settle minor conflicts.
- Discontinue background information.
- Quit introducing new settings.

Following these guidelines will certainly help to focus your novel, but it won't necessarily contribute to your reader's desire to keep reading. Not only do you want to focus your reader's attention on that climactic point in your novel, but also you selfishly want them to ignore everything else in their life while they continue reading, mesmerized by the awesome fictional work you've created. The most reliable way to do this is by increasing the pressure on your hero by:

- Decreasing the time he has to resolve the main conflict
- Boosting the motivation he has for resolving the main conflict
- Having one of his attempts to resolve the main conflict result

in a costly failure where one of the supporting characters dies or the hero experiences some other form of significant loss

- Changing your hero through a process of growth that allows him to become the person he needs to be to defeat the villain and conquer the greatest obstacle blocking his path
- Increasing reader certainty that no possibility exists for the hero to succeed

If you do this right, you'll create a tangled web of interlinking events that combine to heighten the pressure throughout the last third of your novel.

All plots are limited in how hard the dramatic envelope can be pushed before the story collapses into farce. What you're looking to do is push that envelope while accounting for the elasticity of the novel's overall tone. For example, in Jane Austin's *Pride and Prejudice*, the novel's convergence occurs during Elizabeth Bennet's trip north. Several unlikely factors came together to deliver Elizabeth to exactly the point she needed to be so that she could hook up with Mr. Darcy. First, Elizabeth's Aunt and Uncle invited her to go with them on vacation, which is the mundane, non-coincidental, completely believable event that starts Elizabeth on the right road. Elizabeth's Aunt just happened to hail from the village of Lambton which was conveniently located near Pemberley (Mr. Darcy's estate). When their trip to the Lake Country had to be shortened, they understandably went to Lambton instead, which was only five miles from Pemberley. When her aunt and uncle wanted to visit the nearby great estate, Elizabeth would have refused, except that she was told the family (meaning Mr. Darcy) was away for the season and could be counted on not to be there. Except that Mr. Darcy comes home a day early and encounters Elizabeth right where he needs her to be to move the story toward its conclusion.

If examined objectively outside the story, several of these coincidences seem far-fetched but certainly not impossible. For the readers of *Pride and Prejudice*, who are immersed in the story as all good readers are, they don't object to these few paltry coincidences but rather expect and enjoy them as a necessity.

Compare those events to the ones in *Indiana Jones and the Raiders of the Lost Ark.* In the latter part of that movie, Indiana Jones finds an ark that's been lost for millennia, escapes an Egyptian chamber filled with deadly snakes, gets beaten up by a burly Nazi only to have the guy fail to notice he's about to be Cuisinarted by a plane's propeller, defeats an entire truckload of German soldiers, rides a ***submarine*** to a hidden island base, and remembers to close his eyes as the spirits of the ark melt an entire Nazi regiment. These events are pretty crazy, but they're taken in stride because of the action-oriented nature of the picture. Granted, if you wrote a novel like this, it would be rejected because of its *deus ex machina* ending. After all, Indy doesn't do any-thing—God's badass spirits take care of the Nazis for him—but with big budget movies, especially movies from the 80s, you could get away with stunts like that. The point is that most of the events are well beyond the realms of logic and known possibilities. We accept those events because they're normal for that genre.

Finish It Already!

You've been building up to your climactic scene since page one of your novel. Now its time has come. The stage is set, the actors have taken their places, and the audience knows what's at stake. The direc-tor yells, "Action!" and your big finale is under way.

This scene is the payoff your readers have been waiting for. This is when you satisfy their greatest emotional craving. This is when you prove your worth as a writer. This is when you convince them to buy your next book. If you've done your job well, the anticipation your readers feel is the greatest they have felt so far in your novel. They want to finish your book. They ***will*** finish your book, and they will finish it ***now!*** Sleep, work, spouses, and children be damned!

If you've crafted your novel well, you've focused your story until all that remains is this one scene. You're ready. The reader's ready. So let's get this show on the road.

If you want the end of your novel to be as successful as possible, typically your final scene:

- Takes place at a previously used setting
- Happens either on an epic scale (think massive battle) or an extremely focused scale (think Jodie Foster in *Silence of the*

Lambs pursuing Buffalo Bill around his maze of a house until Buffalo Bill traps her in a pitch black room)

- Expands time, meaning the scene takes place over many pages but involves a relatively short passage of time
- Involves mostly main characters with minor characters playing only the least important roles
- Is driven by the hero's own efforts, sacrifices, and motivations
- Is an all or nothing situation
- Works best if the hero goes beyond what he thought was possible or does what he once believed could not be done[10]

The reasons for these requirements are straightforward.

Familiar Setting

If the scene takes place in a location we've never seen before, you need to spend valuable time setting the scene. Since scene setting is never dramatic, you're weakening the tension of your final scene by detracting from the action. You can get around this by using a cliché setting: An abandoned factory, an empty plain, a mall. If simply naming where the scene takes place allows your readers to fill in the details without further elaboration, your scene setting, if it exists at all, is minimal, yet reliable. A famous pair of examples that demonstrate this well come from the first two Terminator movies. Both had endings that took place in non-descript factories. What type of factories, where the factories were located, and why they had such lax security are never mentioned or relevant. They're empty but fully functional factories. That's all the readers (or in this case, the viewers) need to know.

Epic or Intimate

Most novels typically follow two main paths for the last scene. Either the last scene is vast and sweeping, encompassing everything and everyone of import touched by the novel, or the last scene is narrowly focused on the main character and the villain or perhaps the two

---

10. A graphic and humorous example of this comes from *Ghostbusters* where Egon had warned Peter and Ray that they could never cross the proton streams from two particle throwers but for the climactic moment, that's exactly what they do.

main characters and the great obstacle separating them from success. In the movie Titanic, it's just Jack and Rose out there in the vast Atlantic ocean freezing to death. Well, Jack was freezing to death. Rose was saying she would never let him go. And then, of course, she let him go. Hey, circumstances change. The point is that last scenes tend to be inclusive or exclusive. Either most folks are on the guest list or it's just the stars of the show. Even when everyone's on the guest list, the spotlight nearly always focuses on the two main characters for a final climactic moment.

Expanded Time

If you've designed your plot correctly, everything is happening in your last scene: Your three main characters are resolving their love triangle, they're fighting the evil demons who seek to wipe out all sparkly vampires everywhere, the planets are experiencing a once in a century conjunction in the night sky, aliens are attacking from Mars, and riddle-speaking aliens from the future are injecting their advice at every opportunity. Although this example might be extreme, if your last scene is done right, it's going to be a big scene. That means lots of pages. Few results disappoint a reader more than a climax that's reached too quickly. The tension should build throughout the scene (as it has throughout the novel) until it becomes almost unbearable. Finally, when you trigger that last release, the reader is more than ready. For example, consider the *Silence of the Lambs* example from earlier. If Buffalo Bill had been standing in a different place or had gone for his gun when he first realized Clarice was on to him (both logical and plausible possibilities), the scene would have been a couple minutes long. Viewers would have felt cheated. One important caution: You don't make your climactic scene better by making it longer. You pack more excitement-generation drama into the scene, which requires a longer scene.

Stars of the Show

Your last scene almost always centers on your main characters. They are the stars of your show. Why wouldn't you want them to be the center of attention during the most important moments of your novel? Often secondary characters are mentioned, and sometimes the spotlight shines their way for a few brief moments, but even this brief attention usually links to the hero's success or failure. For example, it's not uncommon for secondary characters to drop like flies in the final scene as each makes the ultimate sacrifice to further the great cause. Having your last scene comprised mostly of main characters is simple logic. You chose your main characters for a reason. You've given them the most attention, detail, and scenes throughout your novel. Now, here at the end, they need all the love you can give them.

Proactive, not Reactive

If your villain is a worthwhile obstacle, at various points in your novel, your hero has been forced to respond to the villain's evil machinations. Even if you're writing a person against nature novel, your hero's been forced to respond to mother nature's fury. But in your last scene, the hero has taken control. The parameters of the showdown may been specified by the villain, but your hero sets out to make the final scene his own. He comes up with a desperate, far-fetched plan for ultimate success. He acts intelligently, resourcefully, and brings to bear every capability and asset he can muster. And lest you think these descriptions are relevant only for action novels, even *50 Shades of Grey* demonstrates this take control attitude, which is interesting because in that story, Anastasia's taking control is represented by her finally agreeing to be Christian's submissive. At the same time, this is her last ditch, ultimate effort to break through the emotional walls Christian's created to protect himself.

All or Nothing

In your climactic scene, there are no second chances. That doesn't mean your character can't get a second chance to defeat the villain within the last scene—that's actually quite common—but rather it means that your hero knows that if this attempt fails (meaning this encounter with the villain fails), all is lost. As a result, nothing is held back. There are no thoughts of turning back, no possibility of giving up, and no acceptance of failure. Note that it's not necessary for this to be the case when the scene starts. It can be an all or nothing situation from the get-go, or something can happen during the scene that removes all possibility of retreat or escape. What's important is that your hero has no options other than to give the scene everything she has to give. For many novels, this means the hero is facing her own mortal peril for the first time. Perhaps she was an amateur sleuth who has grown too close to solving the mystery, so the villain must kill her to escape justice. Instead of solving the mystery, she now finds herself running for her life.

Impossible Now Possible

In your climactic scene, events will not unfold as your hero planned or foresaw. At some point late in the scene, all will look hopeless. The hero realizes that the desired outcome he's been fighting for over the past 300 pages is lost forever. In that moment of desperation, your hero will reach inside himself and pull forth an inner strength, or an inner ability that seemed beyond reach when the scene started. As a result, the hero might perform some action thought to be impossible or unthinkable only moments before. The key is that the hero is the one who makes this happen, and after it occurs, it is **not** a reach. The action is completely plausible and in hindsight, even expected. Of course the hero sprouted wings and flew up to drop a giant boulder on the villain's doomsday machine. Hadn't he mysteriously started laying eggs only a few chapters before? And back in Chapter Five, hadn't the old wise woman told him that his mother was a duck and that he might share more genetic traits with her than he previously thought? More often, a secondary reluctant hero charges in to tip the balance in the hero's favor. In *Star Wars*, this was Han Solo, who had sworn not to get involved, dropping out of the sun to disable Darth Vader's TIE fighter just as Darth was about to turn Luke into a special effect budget overrun. Or it was those spirits emerging from the ark to destroy all the Nazis in *Raiders*. Personally I prefer stories where the hero solves his own problems, but sometimes that lacks believability. While most of what the hero accomplishes is all hero, sometimes it's useful to have that secondary hero who we thought was dead crash through the barricades and whisk the hero and her lisping daughter away to safety.

Not Quite Done

At this point, we know one way to make a great ending. What I haven't covered are the hundreds of other types of endings that work just fine but that violate everything I've already said. In truth, endings can be tricky beasts if you don't want to follow the easiest path to success. Additional complications are caused by huge cultural bias against or acceptance for certain types of endings.

People often complain about Hollywood happy endings, but they ignore that most Hollywood pictures have happy endings because that's what most Americans like. Many people say, "In real life we experience more than enough misery. Fiction is an escape." But people who exclusively enjoy happy endings are only one type of person. Take writers, for instance, who tend to be a grumpy lot. George R. R. Martin doesn't consider it to be a successful day unless he's killed at least two characters before breakfast[11]. Writers tend to gravitate to "more realistic" or "more artistic" endings than the big blockbusters coming out of Hollywood. Sometimes their instincts are good. Other times perfectly good novels are ruined because the author decided to make the ending "more realistic," and as a result, created a downer ending that only the author could love.

I'm not saying you shouldn't pull and push and twist your ending until it fits your novel. But even if you create an atypical ending, most of the advice I've provided still works. The vital concept is to make sure you nail the big climactic scene at the end. Barring any possible epilogue or denouement, it'll be the last thing your reader digests before they decide whether they enjoyed your book.

Check Your Climax

Your goal is to create a great ending for your novel, but all writers struggle to make the climactic scene the best it can be. If your final scene seems flat or just not as powerful as you believe it can be, here are some questions you can ask yourself that may help you to sharpen your focus:

---

11. Just kidding, George!

- Why is the end the end?
- What makes this ending more exciting than any other scene in the book?
- Does the ending have a satisfying sense of finality?
- Will the ending leave the reader wishing there were more without feeling there should be more?
- Are all of your main characters involved in the final scene? If not, why not?
- Are the main characters at peace?

The answers to these questions should help you to pinpoint where your problem area lies.

<u>Why is the end the end?</u>

When you first came up with the idea for your ending, why did you decide on the ending you did? For many writers (including myself), the ending of the novel is the whole reason for writing the book, but we don't often ask ourselves, "Why?" What elements of this ending make it the "right" ending? Sometimes we can keep the core elements of the ending that make that ending important to us while changing other parts that result in a better ending overall.

<u>What makes this ending more exciting than any other scene in the book?</u>

If you still have readers by the time they reach the final scene of your novel, it's almost guaranteed that your hero has faced difficult obstacles and overcome at least some of those obstacles. What makes this final obstacle larger and grander than all the others?

<u>Does the ending have a satisfying sense of finality?</u>

Even if you're writing a novel that's part of a series, I believe each novel should have its own ending. While the story may indeed continue, the ending of a series novel represents a temporary respite. This sense of finality should be felt by your readers, who should feel that the story (at least temporarily) is at an end.

<u>Will the ending leave the reader wishing there were more without feeling there should be more?</u>

The key word in this question is "wishing." Your readers should feel like the novel is over, but they should *wish* for more because they've been enjoying your characters and your story so much, they hate to leave them behind. They still want to know what happens next without feeling like they're being cheated by the author when they're *not* told what happens next, at least not without buying the next book.

Are all of your main characters involved in the final scene? If not, why not?

We discussed the benefits of having your main characters on stage for the final act in the "Finish It Already!" section, but what if your novel is different? What if you populated your climactic scene with walk-on players? If so and your ending still isn't working, it's time to examine why you chose to keep the stars away from their biggest scene. Usually the answer to that question will help you determine if you had a good reason for what you did or whether you're about to experience an, "Oh, God, what was I thinking?" moment.

Are the main characters at peace?

I'm more than old enough to remember when *Star Wars: The Empire Strikes Back* came out. (Yes, I know, quite ancient.) I cite this movie because it's one of those that has changed greatly with time. Many critics blasted the film when it was first released because it had no ending. It was the dreaded middle episode of a trilogy. But in the years since its initial release, a strange transformation has taken place. Most critics now name this film the best of all *Star Wars* movies ever made. What changed? The film certainly didn't. To understand the initial negative reaction, you need to imagine yourself in the place of those original viewers. They'd waited impatiently for three years to see this movie. They knew it would be at least three years before they could see the next part of the series. They desperately wanted an ending. And they didn't get one. That's because the end of the film had Luke pondering the big reveal of the whole series, Han Solo had been kidnapped and a rescue attempt was being mounted, and none of the characters felt at peace. Each of them felt as if they were still smack dab in the middle of the conflict (which they were). Since none of the characters felt at peace, the viewers didn't feel at peace—and they felt like they'd been cheated out of an ending. Only in retrospect are viewers able to recognize that several plot points have been resolved and that the end of the movie is indeed a good stopping point. And before you decide that since all turned out well for *Star Wars*, you too can leave your novel without an ending, realize that if *Star Wars* hadn't been such an overwhelming success and huge money-maker, there's little chance that the last film in the trilogy would have ever been made.

The Power of a Captive Audience

Pull some writing stunt at the beginning of your novel and your reader's likely to throw your book against the wall (or in today's terms, the reader highlights the title of your novel and clicks "Remove from Device"). Either way, that reader is finished with your novel and probably you as a writer.

Late in the novel, the rules change. If you've done your job correctly, you've ensnared the reader to an extent that he will let you get away with minor irritations. That doesn't mean that you should go out of your way to irritate your reader—far from it—but sometimes in order to heighten the tension toward the end of the novel, you'll intentionally frustrate your reader to encourage them to keep reading.

Well-known examples you would normally avoid but that become viable in the latter part (normally not final scene) of your novel are:

Meaningless dream sequence

Authors love random dream sequences that only they understand; readers often hate them.

Perfect plan

The hero tells another character that he's figured out the perfect plan to defeat the villain and says he'll explain it in full—just before the chapter ends (and the reader is never told the plan).

Carrot dangling

The author intrudes with a promise of something exciting to come. For example, at the end of a chapter, a character says something like,

"If Sandy knew then that she would never leave the house alive, she never would have entered the front door."

Fake death

The hero is killed, except not; for example, the hero plunges over a cliff into the churning water below and is presumed dead—but later shows up alive and fine.

Extended cliffhangers

The hero's in the middle of an exciting situation and focus shifts elsewhere (somewhere also exciting). Focus stays away for pages or even chapters.

Plenty of writers use these throughout their novels, never realizing or caring that they're frustrating their readers. If the writers are good writers, meaning they create interesting, exciting fiction, they can get away with these anytime they feel like it. Too often, writers of lesser caliber copy their writing heroes and use these early in a novel without realizing they're losing readers. Even late in a novel when the readers are properly ensnared, the above techniques should be used cautiously and with purpose. The reason to avoid these is that they're usually not needed. Even with the "Perfect Plan," any unexpected alterations or derailments are more interesting if the reader knows what the hero was trying to do originally. Readers don't want every detail, but it doesn't hurt to let them know whether you're charging in the front gate at dawn or sneaking in the back while it's still dark.

One Step Too Far

Some writers just don't know when to shut up. As readers, we all recognize the perfect last line when it hits us. The novel is over. We rejoice! Except that it isn't over. The dunderhead of a writer has prattled on, not seeing the last line for what it was, not realizing that stuffing several extra paragraphs or even pages down our throats degraded a beautiful and intimate moment that would have immediately driven us forth in search of his next novel. Instead, when he finally releases us with "THE END", we shrug and think it was a decent book and that maybe we might buy another one from him someday with emphasis on *someday*.

So what is the perfect last line? Ideally it holds some mention of the future. Often it captures the current happy moment with an implication that the moment will continue. Many times it reflects a tiny flash of the entire novel. In the best circumstances, it will be simple: "He had never seen a mountain." or "She was going home." or "He loved Big Brother." or "After all, tomorrow is another day." or "All that was left was love and wonder." Sometimes great final lines are complicated, but for most modern books, these are often mere overplay by the author.

From a practical standpoint, the great lines of novels are recognized as great because they came at the end of great books. Great lines at the end of lousy books are never recognized as great. This is the reason why you should end your novel as soon as possible after the climactic scene has been resolved. Anything else is just self-satisfaction.

So finish it already.

There is too much. Let me sum up

Endings are more important than any other section of your novel. Allow your entire novel to contribute to your ending. Most important, make sure you have an exciting and satisfying climactic scene. Don't be afraid to craft an ending that's totally your own, but don't deviate from tried-and-true techniques without reason.

- The most important part of any novel is the ending.
- Discover your ending as soon as possible.
- Dwell on that ending as you write your novel.
- Keep your ending flexible and improve it as the full novel takes shape.
- Readers are most often satisfied with an ending when that ending provides the main character with a sense of satisfaction.
- The ending of a novel starts at the point where the novel's complexity quits increasing and continues throughout the novel's tightening and narrowing process all the way through the climactic scene.
- To create the ending for your novel, narrow the novel's focus by eliminating minor characters, concluding minor plot lines, settling trivial conflicts, and discontinuing the introduction of background information and settings.
- Increase your ending's level of excitement by constraining your hero's available time, increasing your hero's motivation, allowing your hero to experience a costly failure, expanding your hero's capabilities, and convincing the reader the hero can't succeed.
- Fit your ending within the constraints of your novel's genre.
- For the ultimate climactic scene, use an existing setting, go epic or intimate, expand the drama, use main characters, allow your hero to drive it, make it an all or nothing situation, and allow your hero to go beyond what even he thought was possible.
- There are as many different types of good endings as there are writers, so if your ending works, use it.
- Don't force your ending to be a realistic downer, but don't shy away from that realistic downer of an ending if it's the

one that works best.

- If your ending isn't working, ask yourself a series of questions that should help pinpoint the problem.
- If your novel demands that you take advantage of your reader, your ending is the most likely place where you can do it without losing the reader entirely.
- End your novel as soon as possible after the climactic scene's resolution.
- Don't worry about coming up with a great last line, because great last lines are simply the last lines from great novels.

Chapter Six:
Nuts and Bolts

How Do We Turn This Thing On?

So far we've covered beginnings, endings, story, characters, and the golden rule of writing, which is to write as much as you can. If you're a master in these skills, meaning you're a productive storyteller featuring great characters who knows how to snare a person's attention, keep it for as long as you like, and send them off with a satisfied grin on their face, then you have the overall skills you need to be a great writer. Everything else is details. But as they say, the devil is in the details. By the devil, they mean the lion's share of your available time and mental faculties.

What about when it comes time to put pen to paper? Or finger to keyboard? Or stylus to notepad? Or whatever the modern phrase would be? What then? We've talked about where to start, how to introduce your characters, get your story going, and how to finish. But the words, oh wise and powerful Oz, what about the words? And the sentences? And the paragraphs? And the scenes?

How do you actually do this thing called writing?

Be Yourself

A lot of writers talk about style as if it's the holy grail of writing. In some ways, it is, but it's not something you can manufacture. When they tell you, "Your writing should reflect your unique style," they're not giving you directions on how to make that happen. That's why so many beginning writers have prose that sounds like William Shatner at his cheesiest doing Hamlet:

> But, soft! What light ... through yonder window ... breaks? It is ... the east, and ... Juliet ... is ... the sun.

In reality, I believe William Shatner could have done Hamlet quite well when he was at the right age for the part. But those classic William Shatner halting speech patterns made famous from his days on Star Trek playing Captain Kirk form a recognizable style. In a real sense, when you're talking about having a unique style as a writer, this is what is meant. You just do what you do and readers recognize your unique twist on things.

Here's my take on style:

- Don't worry about it, meaning don't effect a style; just be yourself and eventually your style will manifest itself.
- Write as much as you can, always striving to be as interesting as you can be.
- Allow your true self to come out and edit away any rough spots.

This last one is important. Most new writers don't have style because they're on their best behavior. It's like they've all been trotted out on stage buck naked and told to stand at attention while reciting the Gettysburg Address. This is never good. At least not in terms of style. And yet this example holds the key to your success. Practice while endeavoring to succeed. If you did 100 performances of that Gettysburg Address in the nude, and the level of your performance reflected how many raw fruits and vegetables the audience tossed your way, chances are good you would either learn how to perform well (or at least in an interesting way) or you'd end up in the hospital.

Writing is similar. You try your best. Either you succeed (readers like you) or they don't. Both results are acceptable. Not everyone will like you, meaning not everyone will like your style. Chances are good some people will. That's what you're going for. Fans. The worst result you can achieve is indifference. If you're forgettable, you will be forgotten.

Your unique take on everything is the most powerful asset you have to bring to the table. No one can match that. No one can take it away. The trick is believing that you are worthwhile.

I guarantee there are tons of writers who hate this book you're reading. They don't like my approach or my tone or my advice. But it's all me. That's what matters.

This doesn't mean you don't try your best. Tell the best stories you can in the best way you know how. But don't be afraid to be yourself. You can't capture lightning in a bottle if you're not willing to brave the thunder.

Diction

Remember that editor who told me that diction was the only thing that editors couldn't fix? While the dictionary definition of good diction is all about the proper choice of words, that's misleading. This editor wasn't saying you had to be proper, but rather that you must show control and you must communicate effectively. If the reader can't understand what you're saying, all else is lost. A famous saying is often attributed to Winston Churchill related to the edict not to end your sentences with prepositions:

> This is the sort of bloody nonsense up with which I will not put.

Darn tootin'. Whether Winston really said it is irrelevant. It's a better story if he does. And what he's saying is that a writer's (or speaker's) most important job is to communicate effectively. It's about flow. It's about being understood.

Unfortunately many writers, even experienced writers, don't understand this. I've even had a writer (who commented on my manuscript) use a version of Winston's quote as a reason why she had changed my sentence so that it didn't end in a preposition. Really? It's this lack of understanding that I believe is what my editor friend meant when she said you needed good diction. Learn how to communicate your ideas effectively, but above all, be yourself.

Elementary

Oh lordy, how writers do love to redefine what words mean! Techniques, modes, elements, parts, pieces, remnants, tatters, blah, blah, blah. I wouldn't bother to attach a name to this section at all, except that a blank section name looks a lot like a blank page.

Never fear. All I'm doing here is discussing various parts of fiction writing, such as:

- Dialogue
- Action
- Narration
- Introspection
- Foreshadowing
- Description
- Recollection and Flashback
- Transitions

In all honesty, these words are just handy tags we attach to the ears of our fiction so we can talk to other fiction ranchers about what's going on with these herds of words we call our novels. By themselves, your understanding of these terms don't help you write better. They allow you to frame the questions you ask yourself and others when you're writing your novel. They also allow folks who talk about writing (like me) to gather together our ideas about a particular aspect of writing and bind them into a tidy package for your benefit.

The list above is roughly ordered by my view of their importance. Story and characters are the two great cornerstones upon which everything else is built. From that viewpoint, all the elements listed above are merely assistants designed to increase the emotional impact of your story, your characters, or both.

Dialogue

Dialogue says so much.

As readers, we often decide how much we like a character by how they talk, by what they say, and by the conversations they have with other characters we like or dislike. Dialogue helps sets the mood. It can make us laugh. It can make us cry. It can convince us to fall in love. Above all, it's one of the most powerful tools in helping us to feel what the characters feel and allowing us to step into the characters shoes and walk around the story.

What is dialogue then? It's the words your characters say, obviously, but it's more than that.

Impression Is Everything

Writing good dialogue isn't about capturing reality. The words you put on the page aren't meant to represent the way people talk in real life. Why? Because real life (and real dialogue) is boring! I could give you plenty of examples here, but it's easy to hear plenty of "real life" examples every day: Just listen to the folks around you the next time you're waiting in line.

What's interesting to me is that many writers who write great dialogue claim they learned to write dialogue by listening to other people talk (and they will recommend that you learn to write dialogue by listening to people talk). This is a truth, but it's not the only truth, and it's certainly not the whole truth. When learning to write dialogue by listening to people conversing, think of yourself as a reporter. You've decided to include a couple of short quotes in an article you're writing about underwater basket weaving for the social page in the local weekly. But the whole article's only 250 words long. At the weekly meeting of Underwater Basket Weavers Anonymous, you hear about 6,000 words spoken in the hour you're there. You can use maybe 25-50 of those for your article. That's less than 1%. Think you'll pick the most boring and least informative 1%? Not if you're any good at your job.

The same situation holds true as a writer. If you want to learn how to write dialogue, it doesn't hurt to listen to real dialogue, looking for that sparkly gem among the mounds and mounds of julienne dribble, but it's a lot more efficient to listen to (or read) great dialogue in genres similar to the one you're writing.

The key when writing dialogue is that you're not trying to write a real conversation that anyone would ever have. You're trying to create an impression of reality. The conversation you create should feel real. If you're successful, your fictional conversation will feel more real to your readers than the conversations they have with flesh and blood people. Who knows? Maybe those readers will even start quoting your dialogue in everyday life.

Here's another secret. Great dialogue in fiction is rarely great dialogue anywhere else. It's the story and the characters who make a line of dialogue hum. That's why great movie quotes are typically great only if you've seen the movie. Take these famous quotes, for example:

- "Of all the gin joints in all the towns in all the world, she walks into mine."
- "I'll be back."
- "Frankly my dear, I don't give a damn!"
- "You talkin' to me? You talkin' to me? You talkin' to me? Well, who the hell else are you talkin' to? You talkin' to me? Well, I'm the only one here. Who the fuck do you think you're talkin' to?"
- "Toto, I've a feeling we're not in Kansas anymore."

There's nothing special about these quotes beyond the stories (films) that contained them. Like so much of fiction, if you want to write great dialogue, create a slew of great characters and release them into a great story. If you do that, the dialogue will almost write itself. Your job then is to get the hell out of the way and let it flow.

Work It, Work It Good

Unless you have an excellent reason to the contrary, all dialogue should be interesting, understandable, and easy to read. Go beyond that minimum benchmark by creating dialogue that functions on as many levels as possible:

- Identifies the character speaking
- Conveys information

- Specifies motives
- Provides descriptions of characters and settings
- Increases conflict
- Keeps the novel moving

We'll cover each of these individually, but good dialogue will be a mix from the list above and your best sections of dialogue will include all of these.

He Had a Way with Words

Characters should be recognizable by what they say and how they say it. This will rarely be 100% foolproof—that's why we attribute a line of dialogue with a "he said" or a "she said—" but normally a reader should be able to match a line of dialogue to the correct character if they spend a second thinking about it. We provide attributes so that readers don't have to waste that second thinking about it. The last thing you want is for readers to stumble along not sure who said what because you never use any attributes, unless, of course, you're Elmore Leonard. No slight to the late, great Elmore Leonard, but a dislike of attributes isn't what I'm talking about here.

Your characters should have speech patterns that are comprised of the words they use, the topics they choose to talk about most of the time, the length of their sentences, and the tone of their conversations. More than that, their speech patterns should change when they're under duress, when they're excited, when they're in love, etc. Even so, at all times their speech pattern should be uniquely theirs. While it's true that family members and close friends will often share a few speech similarities, all of your characters should be unique. Most of the time, they should talk like it.

But That's What She Said

We all know that person who talks just to hear themselves talk, but typically the purpose of the spoken word is to convey information. No surprise then that most dialogue in a novel also conveys information. As in real life, that information might be accurate or inaccurate. Typically people speak a version of the truth unless they have a reason not to. Characters do the same. In many genres, it's expected that a good share of the people our hero encounters will be deceitful at some level. When our viewpoint character is deceitful, it's normal practice to let the reader know about this deceit through introspection or through later dialogue with a trusted confidante. In a similar way, if our viewpoint character believes he's talking to someone who's lying, our viewpoint character typically reveals that information to the reader through introspection or as part of the dialogue:

> "I never saw that woman before in my life."
>
> "You're lying!"

Not exactly subtle. But it works. That's just one of the reasons that many viewpoint characters are somewhat rash and outspoken. It's makes the author's job easier.

Overall, most dialogue will be relatively accurate and truthful. This isn't a writer-held belief in the greater good. Having characters speak the truth is necessary for the sake of efficiency and clarity. Plus it makes their lies more meaningful. If a character lies constantly, all the lies blend together into insignificance.

It's What I Want

Motivation is vital to conflict. Without motivation, your characters just sit there. To understand the conflict in your novel, readers need to understand the motivations of your main characters. Obviously you could just tell the reader through narration, but showing is usually better. Dialogue is one good technique for revealing motivation (the other is action). But it's usually not as simple as your main character saying something like, "I want to get off this rock because I find it incredibly boring here. I want adventure and excitement!" This is what Luke could have said in the first *Star Wars* movie. Instead, he talked about droids and transferring his application this year instead of next, and how if there was any excitement in the universe, this was the furthest place from it. The dialogue was spread over multiple scenes and spoken to multiple people. That's what you're looking for. Give your characters motivations. Then allow those motivations to reveal themselves naturally through what your characters do and say.

<u>She's a Looker</u>

I detest novels that have the main character admire herself in the mirror early in the first chapter, especially when that seems to be the main (or worse, sole) purpose of the opening scene: to give the writer the chance to tell us what their main character looks like in gory detail. A character's physical appearance is important. It determines how other people treat them. It limits or expands their options in certain situations. But too much detail about a character's appearance can be a bad thing. After all, when they make your novel into that blockbuster movie, they might not be able to find an actress who looks the part.

Describing what a character looks like using dialogue works wonders when it comes to protecting writers from themselves. It's hard to have a paragraph of dialogue like this:

> Sara said, "Nancy, even though you're staring at the bedroom mirror, I bet you don't notice the frizz of your wet, curly, brown hair, the flush of your skin, or the ripple of your well-defined muscles that are exposed because you're wearing nothing except your black sports bra and training shorts."

And yet, many writers seem to feel it's okay to share this kind of crap with their readers directly by using narration. Never mind that it's a loss of viewpoint. If a character looks in the mirror and doesn't notice something, then how are they reporting it to the reader? Oh, right, they're not. The writer's using an omnipotent viewpoint, often unintentionally, to tell the reader something that the writer probably should have kept to themselves.

The great thing about describing characters or places through dialogue is that you get to the true purpose of the writer's intent without any guesswork. If you want your main character to be gorgeous, simply telling the reader in narration that Julie was gorgeous is considered cliché and without much meaning. But if Julie's good friend Linda says to her, "What are you worried about, Julie? You're gorgeous. He'll be falling all over himself to ask you to prom," then the reader conjures up a mental image of someone they find gorgeous.

The same is true if a character says, "Kanona? Why would you want to move to Kanona? It's not even a wide spot in the road." Immediately the reader knows that Kanona is some incredibly tiny town with little of interest.

The Hell You Say!

There are many ways to heighten conflict in your story, but dialogue is one of the more powerful and natural ways to increase conflict and heighten tension in a novel. Take the following example:

> "How was the library?"
>
> "Good. Quiet."
>
> "Did you finish your report?"
>
> "Almost. I got all the references I need. Now I just need to type it up."
>
> "Bullshit!"
>
> "What?"
>
> "You heard me. You weren't at the library. I was at the library. For hours I was at the library, waiting for you, waiting to give you this!"
>
> "A ring?"
>
> "An engagement ring."
>
> "But we promised we wouldn't get serious. You said you didn't want to get married."
>
> "Well, I damned sure don't now!"

This passage is less than 100 words long, but it conveys a lot of information. Dialogue, if done correctly, is always a form of showing. It allows tension to form naturally rather than being painted on with the wide brush of a clumsy writer.

Where Did He Say That?

We live in a video world. In a video world, dialogue is the fuel that drives our stories forward and completes the character portraits we've painted. Did you know that a lot of modern readers simply skip long passages of narration? If you want to guarantee a reader will notice a vitally important piece of information, put it in dialogue form. More than that, make it catchy, interesting dialogue. Imagine the following conversation:

>"Get your filthy hands off it!"
>
>"Whatever you say. If you touched it, I certainly don't want to."
>
>"It's broken! I can't believe you broke it."
>
>"Of course I didn't break it. It was that way when I walked in."
>
>"Liar!"
>
>"Oh, don't be so melodramatic. It's only a cookie. Still perfectly edible."
>
>"Not after you touched it."
>
>"Hmmm, then can I have it?"

Just pure dialogue. And yet, it's not only much more dramatic than the same scene as pure narration, but also the same scene as narration would be almost impossible to pull off. Granted, we could make this conversation better with a few attributes, a few actions, perhaps a bit of introspection, but readers have a much better chance of remembering this argument over the broken cookie if it's presented through dialogue than they would if it were recounted as narration.

Attributes

Dialogue is much more effective when we know who says what. The easiest way to be sure the reader knows who's talking is to slap an attribute on your dialogue. In most circumstances, that attribute is going to be "he said" or "she said." Does that mean we slap an attribute on every line of dialogue? No. It means we give the reader information that allows them to recognize who's talking. This recognition should be automatic, requiring minimal effort on the reader's part. What you don't want is the reader counting back from the line they just read to one that had an attribute nine paragraphs earlier, then gradually tracing their way through the minefield of talking heads to figure out who said what.

Many ways exist to clarify who is speaking. The following sample of methods are ranked in order of preference:

1) Action
2) Context
3) Unique style of speech
4) Direct attribute (he said, she said)

If you have a paragraph with a character action immediately followed by a line of dialogue, the character who performed the action is the same as the one who spoke. Action implies speech if it's in the same paragraph. If it's in the next paragraph, it implies a different person spoke from the one who just performed the action.

> I kept walking. "How long before we get there?"
>
> vs.
>
> I kept walking.
>
> "How long before we get there?"

If you only have two people in a scene, the two-paragraph example above a is legit way to identify that it was not "I" who spoke. "I" was walking. It's the other (currently nameless) character who spoke. For the one-paragraph example above, the viewpoint character "I" is clearly the one who asks how long it will take.

Character action is one of the most common ways to identify the speaker for a line of dialogue.

Context can uniquely identify the speaker. The most obvious context example is the two-person scene where one person is clearly identified as the speaker for the first line of dialogue. The second line of dialogue (in a new paragraph) is then unquestionably the other person in the scene. Unless told otherwise, most readers will assume a conversation goes back and forth, so alternating is expected.

A somewhat more complicated context is when one character just got hit by a truck and the other characters in the scene are trying to help.

> "Are you okay?"
>
> "Can you move?"
>
> "Of course not! Has anyone seen my leg?"

It's not hard to guess who's the injured party here. That's context.

While I believe all characters should have their own mannerism and patterns of speech, identifying a character quickly and easily from their dialogue alone is always risky. If you use that technique, it should be immediately obvious who spoke from what was said. If the reader has to think for even half a second to figure it out, that's way too long.

The last and easiest way to identify the speaker for your dialogue is the direct attribute. For the most part, this means the verb "said," but other attributes are sometimes appropriate. "Shouted," "whispered," "sang," "asked," and "yelled," are all valid. Don't let anyone tell you otherwise, provided you've used them sparingly and as they were intended. For example, "Where are you going?" Mom asked. "To the mall," we all sang out together. This works for me, but I can see where it would be abhorrent to many writers. On the other hand

> "Dashing through the snow, in a one-horse open sleigh," he sang.

is going to be acceptable to nearly everyone.

There are folks who hate all attributes, most attributes, particular attributes, etc. Don't worry about those people. They're fanatics. They're entitled to their opinions, but it doesn't mean they're right.

Consider our most recent example.

> When I walked into the kitchen, I found Sara Lee. I couldn't believe what she was doing and shouted before I could stop myself. "Get your filthy hands off it!"
>
> She shrugged. "Whatever you say. If you touched it, I certainly don't want to."
>
> Allowing her wrist to go limp, she opened her fingers. It fell.
>
> I rushed forward and looked down. "It's broken! I can't believe you broke it."
>
> "Of course I didn't break it. It was that way when I walked in."
>
> "Liar!"

Spittle flew out along with the word.

"Oh, don't be so melodramatic. It's only a cookie. Still perfectly edible."

I groaned and sunk to the floor. "Not after you touched it."

She grinned. "Hmmm, then can I have it?"

Notice that we haven't used any direct attributes at all in this passage. This is the norm for most of the modern fiction I read. Action and context. Not that you can't throw in a said or shouted once in a awhile when it's awkward not to do so. It's worse to spend time thinking about it and slow down your writing than it is to use a few attributes.

There's nothing overly complicated about it, but a lot of professional writers hate using attributes. When we talk to people, write them texts or emails, put stuff out on Twitter or Pinterest, or even send them an old fashioned letter, we're communicating. For all its literary pretention, fiction is just another form of communication. If your reader doesn't understand what you mean, they're not going to appreciate all the subtle humor and plot twists you've so carefully devised. Beyond anything else you do, you must communicate.

What you're looking to avoid is having a dialogue tennis match.

"Get your filthy hands off it!" I shouted.

"Whatever you say," she said. "If you touched it, I certainly don't want to."

"It's broken!" I replied. "I can't believe you broke it."

"Of course I didn't break it." she said. "It was that way when I walked in."

"Liar!" I shouted.

She said, "Oh, don't be so melodramatic. It's only a cookie. Still perfectly edible."

"Not after you touched it," I said.

"Hmmm, then can I have it?" she asked.

Not only are most of these attributes not needed, they're clunky and repetitive. It's passages of dialogue like this that led some writers to swear off attributes entirely.

You may have noticed that I didn't mention speaking a name as a way of identifying who was talking. That's an overused technique that sounds nothing like a real conversation. Most people can talk to their best friend or a sibling for hours and never mention the other person's name. Names aren't used in place of attributes. They are used for emphasis, the same as we do in real life.

> "This new XR-7 autoflight 3000 is a beauty. If you fly around town in a vehicle like this, Jack, you'll feel like a new man."

Salespeople use names of clients in dialogue all the time. Research indicates that most people are flattered when someone they don't know well remembers their name. Another example is when a kid gets in trouble.

> "Marty Michael Vincent, get your ass in here before I paddle your hide within an inch of your life!"

Sometimes a person will use a person's name when they're trying to break into a conversation.

> Mary touched the waiter on the arm and gave him her best coy smile. "Oh, you are so funny!"
>
> He leered and leaned in close to whisper something in her ear.
>
> "Mary," I said, "we're leaving."

People also use the name of someone they care about deeply in tense moments.

> "I just don't know, Shanice. We've tried to make it work three times now. I'm not sure I can try again."

Most writers overuse this technique. Don't increase your usage by using it for attributes as well.

As You Know, Bob

Another mistake to avoid is having fake conversations. This rarely happens if you remain tightly inside the head of your viewpoint character. If you do that, when you try to have that fake conversation, your viewpoint character will look at you in disgust and declare, "I'm not saying that, you twit. I already know the information we're discussing and so does the person I'm talking to."

The temptation to use an "As You Know, Bob" passage comes from the need to get information to the reader and the inherent laziness or ever present lack of time that prevents our inventing an imaginative way to do so.

> "You, as my underling, have been working beside me for eighteen months, but right before we detonate the secret weapon, I think we should go over how it works one more time."
>
> "Yes," Kelly replied. "We'll need to make sure we transport the device packed in liquid nitrogen, or it could go off prematurely."
>
> "Of course, you're right," I said. "The RS 232 isotope we developed may sound like a communication protocol, but it's really an unheard of power source that will allow us to conquer the world. Tonight's destruction is just the first step on our path to absolute power."

This example's hokey, but beginning writers make this mistake often enough that it has its own name: "As You Know, Bob."

A similar technique is to say the same thing in monologue.

> "As you know, Bob," I said to myself, "I need to make sure my underlings know the device must be transported packed in liquid nitrogen, or it could go off prematurely.
>
> "The RS 232 isotope I created is no communication protocol. It's the unheard of power

source that will allow me to conquer the world. Tonight's destruction is just the first step on my way to absolute power."

Action

This category is not about scenes, as in action scenes or fight scenes. By action, I mean the actions your characters take. In its simplest form, this is prose that lets the reader know what your characters are doing. This includes facial expressions, body language, and physical movement.

When writers or editors instruct you in deafening shouts of "Show! Don't tell!" they are referring in part to action. If you reveal what a character is doing by specifying their actions, you're showing. Compare the following examples.

> Showing: Dorothy twirled, her dress billowing, the heels of her silver shoes clacking on the yellow bricks of the winding road.

> Telling: Dorothy's elation at being able to go home prompted several seconds of dancing.

Actions let the reader know what's happening at any given moment. They're concrete rather than abstract. Another way to think of it is that actions are process rather than result. For example, "Captain Kirk escaped the Gorn's grasp," is not action, because it specifies a result rather than a process. "Captain Kirk scrambled backward in a shower of gravel. The Gorn closed its massive arms on the spot Kirk had been a moment before." That's action.

Actions can be as simple as "He frowned," "She smiled," or "They sat on the couch," but those aren't as specific as "His brow wrinkled and the corners of his mouth dug into this chin," "Her teeth flashed as her cheeks dimpled," or "They collapsed in a heap, crushing the cushions of the couch."

However, this kind of overwriting can get old quickly. If you find yourself writing "he smiled" or "she smiled" too often, consider removing the actions instead of doctoring them into a blow by blow progression of facial muscle movements.

The same goes for finding that perfect verb instead of avoiding the dreaded adverb. Many writers will struggle to find just the perfect way to say, "He raised his arm slowly," when sometimes all the writer is really trying to say is, "He raised his arm slowly." Having said that, adverbs can get tiresome. "He ran quickly," is stronger as, "He sprinted." "She walked slowly," is often a weaker way to say, "She ambled."

Actions are sensory. If a character does something that another character (or the reader) can see, smell, hear, taste, or feel, it's usually an action. Typically actions support dialogue. The exceptions happen in action and fight scenes where dialogue often supports actions or introspections.

Narration

Despite all the advice to the contrary, telling (rather than showing) holds an important place in your novel. If you show every little action, if readers gain most of their information through dialogue, the novel slows down. This is because some actions and information aren't important enough to justify the space it would take to show that information rather than telling it.

And that's what narration is: telling. Note that I call it *narration.* Other writers might call it narrative, or even narrative summary. A few might call it exposition, narrative exposition, or summarization. The key is that if you narrate something, you tell it.

The problem with telling rather than showing is that narration robs your scenes of their emotional punch. Readers read because they enjoy experiencing the story as it unfolds. Put another way, they feel what the main character feels. Those feelings are what keeps your readers turning pages.

But not just any feelings. As a writer, you should concentrate on feelings related to your story. For example, driving in rush hour traffic when you're late for an appointment can be frustrating and infuriating. Those feelings only matter if they relate to our story. For example, if our serial killer just called our heroine and told her he'd drugged her boyfriend and dumped him in a low lying ravine just before the start of a major thunderstorm, it's vital to the story whether she makes it across the city in time to save him. As a writer, you should show that drive in L.A. traffic. But if our hero is late for an anniversary dinner with his wife, the fact he's late is more important than his turn by turn attempt to make it on time. In that case, you might narrate the following:

> Jethro fought the L.A. rush hour traffic for two hours and arrived fifteen minutes late to Chez Pricey. He fought his way through the crowd near the maitre d' and found Delores already seated at their favorite table.

The emotional impact to the story will happen after Jethro approaches the table and Delores lets him have it for being late and not calling.

His harrowing journey across town is important, but only as a background fact.

Narration is typically used to:

- Summarize an event that has no significant emotional or informative benefit if presented to the reader as a scene
- Connect two disparate sequences of time during an interlude where little of import happens
- Provide a block of background information related to an object, person, or place in the current scene
- Describe a gradual, incremental transition that happens over an extended period of time where isolated individual changes have no meaning, but where the collective changes result in a major character or environmental alteration

The power of narration stems from its high signal to noise ratio of information. With all narration but humor, your goal is to convey as much information as possible in as few words as practical.

Writing narration doesn't relieve you from making what you're writing as interesting as you can. The less interesting it is, the shorter it should be. But sometimes a reader just needs to have the story told to them, the way your retired mother tells you about the strange neighbor lady who just moved in and likes to nude sunbathe in her living room in the middle of the night, shades up.

For example, consider the following extended bit of narration.

> "Don't tell me I have to take the Buick?"
>
> "What else?"
>
> The Buick was a long-running family joke that everyone had heard too many times. A 1959 Buick LeSabre, barely used, purchased by my grandfather several years before I was born. From him, it fell to my dad. Then it fell in my lap like an extra large, extra hot coffee from McDonalds. Long ago, the car had been white. Whether that was the original color, I had no idea. Not that it mattered. The white had chipped off long ago. Now the car was rust. Not the color of rust. Just rust. Literally. It still drove. That's the thing about those old Buicks:

They're impossible to kill without a brick wall and a lot of speed. But I hated that car from the moment dad first said, "She's yours!"

Who could blame me? A teenage boy in the early 2000s driving a beat-up wreck so old nobody even knew what it was. And the mileage was measured in gallons per mile rather than miles per gallon. It was all I could do to keep enough gas in it to drive it twice a week. And that's when gas was cheap.

And now, freshly graduated from college and back for my last visit before I join the prestigious law firm of Harry, Harry, Harry, and Smith, I want to spend one last night on the town. But I can only do so if I take the Buick.

I hated the Buick.

There's no reason to show any of this background information related to this old car, but the reader needs to know it, either for its quirky prop value or because the old Buick gets hit in the next chapter by a warhead fired by an RPG. Nearly unbelievable, the Buick is still drivable after that. The reader needs to know about and appreciate that old Buick. Giving them a bit of its history helps them to do that.

Most stories you write will need this kind of background information. Note that if the background information provided stretches on for a page or more, you should consider putting a scene break before and after the narration. This lets the reader know that you're about to do something different. In this case, you're going to tell them the story of the old Buick. Sit back, relax, and listen until the next section break, when we return to our regularly scheduled programming.

Introspection

Movies are visual. Novels are mental. That makes sense given that most writers are mental. Okay, maybe just the ones I know. And yes, I'm including myself in that group.

Films have a power that novels can't match. In a film, you see and hear what's happening. It's right there in front of you. As a result, the most mundane story element can be stimulating. Take the typical car chase. It may suck up fifteen minutes of the movie, but in terms of story, literally nothing happens. Our protagonist chases our antagonist across the city. The screen is filled with crashes, explosions, and impossible stunts, all of which are punctuated by a couple of humorous one-liners. In the movie *The Rock* starring Nicolas Cage and Sean Connery, the main car chase scene takes up 5% of the movie, more if you throw out the credits. Yet nothing story-wise happens beyond flashes of pictures that drill straight into a viewer's brain and make it all seem so exciting.

But novels have something films don't. Introspection. Sure, our film private eye can say something along the lines of,

> "She walked through my door like a soccer mom bent on retrieving a toddler from day care on the day of her big dinner party. Dressed to the nines in stiletto heels that somehow matched her business suit, she looked right through me like I wasn't there. Perhaps I wasn't. I don't know. I haven't been on camera yet."

The difference is that voiceovers in film, especially voiceovers that tell exactly what a character is thinking, are inherently cheesy. The difference comes from the fact that a viewpoint character in a novel is our only source of information. Provided the writer doesn't slip into omnipotent viewpoint, we hear, see, taste, smell, and touch everything through the senses of our viewpoint character. Having that viewpoint character reveal his thoughts is as natural as being told that he's breathing hard after that long chase on foot. It's natural. It's expected. And it's powerful.

A reader and a writer share a special bond. A writer creates a story and conceives characters fully formed, but a reader gives them life. Everything about the fictional world from a novel is created in the reader's mind. That's why introspection goes straight to a reader's brain the way those exciting pictures and sounds go straight to a film goer's brain. They connect reader with viewpoint character in a way nothing else can.

What Is It?

Introspection are thoughts. They can tell us anything that a character knows or suspects or feels. When done correctly, a reader gains more understanding about a character from their introspections than from any other source.

The amount of introspection and the way you convey that introspection are dependent upon your own style and upon the type of novel you're writing. A handy guide to keep in mind is that you should typically use more highly emotional introspection than you do non-emotional introspection. Plus the more introspection you use, the more tightly your reader will connect with your viewpoint character. Imagine the following scene snippet:

> Stevan wished he were back in bed, dreaming of happier days. Bruised and bleeding from his desperate escape through the hole in the chain link fence, he crawled toward the underside of the dump truck, hoping against all logic that the shadows would hide him. The gravel beneath his raw hands cut into his palms and it took all his willpower not to slow down or cry out from the pain.
>
> Just a few more feet.
>
> Minutes ago he had been confident. Jubilant even. The deal was going exactly as he'd planned. Now his financial future was ruined, and his life balanced on whether he could reach safety in time. The sharp tang of gasoline and the musty smell of axle grease tickled his nose. He prayed he wouldn't sneeze. In surprise,

```
he realized he was grinning at the ridiculous
thought of his life lost because he'd failed to
take an allergy pill this morning.
```

The above passage is laden with introspection of different types. While we have no dialogue and very little action, the passage draws the reader in. An empathic reader feels Stevan's pain and desperation. These are emotions. Sharing those emotions with a viewpoint character is why most readers read, and introspection is the bucket you can use to draw those emotions up and pour them onto the reader. While it's true that you can create powerful emotions in a reader without the slightest hint of introspection, it requires more effort, both on your part and on the reader's part. By contrast, introspection is a gift that keeps on giving.

Many writers will go on to make up a bunch of rules regarding introspection. Things such as "Never reveal emotions directly (Stevan felt more afraid than he ever had before)," "Never use the words 'she thought,' (That's the silliest dress I've ever seen, she thought)," or "Never put a character's direct thoughts in italics." While these are decent recommendations, the truth is that none of them matter much as long as you're consistent and you have a great story populated by great characters. That's because introspection is used to get a reader's juices flowing. If the reader isn't into your story, all introspections are likely to seem contrived and cheesy.

A few introspection guidelines seem worth your attention:

- Only your viewpoint character is allowed to introspect. If you're head-hopping like a crazed Jack Russell Terrier begging for treats, you can introspect with any viewpoint character you have, but those hoards of introspecting characters still need to be genuine viewpoint characters and not innocent bystanders.
- For third-person, past tense points-of-view where you have a first-person direct thought, that thought should be in present tense. For example, "When Jack returned from the airline bathroom, he groaned at the site of the emergency door open and everyone wearing a parachute except him. Why am I always the last to know about these things?" If it's not a direct

thought, then it would be past tense, just as with the rest of your normal prose.

- Italics are not necessary in today's world, but if you use them, the only introspections you should italicize are direct thoughts. For example, you could have italicized the "Why am I always…," thought in the above bullet item.

- The more intense and emotional your introspections, the less grammatically correct and formal they should be. In the scene snippet above, "Just a few more feet," is a sentence fragment, but the fun and games don't stop there. If someone's in a highly emotional state, they aren't thinking clearly. Any confusion and excitement should come out through the language used to express their thoughts even more so than the thoughts themselves. Repetition, incomplete sentences, exclamation points, and a general narrowing of focus to a pinpoint are the order of the day. Consider the following example:

> No, damn it, not Juli. Not Juli! It can't be.
> If only— Not too late— But cold. Lifeless. Dead.

- Unless you're employing some advanced artistic technique best saved for attempts to win a prize rather than satisfy your reader, introspections should always be accurate and truthful. The other characters aren't getting this window into your viewpoint character's thoughts. Introspections are aimed squarely at the reader. Lie in an introspection and you're lying to your reader. Do that and you breach reader trust, which is a bit like crossing the streams in the movie *Ghostbusters*— only much worse.

Characters are people, and like people, they don't always tell the truth or reveal exactly what's on their minds, unless that character is introspecting. One of the main ingredients that makes introspections so powerful is that you're giving the reader a glimpse into a character's mind. If you've done your job right, your reader cares about your viewpoint character and is therefore naturally interested in what they're thinking, feeling, and experiencing. And they want it in the non-filtered way that only introspection can provide.

Foreshadowing

As writers, we wave our magic wands and create entire worlds out of nothing more than words. It's a crazy concept that's driven by a reader's suspension of disbelief. It's a game every reader plays. They know what they're reading isn't real. They know every novel has a beginning and an end. Deep down, they know these characters that they love aren't real. They pretend that they are because it's a heck of a lot more fun that way. If your reader is constantly thinking, "What a load of crap!" because your story or your characters are unbelievable, chances are pretty good you're not selling another novel to that particular reader.

Foreshadowing is one of the techniques that helps your reader suspend their disbelief. In *The Lord of the Rings,* when the Balrog rises from the depths of the mines of Moria and fights the seemingly invincible Gandalf to a draw, it's much more believable because the reader has already been given many hints about the great evil that lurks in Moria. Gandalf himself told them, "There are older and fouler things than Orcs in the deep places of the world." When the Balrog finally appears, not only does the reader believe a beast such as the Balrog can exist, they've been waiting for it to show up.

Such is the power and the necessity of foreshadowing.

While the need for foreshadowing is clearest in the fantastical genres, it's equally necessary in the real-life settings found in police procedurals and romance novels. If the heroine in a romance novel is going to fall in love with that guy she hated when she met him in Chapter One, the reader has to be given a basis for that change of heart. Maybe the heroine has always longed to meet a tall, handsome, mysterious stranger. Granted, the one she pictured in her head wasn't a complete jerk, but the seeds are there. Readers sense the rightness of it because the writer prepares them to accept the transformation in the heroine's feelings.

Foreshadowing is typically reserved as preparation for large changes. If our heroine always wanted to be a surgeon, but is going to give up her dream in Chapter Twenty-three to become a stay-at-home mom, that level of unbelievability takes a ton of preparation.

If most of our novel is set in the world as we know it, but aliens show up in the last chapter, the reader needs to be primed to accept and possibly expect their appearance.

To a lesser degree, foreshadowing can also be used to heighten reader interest or for humorous effect. These are valid uses, but typically their use is more style than necessity.

Priest of Janus

Creating great foreshadowing is a bit like playing with time. Information is given to the reader that makes sense in the current scene but that also plants seeds that produce fruit ready to harvest in later scenes.

Foreshadowing can be direct or indirect.

The Lord of the Rings example concerning the Balrog is direct foreshadowing. It usually comes up in dialogue and it often comes up as a warning or an apprehension. "I wouldn't go campin' up at that lake if I was you," the old man says. This immediately tells the reader something bad is going to happen up at the lake. That's direct. It also warns the reader that they're going to lose at least some of these characters, so be prepared for it.

Chekhov's Gun is a classic example of indirect foreshadowing. If you have a gun in a story (or a harpoon, or a joy buzzer), someone is going to get hit with the object in question before the end of your novel. Some objects are used more than others (such as the antique rifle hanging on the wall that our crusty old secondary character says he keeps loaded to remind himself of younger days). When the reader is told about that rifle, the reader expects that rife to be used. Granted, in today's world, our hero might try to use the rifle, have it fail to go off, and use it to beat the villain senseless instead of shooting him. It still gets used.

Anticipation

Have you ever read a novel where a cliffhanger at the end of a chapter starts with something like, "If she only knew then what would happen, she would have never …." This is an example of direct foreshadowing being used to increase anticipation. I wouldn't recommend using this exact technique, but the example is clear enough. The writer lets the reader know that *something* is going to happen. This kind of foreshadowing is done for immediate effect. In essence, the writer is begging the reader to keep reading.

A more subtle and effective form of foreshadowing can be used to build reader anticipation for a final climactic scene. To demonstrate what I'm talking about, I can draw on U.S. history.

Let's say the Battle of Gettysburg was actually a novel. In the beginning, a major battle is foreshadowed, because that's what the two armies were doing in Pennsylvania. General Robert E. Lee wanted to draw the Union Army from its strong defensive position, so he could destroy it. General Joe Hooker wanted to keep his army between Lee's army and the capital of Washington, D.C.

In the actual history, neither army planned to fight at Gettysburg before the battle started: They just knew they would fight eventually. Initially the battle started with a skirmish between just a few units. As the battle progressed, each side brought more and more men into the fray. With each scene in our imaginary novel, we can build information crucial to our final scene. The Union has the high ground. The Confederate forces must take it from them. The Union's flank is growing longer. The Confederate forces must get around it and roll up the line to route the whole force. Each scene we write works on its own, but each makes it clear that if this attack doesn't succeed, desperate measures will be needed. Then those measures become more detailed based on events that are happening. Fresh troops will be needed to succeed. A massive artillery bombardment is the only way to soften up the entrenched positions. Coordinated movements will be required. Diversionary attacks are the only way to hide the true plan.

Then, when the climactic attack finally takes place, the reader's on edge. This is what they've been waiting for. Not only are they eager for the final charge to begin, they understand the positions of both armies, what's at stake, and the plans of attack and defense.

This information isn't all foreshadowing, but much of the anticipation comes from foreshadowing. Hints are given about what might go wrong and what might go right. Readers want to know which it will be. Will the attack happen the way the leaders envision? What unexpected problems will crop up? This heightened drama comes from an abundance of information and a clear understanding of the motivations on each side.

Flashback scenes also benefit greatly from foreshadowing. Before the flashback takes place, you want the reader hungry for the information you will provide. If they're eagerly anticipating the scene, they are much more willing to travel back in time to witness an event that's already occurred (and is therefore less dramatic). If you then do your flashback well, they are satisfied and happy to return to the present to continue with your story.

Humor

It might be better to label this type of foreshadowing as amusing rather than humorous. On rare occasions, particularly clever foreshadowing can cause a good belly laugh, but what we're usually going for here is an extra bit of entertainment for readers who are paying close attention. In essence, some tidbit of information exists in an earlier scene that hints or predicts later events. Like much of the foreshadowing we do, these bits of info are only recognized as foreshadowing after the predicted event takes place.

Here's a couple quick examples from well-known films: In *Psycho,* Norman Bates says that his mother's as harmless as his stuffed birds. This is fitting because his mother is actually stuffed. In *The Empire Strikes Back,* Luke kills Darth Vader in a vision and sees his own face beneath Darth Vader's mask. This predicts Luke's discovery that Darth is indeed his father.

One of my favorite humorous foreshadowing examples is from an old John Wayne movie that few of you have seen called Big Jake. In it, John Wayne plays Jacob McCandles, who everyone seems to have heard of a long time ago but hasn't heard anything about recently. As a result, whenever they realize they're talking to *the* Jacob McCandles, they're naturally surprised. Each can't help saying, "I thought you were dead." The next to last time this happens in the movie, John replies, "Dead? The next person who says that, I'm going to shoot, so help me." And so he does. the humor comes from an exchange of cause and effect. John Wayne is trying to rescue his grandson and shoots the main villain as part of that attempt. Only after the villain is mortally wounded does he ask John for his name and make the expected comment about thinking he was dead.

Humorous foreshadowing is used mainly to reward careful readers and to encourage other readers to mimic their example. Think of this kind of foreshadowing as a combination of self-gratification or self-amusement as well as a reward for good reader behavior.

Use Your Powers for Good

One of the big differences between a writer and a reader is that the writer knows how the book is going to end. More than that, the writer knows everything that's going to happen. This omnipotence can create problems. Sometimes writers think they've given readers information that hasn't been made clear. Sometimes writers are too easy to predict. Taking a break between your finished drafts can help you to spot these problems.

But omnipotence can work in your favor. After you've finished your novel, you know what information your reader needs in Chapter Three to understand and appreciate what happens in Chapter Twenty-Three. The key is that you should never plant information in earlier parts of your novel. If you need your main character to learn how to shoot a crossbow early in your novel to explain why they survived a fight later in your novel, create a desperate need for them to gain that skill when they do. J. K. Rowling is a master at this kind of preparation. An entire book could be written on all the events that happen to Harry in earlier novels that allow him to succeed in subsequent ones.

You can test if your foreshadowing is natural or forced. If you have natural foreshadowing, it will satisfy the following two requirements:

- The information is an intrinsic and necessary part of whatever scene contains it
- When the novel (or series of novels) is finished, your foreshadowing no longer looks like foreshadowing

When I say your foreshadowing no longer looks like foreshadowing, I mean that readers can't reliably predict whether a particular action or bit of information foreshadows a future event. Also, it means that your foreshadowing directly changes your novel. An especially meaningful bit of foreshadowing can grow into a novel unto itself.

When I compared foreshadowing to time travel, this is partly what I meant. If you go back in time and change an earlier part of your novel, it's much like going back in time and killing a historic figure when they were just a child. Everything is changed by that triggering event. In effect, your foreshadowing ripples forward across the rest of your novel.

In practical terms, this means you should foreshadow events only when necessary for believability, when the resulting humor is worth the expense, or when that foreshadowing is heightening suspense by establishing parameters for a final climactic scene. No need to create a time paradox when it's not necessary.

Description

If you've noticed a common theme with this book, it's emotion. Your readers want it. You better create it if you want those readers to come back. Nothing captures a reader's attention quite like dragging them so deep into your story and your hero's point-of-view that they forget they're reading a book. You want your readers to live your story, not just hear about it secondhand. And nothing feels like hearing about it secondhand more than blocks of description.

Need to Know

Some writers regimentally describe every character they introduce.

> Nancy stood five foot seven in her bare feet. Slender but athletic, she had long legs and a short torso. Her brown hair, parted in the middle, fell to her shoulders and framed a heart-shaped face. Blue eyes peered out from behind thick glasses that were perched on her button nose. She had tiny ears and a delicate, perfectly shaped mole on her left cheek.

The problem with a description like this is that the reader's unlikely to remember much about it if this is the first they've heard of Nancy. They don't know who she is or why they should care. This apathy gets worse if you introduce every character this way. Soon, your readers are barely paying attention to any of your character descriptions. If you let them read for another chapter and then ask them questions about Nancy, they probably won't know the answers. What color was her hair? What style? What color were her eyes? On which cheek was her mole? Does it matter?

No. It doesn't.

It doesn't matter because you haven't given the reader a reason for it to matter. While it's true that a few readers live for descriptions and carefully read every word, most just skim paragraphs like the one above and forget every physical detail you gave them by the next page.

That changes when Nancy has already been on scene for a few pages. While I don't recommend this kind of blocky physical description even when the reader knows how important Nancy is, the chances that a reader will remember descriptive details goes up with their need to know.

What if the first few pages of a chapter had your heroine at a murder scene and an eye witness had given a description of the murderer? They said she was female, brunette, a bit taller than average, athletic, and wore glasses. If we then start our next chapter with the example description of Nancy, chances are better that the reader will pay attention.

The same ideas apply if you're describing a location. Start each chapter with a couple paragraphs describing the landscape and there's a good chance your reader will remember few if any of the details you so carefully crafted.

The best way to create a need to know for descriptions of both settings and characters is to make those descriptions intrinsic to your story and reveal them through the eyes of your viewpoint character.

Blue Screen of Death

In today's world, most actors are familiar with scenes shot in front of a blue screen (or a green screen). The solid color allows the post-production team to replace the blue with whatever images they want. As writers, we don't have a post-production team to take care of our settings. While describing too much is ineffective, you must have a minimum amount of character description and scene setting. When your descriptions are balanced, your readers will be focused on your characters. They'll see the objects those characters touch, get a glimpse of the people they meet, and see the streets and forest paths they walk upon. What they won't see is you, the writer, barging your way into their world.

The only reliable way to do this is for you, the writer, to live in your character's world. You see, hear, smell, touch, and taste what your viewpoint characters do. But even your characters need to be standing somewhere. Describe your characters, your settings, and your props, but don't divert your reader's focus from your story and characters. To do that, sharpen your descriptions to a razor's edge such that they're interesting but don't slow down your progress. You want your reader to feel like your entire world exists without distracting them.

I'm Ready for my Close-up

The easiest way to balance your descriptions and settings without having your characters flounder on that blue screen of death is to zoom in on who they are and what they're doing rather than what they look like or where they happen to be standing. Consider the following:

> Walter Wyley was sixty-eight with a face no one had ever loved. Silvery stubble dotted his chin and covered his rosy head like mold on a strawberry. Retired now, he had worked as a welder in the Norfolk Naval Shipyard for forty years. Barely able to afford his two bedroom condo that perched beside the Elizabeth River, he hated his life, hated caring for his invalid mother, and hated the children that shrieked in play outside his window at all hours of the day and night.

Let's look first at physical details. What does Walter actually look like? We know he's sixty-eight with short cut, gray hair and that he hasn't shaved for a day or two. We suspect he's ugly, but we don't know that for sure. Beyond the way he looks, we know that Walter lives in Norfolk in a two bedroom condo beside the river. He worked as a welder for forty years. He's struggling to make ends meet, and the joy exuded by the children who play outside irritates him. He has little love for his invalid mother. Coupled with the earlier comment about having a face no one had ever loved, it's likely his mother was cruel or uncaring toward him when he was a child, supporting his resentment of the happy children now. The moldy strawberry comment evokes a feeling of rot and decay. Above all, we understand that Walter's unhappy and bitter.

As readers, we feel like we know this Walter guy. We may not like him much, but we see him in our mind.

Imagine Walter trudging into the smaller bedroom to see his elderly mother. What do you think we'll find there? The smell of urine and feces blanketed by an overwhelming tang of bleach? A grim-faced old woman with gnarled hands and thinning unkempt hair? Sounds possible, doesn't it? And yet nothing in Walter's description said his mother even lived with him. By concentrating on emotive details of characterization, we invite the reader to join us in creating our world. We have a base from which to work. That base is Walter.

Having said that, this kind of block description isn't usually the best way to describe your characters or set your scene, mainly because Walter isn't doing anything. He's not on scene. We're simply talking about him as if he's waiting in the wings, ready for his cue to enter, stage left. Often such descriptions work well for a first draft. They allow you to get a clear picture in your mind of the character. When you expand that first draft, you crumble this chunk of description into bits of information that you sprinkle into a scene that shows more than tells.

While we don't normally dump a description on our reader in a block, we still need to cover the basics (who, what, when, and where) as quickly as possible. And sometimes, if the situation warrants it to avoid reader confusion, a short block of description can be the most effective way to give the reader the information they need. Just make it interesting.

Basics

When it comes to descriptions, my overriding principle is to filter everything through your viewpoint character. If you're living your scene the same way that this viewpoint character is living the scene, you report on what your character is experiencing as they experience it. You know what descriptions are important because they're descriptions of the people and objects your character finds important. You are also limited by what that character knows, recognizes, and notices. Every description you give is tinted by the lens of your viewpoint character. From our example on the previous page, it's easy to imagine that Walter would see everything in a dim and pessimistic light. If our viewpoint character was one of the kids from outside, their description of the same people and places would be uniquely theirs and completely different from Walter's.

Verbs, Words, Adjectives, and Other Nouns

Many writers make a big deal about adjectives and adverbs. They do this because so many beginning writers don't utilize their verbs to their fullest potential, they use adverbs where they're not needed, and they hang strings of adjectives everywhere like popcorn garlands. Unfortunately many writers go too far. They claim everyone should avoid adjectives for the most part and shun adverbs as if they're radioactive death. The true answer lies in strong verbs. By strong verbs, I mean verbs that are more specific than weak verbs. Take the weak verb "to go." It can be a useful way to say somebody went somewhere, but if you look in the dictionary, the plethora of definitions for go can fill a couple pages. That's how beginning writers end up with "she went to the store," "the interstate went near the city," and "the string went between the cans," instead of "she drove to the store," "the interstate skirted the city," and "the string connected the cans."

What you're looking for is a standard frequency pyramid with a wide layer of verbs on the bottom, a narrow layer of adjectives above it, and the section for adverbs capping the pyramid.

Everything and Everyone in Proportion

It's been said that William Shatner, when filming the Star Trek series, liked to steal lines and valuable screen time from his fellow actors. While I don't know whether that's true, you don't want this to be true about your viewpoint character. That person is the star of your show and you need to treat them like it. What they think is important (people, places, or things) is where you focus your descriptions. In general, it's proportional. If your hero visits a roadside café that will never be seen again, it may get a line or two. If that same café is the setting for half your book, your readers should believe they know what it looks like by the time your novel's done.

Similes Are Like Metaphors

There's not much separating a simile from a metaphor. Both are used to relate different items that share some common characteristic.

She was a snake.

or

The undertaker swooped into my father's
house, a vulture preying on the dead.

These are metaphors. All comparisons of dissimilar objects or ideas that transfer the meaning of one thing to another can be labeled metaphors, but if we look at the base of the words, metaphor is more about transference and simile is more about comparison. It's no surprise then that similes contain words such as "like" or "as."

That elephant was as big as a mountain!

or

The restroom at the all night truck stop
smelled like an outhouse.

Similes and metaphors tend to be the most powerful descriptive techniques in our arsenals. That's why people use them so much in everyday life. As humans, we're naturally prone to comparison. In everyday life, metaphors are often exaggerated. For example, "Hot as hell!" When used as description in prose, metaphors are typically accurate. They are used as a shortcut to clarify complex ideas or objects into easily digestible symbols that allow the reader to understand.

My old writing instructor used to say, "Every writer should have at least one image per page." He used the word "image" for "metaphor." Don't ask. It's a long story. The point is that he wasn't wrong. If you're not using metaphors (images) to engage your reader's brain, your descriptions are going to be flat and lifeless. Just don't overdo it. Metaphors should never steal attention from your story or your characters.

There's Sense In That

One of the first lessons writers are taught is to use all the senses in everything they do. That leads to the inane advice to include all five senses in every description and scene you write. The danger here comes from not using more than sight and sound. In our video world, it's not uncommon for writers to imagine scenes in their head as if they were watching them on TV. That removes the senses of smell, touch, and taste. In video form, these senses are given by the facial expression of the actors. A bad smell equals a wrinkled nose. A touch against smooth skin reveals a look of contentment. A delicious taste of dinner might cause the eyebrows to rise and the head to nod. While you should make use of these visual clues when other characters are experiencing those senses, your viewpoint character has no need for such theatrics. Be aware of the other senses, but don't stuff them into your descriptions just so you can check them off the list.

Details, Details, Details

Often when people are bragging up a great writer, they'll mention that their scenes felt so real. Beyond story, character, and dialogue, many times this sense of realism comes from the details in the scene. When describing your characters or your setting, you're looking for concrete, significant details that allow your reader to immediately understand what you're trying to describe.

> She held her blue dress down against the wind.

vs.

> Her white fingers clenched the hem of her baby blue A-line dress to her knees as she fought a stubborn tug-of-war against a gusting breeze hell-bent on robbing her of her modesty.

I'm not going to claim the second example is great, but it demonstrates a couple of important points:

- The more detail you put into a description, the longer that description becomes.
- Active details are generally better than passive details.
- Good details often provide motivation as well as description.

The key with details is choosing only the details that matter. Since detailed descriptions grow beyond their benefit, it's often useful to overwrite your descriptions and then prune that overwriting down to a couple powerful details chosen from the many.

Creating powerful descriptions is not about throwing details at the reader. Your goal is to limit the details conveyed to ones that convey your message clearly and in an interesting way.

Recollection and Flashback

When you want your readers to know information that happened before your novel began, you can either show an entire scene from the past (flashback) or you can simply state what happened in the past through a bit of narration (recollection). Showing produces more emotions in your reader than telling. so if the information from the past is of great importance, a flashback is going to give you a much better emotional bang, but it will cost more in words. If the past information doesn't demand a scene all unto itself, a recollection should do nicely.

We'll talk first about flashbacks because they're a lot more powerful, much more dangerous, and riskier than recollections.

Haul Your Past to the Present

Unless you're trying to recreate the Carradine-driven Kung Fu series from the 1970s, flashbacks are not needed in many novels, and when they do occur, they are limited to one or two in number. In essence, a flashback is a scene that's out of sequence time-wise with the current flow of the story. If your novel takes place in 1975 and your 35-year-old viewpoint character experiences a boyhood remembrance of the sights, sounds, dialogue, and feelings from a Christmas morning at the end of World War II, that's a flashback.

Flashbacks are tricky beasts that should not be pulled out of the barn for any old thing. Whenever you jolt the reader out of a story to go some place else (whether to another viewpoint character, the other side of the world, or another time), you risk losing the reader. This happens when your past story isn't as good as your present, or your past story is way better than your present, which transforms a satisfied and interested reader into one who is too disenchanted to finish your book.

What this means is that your flashback should be used as an enhancement to the present, not as a replacement for it. Usually a flashback is foreshadowed to build anticipation for the answers it reveals. When the reader finally gets to the flashback scene, they are more than ready to find out what happened that caused the viewpoint character to be the way she is. That's why flashbacks don't work well in the early chapters of a novel. If you want to show a scene that happened before your novel began, either you're starting your novel in the wrong place, you're actually writing a prologue, or you're just flat out wrong about needing the information as a scene instead of recollections spread out over time. I'm sure there are exceptions to this, but I haven't encountered one yet.

Flashbacks typically cause a change in the viewpoint character in the present. Many times this is because the flashback is represented as one character telling another character about a past event. Rather than tell the flashback in dialogue, it is always shown. Only the transitions into and out of the flashback are dialogue. The flashback is a scene whose impact is so forceful that both characters are changed in the present and their relationship is altered.

Oops, I Stepped in my Transition

Transitions are the toughest part of any flashback. Let's face it, a flashback is just a scene (albeit a powerful, emotional scene), but you write scenes all over the place. What's difficult is getting into a flashback smoothly and then getting out smoothly when all is said and done.

As with everything, having an emotive viewpoint character helps. For a character to remember an entire scene from their past (instead of just a few snippets), there should always be a powerful emotional pull to that particular time and place.

I usually like to tell my readers that they're about to experience a memory by using trigger words such as "remember" or "memory." This isn't necessary, but I think it identifies the flashback more clearly. If the viewpoint character is telling the memory to someone (which we will show as a flashback), I mention that other character. Something simple like, "Cyndi settled deep into her favorite armchair and looked at me expectantly."

Give a specific time and a place. The four Ws are relevant here (Who, What, When, Where). We need to know who else, if anyone, is with our viewpoint character in the flashback scene. We need to know what they're doing as well as when and where the scene takes place. All of this information should come quickly, often in one short paragraph.

To get into the flashback (assuming you're writing in narrative past tense, as most novels are), simply write a sentence or two using past perfect tense and then start using past tense.

> Jerry turned the corner. The way the trees framed the old, dusty road brought back memories of the road he followed to school every day growing up. One cold January day when he was in seventh grade, his older sister, June, had walked with him. He loved the way she giggled when he made a joke, like wind chimes in a spring rain.
>
> June quit laughing long enough to get a sentence out. "You're so funny, Jerry!"
>
> Her smile warmed him, even though the cold January wind whipped through their secondhand coats and bit straight to their bones.

You'll notice that I only conjugated one verb (walk) as past perfect It helps that my next sentence (in simple past tense) is emotive. Jerry loved the way his sister giggled. That love is eternal. It didn't end. As such, its meaning works both in the flashback and in the present of our story. This makes it a perfect transition verb. The next sentence about how her giggle sounds also works as both memory and the start of the flashback scene. By the time we reach the paragraph that starts with "June quit" we're fully into our flashback. The reader should have followed us there.

Remember that we've most likely been foreshadowing this flashback for some time. The reader usually knows that something happened between Jerry and his sister. Or happened *to* Jerry's sister. They know enough that when Jerry starts talking about his sister on this road from their youth, the reader thinks, "Ah, here it comes. I'm finally going to find out why Jerry now calls his sister "Jude" instead of "June."

This reader expectation provides a great assist to your transition. If the reader is desperately trying to get through an overgrown hedge, you don't have to cut through many of the branches before they squirm their way through.

When you come out of the flashback, you once again benefit from an emotive viewpoint character. Allow them to latch onto the consequences of reliving that memory. If the flashback was told to another character, one way you show the reader the flashback has ended is by showing the reactions of that character that just heard this story or the reactions of our viewpoint character now that they've finally got that burdensome secret off their chest. If your viewpoint character was alone when the flashback triggered, you show how reliving the memory has changed them in the present.

I usually like to state clearly that the flashback is over by using "now" or "today." While not needed, I think these triggering words help the reader follow where they are.

The mechanics of getting out of the flashback are the same as getting into the flashback. Write a sentence or two using past perfect tense and then start using past tense.

> I can still see the look on June's face as Tommy shoved into her, over and over again. That blank stare revealing a window into a part of her that died that day.
>
> I had never allowed myself to remember that day so clearly before. I wished I hadn't done so now. I shivered, even in the heat and humidity of a southern August swelter. I turned away from the road. I'd find another way to get to where I needed to go.

Notice that I had three sentences with past perfect tense this time, but being a bit tricky, I have one sentence with both.

> I wished I hadn't done so now.

This is our transitional sentence.

As with so much of fiction, if you have a great story and great characters, you can transition in and out of a flashback any way you want, and the readers will gladly follow you. For most beginning writers, these transitions always seem more awkward than they are.

Have faith that your readers will not notice the transitions as much as you do.

<u>My Fleeting Memory</u>

Recollections are the ninjas of the flashback world. They get in and get out: no muss, no fuss, and no transitions. But they have their limitations. Recollections become awkward if more than a paragraph or two long. They aren't powerful like flashbacks, but they're safer and easier to use.

Most of the time, recollections don't have dialogue and narration, because they aren't scenes. However, if you have a line of remembered dialogue that's important to the recollection, you bury it in the middle and call it good.

> Cyndi stepped into the cold water, but stopped, frozen. The last time she entered this lake, it had been to rescue Walter, who was on the verge of going down for the last time. "Oy! Somebody help me! I'm drowning!" he screamed. She had known then that he was in trouble. Now she wished he was still out there drowning. Her foot was already turning blue. If she were to brave these waters today, she needed some incentive.

Granted, this is about as silly an example as you can get, but all the pieces are there. Past perfect tense to enter the recollection, the desired line of dialogue, and a past perfect verb to get us out again. This full paragraph with dialogue type of recollection is what I call an extended recollection. It has all the elements of flashback, except in miniature. With most recollections, this isn't necessary.

A typical recollection is just a statement, image, or line of dialogue regarding the past. This is where the ninja trait of a typical recollection manifests itself. Most readers never notice it as anything other than a tidbit of information.

> Judy opened her front door and allowed Sallie into the small apartment. She hadn't seen her sister for three years, not since she

had walked in on her ex-husband and Sallie doing their version of a nude rodeo.

Sallie stopped in the middle of the room and turned to face Judy. Looking down at the floor, she said, "Grandpa's dead."

Judy started. Of all the reasons she thought Sallie had come, this was not it. She felt tears well in her eyes and saw her and Sallie on Grandpa's lap. As children, they had spent hours, each bouncing on a knee as Grandpa told them stories about his days as a traveling clown. Judy could see his smiling face, smell the sharp tang of his aftershave, feel the warmth of his leg through his old overalls. He'd still worn the round, red nose for their benefit. It was her happiest memory of childhood, despite what her therapist said.

"You're lying!" Judy said. "Grandpa would never die without telling me."

You can pick out the recollections in the above examples as well as I can. The point is that recollections don't break the flow. If we rewrite part of the above example, we can use a line of dialogue instead of an image.

Sallie stopped in the middle of the room and turned to face Judy. Looking down at the floor, she said, "Grandpa's dead."

Judy started. Of all the reasons she thought Sallie had come, this was not it. She felt tears well in her eyes and heard Grandpa's voice. "If I ever die all unexpected like, you done sure better believe your no-good sister, Sallie, done me in."

"You're a murderer!" Judy said. "Grandpa always knew you would kill him."

You can use a similar device to create recollections for any information related to the senses. If your viewpoint character can experience it, he can experience it as a recollection just by letting the reader know it's not happening in the here and now.

Magical Memories

If you would like some great examples of creative ways to do flashbacks and recollections, look no further than the Harry Potter series by J. K. Rowling. Granted, having her characters live in a magical world makes everything a lot easier, but J. K. Rowling employs that magical setting to its fullest. Most of her novels are written in a tight third-person viewpoint. This greatly limits the knowledge Harry has beyond his senses. To get around that, the author invented such wonderful devices as the Pensieve (the Flashback Viewer), the dementor's ability to make people relive their worst memories (the Recollection Giver), and shared consciousness between Harry and Voldemort (the Omnipotent Viewpoint Allower). Because the world of Harry Potter is a rich, detailed place, J. K. Rowling's need to convey huge amounts of information to her readers is enormous. She invented wonderful ways to do this. Don't hesitate to be that creative with your own work if needed.

Transitions

These are not the transitions in and out of flashbacks that we learned about in the last section, although those perform a similar function. In general, transitions take a reader from where they are to some other place (or time), or into some other character's head.

Nothing Means Something

The simplest and most classic transition you can have is a bit of empty space. Often this emptiness isn't completely empty. There will be a page break and a new chapter number or title. There might be three little asterisks or a tiny silhouette of your grandmother in profile. The objective is just to raise a flag and wave it in the reader's face. "Hey! We're doing something different now."

Of course, modern fiction and the need to keep a reader reading has mostly muted the meaningful chapters of the past. No longer are chapters entire little episodes. Instead many chapters today are broken with a cliffhanger. In such cases, you're not taking the reader to another time or place. You're blowing a fanfare on a score of trumpets. "Ta-da-da-daaa! Prepare to be amazed and mystified. Lean forward and hang on to your seat, because you're about to be blown away." Obviously no sane reader can put the book down after that. And so the writer suckers that reader into reading another chapter even though the reader has an early meeting in the morning or the baby's crying or the buzzer on the dryer just went off.

White space breaks come between scenes, chapters, sections, and parts of novels. They are used to denote a transition to a different time, a different place, a different viewpoint, or a different act of the current scene (the cliffhanger chapter breaks mentioned above). The only real guideline with transitional breaks is that you use them when you want the reader to be prepared for something different.

Keep Your Eye on the Watch

One of the most classic transitions comes by using an object that exists in both scenes. By mentioning the object at the end of one scene and at the beginning of the next scene, you transition the reader from one place or time to another. For example:

> As Aaliya reached the top of the summit, she glanced up at the full moon, its bright yellow light surrounded by a mass of star pinpricks in the velvet of night, like thousands of children dancing around a maypole.

*   *   *

> At the western edge of Central Park, Colin adjusted his skirt as he looked up at the moon. It was so full and bright, you couldn't see any stars at all. Not that you ever could, standing under the street lights.

Using the moon as our transitional object is really just a fancy way of saying our next scene takes place at the time or right after our previous scene without literally saying it. But instead of the moon, you could use literally any object that can be seen. In all cases, the transition is saying the subsequent scene takes place at approximately the same time as the previous one. The shared object implies a shared time.

Keep Them Grounded

The main job of a transition is to keep a reader from becoming confused. With white space transitional breaks, readers are expecting something different, so when you give them something different, they're happy. With transitional objects, you give the reader a teddy bear to hold as you take them on a ride from one place to another. With all transitions, you want to establish the four Ws again as soon as you can. Yep, the four Ws again. They are every writer's constant companions:

- Viewpoint character (Who)
- Time (When)
- Place (Where)
- Current situation (What)

Identifying a different viewpoint character is often as easy as giving their name. The exception comes with multi-viewpoint novels when you introduce each new viewpoint character. In each case, you're starting your novel over again and all advice related to beginnings applies.

The time is assumed to be immediately after the scene before the break (if there's a break). If this is true, you don't necessarily need to establish the time again. If you have a buried transition with no break, establishing your time and place is often the whole point of the transition.

> Sebastian lowered the pistol, smoke still curling out its barrel. At last, E.L. Villain was dead.

> Three days later and three thousand miles away, Sebastian patted the pocket with his fateful pistol inside. Just one more shooting and he would finally have time to binge-watch America's Got Fake Special People on NetFilm.

You can also establish your time and place by describing what's happening. If the event has started in a previous scene or been fully foreshadowed, letting the reader know that event is happening establishes time and place.

Putting It All Together

We've delved into the various elements of fiction, but in a novel, all of these elements blend and blur together into a cohesive whole. What makes putting them together tricky is that there's no blueprint to follow. One of the wonderful aspects of writing fiction is that each novel is unique. Even novels that follow a strict formula vary in the details. Like fingerprints, each has its own loops, arches, and whorls, but some patterns are more common than others.

Paragraph Structure

Examining the elements of fiction, we find that some are more likely to be found together than others. For example, the basic paragraph of modern fiction is comprised of dialogue, action, and possibly a bit of introspection. Sometimes the introspection is replaced by a bit of narration, description, or recollection, but those elements also appear in paragraphs by themselves. Foreshadowing is a function rather than a type of prose, so it can take on many guises and appear in many forms. Flashbacks are entire scenes.

While nothing is set in stone, the most common and expected paragraph form for most fiction is:
1) Introspection (optional)
2) Action (optional)
3) Dialogue

A second common and expected order is:
1) Dialogue
2) Introspection or Action
3) Dialogue

All of the following would be examples of common paragraphs structures involving dialogue:

Dialogue Only

Paragraphs of dialogue can be long:

> "I know that was the same person I saw the day before yesterday one week ago," she said. "I can't believe that you would question me on whether I could recognize her. It shouldn't

matter that it was dark. It shouldn't matter that I wasn't wearing my glasses and I'm 20/100 in my good eye. You should just believe me. But that's your problem, isn't it? You never believe me. You never have believed me. You never will believe me. It's just the way you are and the way you've always been. Thank God I'm not judgmental like that!"

Or short:

"What?"

Action/Dialogue

I turned my head and studied the dust cloud on the horizon. "He'll be here in minutes. We need to go now."

Introspection/ Dialogue

I'd never realized how fat I looked until I put my glasses on before I looked in the mirror. Immediately I decided I would never do that again. "Carol, what did you say a person had to do to become a vampire?"

Introspection/Action/Dialogue

Jeffrey concentrated on his hands. Small hands, and everybody knew what that meant. His first three real girlfriends had noticed, and that was before they had slept together. The condoms falling off half the time made everything worse. Maybe he should wear padded gloves to delay the inevitable observation from his blind date tonight. That sounded like a fine idea. He twisted his head and nodded at the sales clerk. "Where would I find the mittens?"

Dialogue/ Introspection or Action/Dialogue

> "I don't know what you're talking about, officer." I concentrated on thoughts of my non-existent innocence. "I've never been to Nacogdoches."

or

> "I think she looks funny." Bertie sipped her soda and made a pouty face. "Don't you think she looks funny?"

Yes, I know I used a lot of questions. They just worked better for the examples. Whether you're exclaiming, interrogating, or stating, dialogue is dialogue for this discussion.

These aren't the only forms your paragraphs of dialogue can take. They're the most common because they're the easiest for your readers to follow.

A third common form is Action/Dialogue/Action/Dialogue.

Many writers will have paragraphs that are Dialogue/Action, but many times those paragraphs read better as two paragraphs. Compare:

> "Everyone lies," I said.
>
> "I've never lied." She shook her head and I wondered if she doth protest too much.

to

> "Everyone lies," I said.
>
> "I've never lied."
>
> She shook her head and I wondered if she doth protest too much.

We're getting subtle here. For myself, I think both forms work, but I've had plenty of editors flag the first example as incorrect. My advice is to use your best judgment. If it reads well to you, it's probably fine.

Talking Heads

Part of putting it all together is avoiding throwing huge chunks of any one type of writing at your reader. Most writers understand that huge sections of narration or introspection or even description are a bad idea, but pages of unbroken dialogue aren't much better. We label this Talking Heads, because all we hear are the words spoken and all we see are facial expressions.

When people are talking, they're rarely just talking. They're moving, they're thinking, they're seeing unrelated activity, or they're hearing sounds from their environment. When you're editing, if you see a large chunk of dialogue unbroken by narration or description, review the passage and see if it makes sense to fill out your environment. Sometimes characters are discussing something so important that talking heads is the way to go, but this shouldn't be the norm.

Variety is the Spice of Fiction

Just as when you're speaking to an audience, you should resist dropping into monotone. In fiction writing, this translates to sentences, paragraphs, or chapters of similar lengths and patterns. In English class, sentence fragments are a bad idea. In fiction, they're a necessity. The same is true for one sentence paragraphs. Both are typically used for emphasis.

> Leafs rustled and branches creaked in the soft breeze. Insects buzzed through the air. A rabbit scurried into the brambles. Patches of blue sky peeked through the boughs overhead and sun filtered down to land on my shoulders like a warm blanket. I breathed deep, soaking in the deep, rich smell of vibrant earth.
>
> I couldn't believe it would all be gone tomorrow.

What you're looking for is a melody rather than the steady beat of a drum. Then when you do start up that drum beat, the reader knows it's intentional. For example, in Winston Churchill's famous speech in early June, 1940, he used this drum beating to great effect.

> "Even though large tracts of Europe and many old and famous States have fallen or may fall into the grip of the Gestapo and all the odious apparatus of Nazi rule, we shall not flag or fail. We shall go on to the end. We

shall fight in France, we shall fight on the seas
and oceans, we shall fight with growing confidence and growing strength in the air, we shall
defend our island, whatever the cost may be.
We shall fight on the beaches, we shall fight on
the landing grounds, we shall fight in the fields
and in the streets, we shall fight in the hills; we
shall never surrender...."

The repeated use of "we shall" forms a steady beat that listeners (or readers) can follow. When used sparingly, this kind of repetition can be extremely powerful.

Humor

It's hard to imagine what life would be like without humor. And who would want to? Genuine laughter is one of the most precious commodities in the universe. So why wouldn't you want to include it in your fiction?

Nobody's Perfect

The first thing you must know about writing humor is that not everybody's going to like it. While most of us seem to accept that not everybody will like our story or our characters or our descriptions or any other part of our novels, too many of us are devastated when even one person doesn't like our humor.

Here's what's important: You're never going to be able to write humor if you're constantly worried about whether people will like it. Humor is an intimate experience. It's a shared experience. It's like making love to strangers, not the way prostitutes do with complete detachment, but with emotion and feeling. When you say or write something funny and a person reacts by laughing, you've invoked real magic that has powers we're still trying to understand.

Create Your Own

One of the most important aspects of being funny is knowing your audience and tailoring your material to meet the needs of that audience. But here's the problem: For most fiction writers, we don't know who our audience is. Male or female? Could be either. Young or old? Could be either. Technonerd or dim-witted jock? Okay, well our chances are better with the technonerd, but there are intelligent, thoughtful, creative jocks who read our stuff. At least we hope there are.

Since we can't know our audience and since we still want humor in our fiction, the easiest way to succeed is to do what all fiction writers do when we need something we don't have. We create it out of thin air. So if you need an audience, write one.

What I mean by that is use the audience you're already writing. Your novel has a cast of thousands, right? Okay, maybe dozens. Or just seven, four of which barely make it into the book. The point is that you have people who are running around your story already. At least one of those sometimes named thousands is your viewpoint character. And this is your audience.

You can count on one certainty in fiction. If a reader hates your viewpoint character, they're not reading your fiction. So if you want to know what your reader thinks is funny, run it by your viewpoint character. If your viewpoint character thinks it's funny, there's a better than 50-50 chance your reader will think it's funny, too.

The cycle of life beauty in all this is that many readers like or dislike a viewpoint character based partly on their sense of humor (or their lack of a sense of humor). Giving your viewpoint character a sense of humor is therefore an organic process. As their sense of humor grows, their personality changes, which changes the type of viewpoint character they are, which changes how they are received by readers.

As writers, it's dangerous to tinker with the natural balance and order of the universe by forcing humor into the mouth of our viewpoint character. What works best is to create a viewpoint character you identify with and then allow them and the characters around them to have a sense of humor. Sure, they're going to say some inappropriate things sometimes. Let them.

Humor is rarely politically correct.

Humor Is Not Happy

If it's happy, it's normally not funny. Human beings are wired to laugh at discomfort. Not real discomfort, but slight discomfort, which is part of what makes humor difficult to write. That sweet spot between unfunny discomfort and humorous circumstance is narrow.

To give your main character a sense of humor, the first thing you need to do is allow them to fail and to do stupid things that aren't necessarily the best course of action if they spent a day or two to think about it. As real people, we don't spend a day pondering our every move. That's one of the reasons we make mistakes. The second trait commonly used to endow humor to your characters is an ignorance or a disregard for social norms. Prim and proper isn't funny until someone who's not prim and proper comes along and points out the ludicrousness of the situation.

Sarcasm

One of the most endearing qualities a character can have is keeping their sense of humor in times of trouble. Not big trouble—if your characters don't take a situation seriously, why should your readers—but little difficulties that are more hassle than real trouble.

Sarcasm is a great equalizer in such situations. By sarcasm, I don't mean the politically correct definition that's full of dire warnings about the harm done to others. I'm talking about the old-fashioned sarcasm, that was meant to criticize in a humorous way. For example, imagine you're stranded on a desert island and a Harvard trained, city-dwelling business executive washes up on the beach. That means another mouth to feed and a strain on the limited water supply. Plus, this stranded executive starts out being condescending because you're dressed in nothing but rags. When this exec asks, "Do you have a boat?" you might reply, "No, I walked here."

Sarcasm works here because it's a stupid question. Your reply, while not drooling with compassion and understanding for the exec's plight, is a lot better than other possibilities. This is because what the exec is really asking is, "Do you have a working boat that can get us off this island?" Obviously, if you did, you would have left long ago.

Friction Between Characters

Characters who respect but don't like each other at first are perfect candidates for humor. Think of Spock and McCoy from Star Trek. Gimli and Legolas from Lord of the Rings. Han Solo and Princess Leia. Murtaugh and Riggs from Lethal Weapon. Normally the characters grow to like each other, but often they keep a bit of that original antagonism in the form of jesting with each other.

Another great candidate for humor is the incompetent sidekick. Think of the original Andy Griffith show. The deputy, Barney, meant well, but he was always overreacting to situations in a comic way. If your characters are smiling and shaking their heads about what Grandma's got up now, there's a decent chance your readers will, too.

Contrary Ridiculousness

One of the most practical ways of injecting humor into your novel is to allow a bit of contrary ridiculousness to creep into your story. The amount of ridiculousness and contrariness will determine the level of humor you're striving for. For most novels, this means just a bit of ridiculousness. Again, it's situational, meaning that the same situation can be humorous in some circumstances and tragic in others.

For example, musicians standing out in ice cold conditions playing upbeat tunes for a bunch of millionaires who barely notice them is tragic, but not too tragic. There could be room for humor there, especially if the musicians start playing "Margaritaville." But imagine those same musicians standing on the deck of the Titanic. Nothing they do will be funny. It goes back to that little bit of pain idea. Slight discomfort: funny. Real discomfort: not funny.

What you're looking for is someone who is acting contrary to how most people would react to the current situation. In most cases, they believe they're acting appropriately. Only other people (and the readers) see the ridiculousness of the situation. This is because the characters are just being who they are. If you create characters that are a bit odd, not only does it make that character more interesting, but also it allows that character to be funny on occasion without meaning to be funny.

Too Much of a Good Thing

Unless you're writing a comedic novel, go easy on the humor. A little humor is vital to most novels, but a little bit goes a long way. If you put in too much humor, you turn your dramatic novel into a comedy sketch. Do that, and the reader starts to view everything as a joke. What you're normally going for in most novels is situations and characters that are amusing—not laugh out loud funny. Granted, you might get a couple truly lol moments in a good novel, but in the best novels, those come from natural interactions between characters that we, as readers, know extremely well.

There is too much. Let me sum up

The nuts and bolts of writing form a tapestry that allows you to tell an effective story. For the benefit of study, we disassemble great writing and identify various elements as if they could ever be truly separate. In practice, every part of your novel influences every other part. While you learn to master the various types of writing, remember that they only achieve their true power when they're combined effectively into a balanced and cohesive whole.

- Style is nothing more than self-based control over your own writing.
- Effective dialogue creates the impression of reality, but good dialogue almost never sounds like any real conversation anyone would ever have.
- Great dialogue is most often spawned by great characters living out a great story rather than by clever or witty wordplay.
- Dialogue should function on as many of the following levels as possible: 1) Identify speaker, 2) Convey information, 3) Specify motives, 4) Provide descriptions, 5) Increase conflict, and 6) Keep the novel moving.
- Clarify who is speaking through action, context, a unique style of speech, or by direct attribute.
- Maintain tight empathy with every character you create so that you avoid writing conversations those characters would never have.
- Actions describe process rather than result, which translates to "Show, Don't Tell."
- Narrate events and information that don't require the emotional punch delivered by a full scene.
- Common uses for narration are 1) Connecting two points in time between which little happens, 2) Providing background information, and 3) Revealing a transition so gradual that only the end result is important.
- Introspections strengthen emotional ties between your reader and your viewpoint character.
- Proper use of foreshadowing builds suspense and increases believability.

- Good foreshadowing doesn't read like foreshadowing.
- Descriptions are best presented (on a desire-to-know basis) using the emotional filter of your viewpoint character.
- Flashbacks are used to trigger a change in a character and answer a burning question the reader has about that character's history.
- Transitions are used to jump to a different place, time, or viewpoint character without losing or confusing the reader.
- Some paragraph structures are more common—and therefore more expected and acceptable—in fiction than other, less common structures.
- Vary length, structure, and word choice for sentences, paragraphs, scenes, and chapters to avoid dropping into fiction-writer "monotone."
- Humor is a powerful tool that improves nearly all kinds of fiction, but the amount needed varies with genre and the overall tone of the novel.

Chapter Seven:
Getting Published (Traditional)

That Way Is a Very Nice Way

For a moment, let's talk about the **easiest possible** road a writer can follow to publication.

First—and most important—let's assume you've spent your whole life preparing to write. That means reading, writing great essays for school, excelling at grammar and syntax, developing a great work ethic, finishing what you start, and struggling through some dark times and coming through them stronger than ever. Second, you have a great idea for a novel or a series of novels. This one is always given too much credit by beginning writers. Yes, a great idea is important, but the way you develop that idea is much more important. J. K. Rowling grossed a billion dollars off her Harry Potter series of novels, but in the hands of nearly any other writer, it would have seen little success. Third, you write the novel to the best of your ability. Fourth, just after you've finished the last polish on your manuscript, you're talking to your neighbor about this great novel you've written and she mentions that her editor cousin from New York is coming for dinner that night and why don't you come over, manuscript in hand? Fifth, you follow your neighbor's suggestion, hit it off with the editor who loves you, loves your manuscript, and has need of a book just like yours to fill a slot in her spring lineup. Within a week after returning to New York, you receive a contract and six-figure check. Sixth, a year later your novel comes out with a novel launch party backed by a million dollar marketing campaign. Seventh, you sit back raking in the dough from royalties and movie deals while you leisurely work on your next book.

Impossible? It would be a bit like winning the giant Powerball lottery, but people do that every year. It's not impossible to win the lottery, no matter what my Statistics professor claimed. It's also not impossible to live the scenario painted above, but it is *incredibly unlikely*. However, it is by far the easiest and quickest road to publication.

That's why I bring it up. If you want the chance to make the most money with the least amount of work on your part, you need to attempt to sell your novel to a traditional publishing house.

Understand that when I say the least amount of work, that doesn't mean that it's a small amount. You still need to write a great novel, you still have marketing to do, cover blurbs to write, interviews to arrange and give, readers and editors to charm, and all the rest. But traditional publishing provides the most help that you can get.

Write First, Sell Later

When I teach my writing classes, everyone always wants to know how to sell their novel. They sit enraptured as I talk about agents and contracts and book signings. They ask detailed questions about whether they need an agent and which publishers would be likely to buy their work.

But they haven't written a word.

There is one absolute universal truth when it comes to writing. You never get a second chance to make a good first impression. Whoever reads your novel, whether it be editor, agent, or glorious reader, they will judge your novel based on what you've written. Granted, they might be predisposed to like it or hate it based on circumstances, but a lousy novel can repel the most eager reader and a great novel can ensnare the most reluctant one.

All of the information provided in this section about Traditional Publishing is only useful after you've finished your book. When you start looking for a market for your novel, that novel should be as finished and as ready to print as you ever plan to make it. If you're not comfortable with the novel you've written going straight to press, it's not done yet. Finish it first, then find someone to buy it.

This advice applies equally well for writers looking to self-publish their work. The difference is that I've never met a writer who planned to self-publish a half-written novel. Beginning writers seem to intuitively know that if you try to sell a reader the first three chapters of a rough draft you plan to someday finish, those readers are going to be unhappy. Strangely enough, these same writers often mistakenly believe that they can sell their ideas or their partial manuscripts to a big publishing house in New York. I've actually had wanna-be writers tell me that they needed to sell the novel they were working on so that their editor could help them finish it.

If you're a movie star who just had sex with the president and you plan to write a tell-all book, that technique will actually work.

But if you're writing a novel, not only should you finish the novel before you try to sell it, but also you should strive to make it as good as you can make it before you let anyone[12] read it.

---

12. If you belong to a writer's group, the other writers in your group may indeed read versions of your first draft. Even in that case, you should still make that draft as good as you can make it. Nothing is more self-centered than asking your fellow writers to critique a manuscript with problems that you know how to correct but didn't bother to fix before you asked them to tell you what you already knew.

Traditional Publishing: What You Get

A respected, long-time chief editor at a major publisher house once told me, "An editor's job is not to buy novels from authors. An editor's job is to sell the novels they've already bought."

This point is often lost on beginning writers. An editor's job is not to discover unknown writers or help those writers publish a successful novel. They are not your friend; they provide one part of a business transaction. Chances are they won't fix your novel, give great advice, or help your book in any way. What they will do is try to sell your novel after they've purchased it. The amount of effort they expend selling your novel depends directly on how much they paid for that novel. If they gave you a million dollar advance, your novel will receive the red carpet treatment. If they paid you the minimum advance they ever give out, you will receive the lowest level of service.

Guess which of those two groups most beginning writers fit into. Hint: It's not the million dollar advance group.

So what services can you expect to receive from a traditional publishing house? In essence, why should you go the traditional route rather than just publishing the novel yourself?

Pros and Cons of Traditional Publishing

Below I've broken out the advantages and disadvantages of traditional publishing. Use the list below to determine whether your best course of action is to try to publish your novel through the traditional model or whether you would be better served publishing your book yourself.

Advantages

- Limted workload after novel is complete:
  1) Correct your manuscript based on editing and copy editing feedback
  2) Create basic marketing materials, such as suggestions for cover, back cover blurb, tag lines, 1-3 paragraph marketing synopsis, selling points, expected market, current competition to your novel, etc.

3) Fill out a new author questionnaire
4) Solicit blurbs from other authors recommending your novel
5) Provide head shot for publicity photos
6) Set up signings, interviews, news releases, and most other forms of publicity

- No need to create or hire someone to
  1) Create cover art
  2) Typeset the novel
  3) Copy edit the novel
- Presence in brick and mortar bookstores and in school and public libraries
- Better visibility on electronic book sites
- You get paid an advance before publication

Disadvantages

- You still need to do all the work listed under the advantages. Further disadvantages:
  1) Limited control regarding what changes to your novel you accept
  2) Little to no control over any of the marketing
  3) Complete blame if the novel fails to make back its advance
- No guarantee you will ever be published
- Limited royalties *after* earning out your advance, typically limited to 8-15% of retail price for printed novels and 25% for electronic novels (compared to self-publishing where you often receive 25% for printed and up to 35-70% for electronic)
- Your printed novels are remaindered after a ridiculously short time
- Impractically long consideration and publication time for first novels, often lasting years

In the Preface, I mentioned that if you put a hundred writers in a room, you'd get ninety-four different opinions. When it comes to traditional vs. self-publishing, we might have to jump that to nine-ty-nine out of one hundred. I can only imagine the pushback you'd get from this chart if you showed it to either editors at traditional publishing houses or to successful self-published authors. One fact is certain: Neither model works for everyone.

Based on my own personal perspective, traditional publishing provides one real and consistent advantage: Big houses have the ability to get your books in front of readers in a way that a lone, beginning writer simply can't match. In decades past, their ability to get your novel in a brick and mortar store was huge. In today's world, those stores are vanishing. If you're writing a YA novel or a children's book, the ability to get that book on the shelves of librar-ies across the country is still a huge advantage. It's no surprise that there are few successful self-published children's authors. But even if we throw out the physical presence on bookshelves, large pub-lishers have a distinct advantage and preferential treatment when it comes to the novels they offer on sites like Amazon. All beginning writers face a serious uphill battle getting their first novels noticed in the marketplace.

As a result, if you are a writer who can't achieve a high level of production (meaning you—at best—write a novel every year or two), traditional publishing might be your best bet. Provided your novel sells well enough, traditional publishers can support you while you gradually build up your readership through years of effort. This doesn't mean you can write a novel once a decade and have high hopes for success, but publishers have clout to get your novel in front of readers even without frequent production on your part. That's nearly impossible as a self-published author.

From the opposite side, traditional publishing has one huge disadvantage: It can take years to get a response from a publisher on a novel you've sent them for consideration. During that time, you're not allowed to send that novel to anyone else. It's an incon-ceivably flawed system that effectively discourages and blocks new writers from publication. Many argue it's necessary, but it's still elitist and wrong—and incredibly prone to mistakes.

In traditional publishing, the only reliable method to avoiding waiting years just to be told no is to short-circuit the system by finding an agent or by making a personal connection to an editor. I would argue that if you have the marketing savvy to do that, you have a good deal of what it takes to be a successful self-publishing novelist. If you can market yourself to an agent or an editor, you can market your novel. But what if you want to buy that lottery ticket that the big publishing houses are offering? In that case, you're going to want an agent—or at the very least, you're going to want to bypass the slush pile wall blocking access to the editor's desk. How do you do that?

Literary Agents

Most writers picture an agent (or editor) as a writer's friend, that person who meets you for lunch and gives you encouragement and advice. They take care of your cat when you have to suddenly fly off to Columbia and rescue your sister from a bunch of ruthless killers. The strange truth is that some writers do have agents who are indeed their friends. Some do provide help, constructive advice, and make a real difference in a writer's career. And then there's everybody else.

Like every other aspect of writing, how much an agent (or editor) is there for you nearly always depends on how much money you've made for that person. Those friends I mentioned above are typically agents (or editors) for bestselling writers. If you're a beginner, chances are you're not going to get much of anything. If you rely on them to take care of your cat, the poor feline is probably going to die. And the odds don't look good for your sister either.

So why get an agent? What use are they?

You certainly don't want them negotiating your contracts for you without looking over their shoulder. And they won't sell your novel for you. Only you (and your novel) can do that. Typically agents know the market better than you ever will (where the market in this case is the publishing houses, the editors who work for them, and possibly what projects they have in the works). Agents also tend to keep a pretty close eye on the money stream after publication. After all, they want paid, too.

That's the minor stuff. For a beginning writer, an agent really earns their money in only one way: They are the only person who can reliably get your novel in front of many different editors in an amazingly short amount of time.

So is this service worth fifteen percent? Absolutely—for your first novel. Without the agent, you probably don't get published—or you wait years to get published. But if your first novel was the first book in a twenty-book series, chances are good the agent just landed the big one. I'm not saying they don't do anything valuable for those other nineteen novels—they certainly will—but whether it's worth fifteen percent of every dollar you are paid is highly questionable.

Agents know this, too, which is why most have contracts that make it difficult to dump them when the going gets good.

I'm not saying that agents don't earn their money. They do. For every novel they sell, they have to handle a ton of turkeys that don't make them a dime. They need to know their markets, maintain contacts in an ever- and rapidly-changing publishing world, and wear a lot of different hats based on what task they're tackling. Why shouldn't they get a big payday when one of those turkeys grows up to be a soaring Hollywood eagle or a perennial bestseller?

Despite all the good things an agent may do for a beginning writer, the only practical reason I can recommend for attempting to get one is the ability to speed up the decision process. In essence, you're hiring an agent for their ability to get that "no" that allows you to move on to the next market.

If you want to sell to the traditional houses, a good agent will give you a better chance to do so. So how do you get a good agent? Can you go online and order one from Agents-R-Us? Not quite. But it's getting closer to that all the time.

Finding an Agent

Like the publishing world, the world of literary agents is ever-changing. That means all of the information in this section is subject to change. Still, the methods outlined here will probably be the same for some time to come. Even so, mentally place "At the time of this writing…." in front of all of the suggestions given below. (It was good advice when I wrote it.)

The process of finding an agent is not a trivial one. You've spent hundreds—more likely thousands—of hours writing your novel. Do the work needed to create a list of competent agents who might be interested in your novel.

The best way to find an agent who might be right for you is the same place we tend to go for everything else: Online.

The best resource I found for researching agents online was QueryTracker (http://querytracker.net). The site is well organized, seems to have good information, and is relatively easy to use. The basic site is free and the premium site was only $25/year. From my perspective, this is the main site you should use to find agents to query.

One of the site's most useful features is under Agents in the top menu bar called "Who Reps Whom." Besides getting their grammar right, this function allows you to find out who represents your favorite authors. If you're on the path to success, you're writing novels that you would like to read yourself. Knowing which agents represent books you like to read gives you a huge advantage in finding an agent who might want to represent you and who has proven they can represent the kind of books you write.

Once you've identified every agent who looks like a good fit for you and your novel, another site can be useful for gathering information about that agent from an agent's or editor's point-of-view. The Publisher's Marketplace (http://www.publishersmarketplace.com) is designed specifically for publishing professionals (meaning agents, editors, and their support staff). Again, the best features of this site come with a paid membership, which is $25/*month*. However, for an aspiring writer trying to find out about editors and agents, a one or two month membership should be sufficient to gather the information you need.

For both of the above sites, you can start out with the free version and make the decision to upgrade to the paid version on your own.

A free resource exists for finding out if an agent you've identified can be trusted. Writer Beware gives information on dangers that writers face, such as untrustworthy agents, scams, and fraud. There are many people and organizations that prey on new writers and on their desire to be published. The Writer Beware can help you avoid some of these pitfalls. These dangers go beyond agents and you should familiarize yourself with the dangers out there.

To avoid scams, follow this key guideline when examining any opportunity: Money flows toward the writer. That means people give you money, not the other way around. If you ever find yourself tempted to spend money because someone promises you they can get your novel published, you are almost certainly being taken advantage of. Run away! Run away fast!

Another couple sites have some useful information:

- AgentQuery.com (http://www.AgentQuery.com)

- Writers Market (http://www.WritersMarket.com)

Since the internet is an ever-changing landscape, your mileage may vary concerning these sites, but a couple Google searches and a few hours you'll never get back should provide you with your own set of the latest and greatest resources for finding agents.

Eeny, Meeny, Miny, Moe, Catch an Agent by the Toe

Agents are shy creatures, seldom seen in daylight and extraordinarily difficult to catch in the wild. Rumor holds that they can be trapped by offering them free lunches and plying them with rounds of alcohol, but since most dwell only in the dark boroughs of New York City, not all of us have the budget to lead a safari into their natural habitat.

While it can indeed be beneficial to meet an agent face-to-face, the classic way to introduce yourself to an agent is through the venerable query letter. In today's world, those query letters are sometimes query emails, but don't underestimate the power of paper. Agents get hundreds of emails today. Why? Because email is easy: Once written, emails cost nothing to generate and send. But letters require work. They require postage. Like the use of typewriters in the age before computers, the effort and expense required to produce a physical query letter guarantees that any prospective agent will receive less physical query letters than they do electronic query letters.

The key to sending a physical query letter in today's world is to *not* include an SASE (self-addressed, stamped envelope), which is what we used to do in the old days. Instead, in your last paragraph, state specifically that you did not include an SASE. If they are interested in seeing a full or partial manuscript of your novel, please contact you at this email (or this phone number). If they are not interested in your novel, no response is required.

There may be a few crusty old agents who get offended by this no SASE inclusion, but for most agents, if they aren't interested in your novel, having your stated permission to toss your letter in the trash is a relief. It's what they were going to do anyway, so it's a nice feeling to have your permission. On the other hand, if they're interested in what you have, they'd rather email (or in rare instances, call) instead of producing a physical letter. We live in an electronic world. You can go outside of that in order to get noticed, but don't ask the agent to put in more work on your behalf. That way lies failure (and wasted stamps).

I'm Special and Here's Why

Have you ever watched a commercial on TV and found yourself wondering, "What the hell are they advertising?" This particular use of the Force must work on at least some of the weak-minded, or why would the marketers use it? For the rest of us, however, the ads that interest us most are ads that provide information about something we want. Maybe we want a cleaner house, a quieter car, cheaper insurance, or less-filling, tastes-great beer.

Most agents and editors would be more than happy to discover the next Dean Koontz, Stephen King or Nora Roberts. But when they read your query letter, they're a bit like a football fan on a Sunday afternoon: They've seen about all the beer commercials they can take. Your job as a writer is to convince them that you and your novel are worth their time.

But just like those ad agencies hawking beer, there are no guarantees. Almost every technique imaginable has worked at some point in time. And almost every technique imaginable has failed. Being especially cute or inventive could work for you, but it's extremely risky. And unlike those folks selling beer, you have an extremely limited set of buyers for your wares. You can literally query every potential market that exists for your novel. That's how few there are.

That means that unlike those commercials mentioned above, you want the person reading your letter to know exactly what you are advertising. The following guidelines provide a safe and reliable approach to querying agents and editors. That doesn't mean you can't be creative or that you should be boring. Be efficient. Be clear. Be interesting. Be informative.

Above all, remember that your query letter is nothing more than a commercial for you and your novel.

The Perfect Query Letter

Take the following information and make it your own. Remember, you're creating a written advertisement for you and your novel. This is equivalent to a TV ad marketing agency creating a TV ad for their services. What you're saying is important, but how you say it is important, too. What I give you below is the nuts and bolts. By necessity, the exact content of your query letter is left as an exercise for the reader—or in this case, the writer, meaning you.

Overall Advice

If you want an agent, your query letter will probably be the most important page you ever write. Be prepared to spend some time making it as good as it can be.

But what do I mean by good? Good is so subjective.

Let's look at it from the agent's point-of-view: You're a relatively successful agent with a few good clients, a few mediocre clients, and other clients who haven't made you any money yet. You get contacted by existing clients and editors, all of which expect a timely response. You need to keep up on all the latest publishing news because the one constant in the publishing industry is that it changes quickly. You also have your job as collection agent which includes reviewing royalty statements and pressuring publishers to find out why your authors haven't been paid on time and oh by the way when can you expect the check? You might submit a book proposal or two, follow up on submitted proposals, placate existing clients who need you for one thing or another, and work on ways to increase revenue for existing clients.

Notice that your focus is on the money because that's how you make your living. Granted, you need new clients from time to time because the existing ones die, quit writing, quit selling, or move on to other representation. But on a day-to-day basis you're not acquiring new clients. If you did, you'd be permanently overwhelmed by new clients within weeks.

So what do you want in a query letter from a prospective client? You want to know that there's a good chance any time you spend on them will pay off. And how can it possibly pay off? They give you a manuscript you can sell. More than that, this will be the first of many high-quality manuscripts they'll provide that will make you a good living for years to come. That means this writer seems professional, competent, and low-maintenance.

For you, as the writer, it means your query letter needs to be:

1) Interesting
2) Efficient
3) Clear
4) Enticing
5) Lucky

The benefits of the first four items should be self-explanatory. As for the last item, your letter needs to be lucky, because even if you write the perfect novel and have the perfect query letter to accompany it, there's an excellent chance the agent you're querying isn't accepting new clients.

What To Include

In your query, include the following:

- Who you are
- What you want (representation)
- Your novel's plot summed up in a single sentence
- Why makes your book a good read
- What qualifies you to write this book
- An offer to send your completed manuscript
- A thank you to the agent for considering your request

The first two items above encapsulate the most basic tenets of cold calling (which is very much the function a query letter performs). Agents need to know you're not trying to sell them Amway products or office supplies. Beyond that, if you can't articulate why they would want you as a client, you probably won't be one. They should understand immediately that you're seeking representation but they also need a reason to keep reading. That's why you tell them why your novel is a novel that will sell, not only to the publishing houses but to the readers, too.

The next to last item is vital. The agent must have no doubt that your novel is finished and ready to sell. The last item is just common courtesy.

In addition to the items above, if a reason exists for your selecting this particular agent, tell them what it is. "My novel is a paranormal western romance. Since you've represented <Author #1> and <Author #2> who also write in this genre, I selected you as the agent best suited to represent my work." Giving specific examples like the one above make your letter personal in a way that will easily allow it to stand out from the crowd. Also, it shows you've done your homework, meaning you know what you're doing in your quest to find an agent. If you know what you're doing in the sales part of the business, it bodes well for you knowing what you're doing in the writing end of the business. Plus everyone likes to feel appreciated. By knowing about the agent's previous work, it shows you've taken an interest in them, which makes them inclined to take an interest in you. But be careful with this one. It's nearly impossible to BS your way into saying why you chose a particular agent if you just grabbed their name because it was the next one on the list.

Know Who You're Writing

Don't step on the agent's face. If you're asking someone to enter into a business relationship—especially one as risky as publishing—the least you can do is get to know the basics about the person on the other end of the request. That means addressing them by name, spelling their name right, and getting their gender right. Doing these represent a minimal level of common courtesy that you should always do whether you're writing an agent or writing anybody else. With the wealth of information available on the internet, you should be able to accomplish all of these easily enough. On the off chance you simply cannot get confirmation of the agent's gender, address the agent by their full name, such as "Dear Jessie R. Agent."

Pointers

Most of the items below are issues of quality. You want your letter to be as engaging as possible without forgetting that it's a business letter with a specific purpose. This is where it would help to be an accomplished ad executive.

- Keep your query brief and to the point (no more than 500 words). If you're sending a physical letter rather than an email, your query should fit on a single page. If you're sending an email, it's best to make it even shorter. Busy people have less patience with electronic communication than they do written letters.
- Construct a friendly and lively letter that captures a bit of your style as well as the essence of your novel. Include humor if possible but avoid being cute.
- Give the agent a reason to request your full manuscript by creating an intriguing impression of your high quality, interesting, marketable novel.
- Remember that you're writing a business letter. If it's a physical letter, get your formatting right. If it's an email, keep your subject short and treat it like the title it is (meaning follow rules for capitalization). Make the subject line specific. You want it to be caught by filters if the agent has set them up. For example: "Established Author Seeking Representation for Paranormal Western Romance" Also, avoid attachments. Most agents have been burned too many times by virus-laden attachments to open yours.
- Don't provide too much information. Often less is more. You want the agent interested, which means rousing their curiosity, not satisfying it.
- Exactly follow any submission guidelines an agency provides. If they've taken the time to create the guidelines, they expect and require them to be followed. Sort of following them (or following most of them) doesn't count.

If you want an agent, your query letter will probably be the most important page you ever write. Be prepared to spend some time making it as good as it can be.

First Sentence

Start your letter with a powerful first sentence. Give your future agent a reason to keep reading. Most of the time that means you're providing a one-sentence summary of your novel or revelation of your unique abilities as a writer.

For example, the easiest way to get an agent is to sell a novel before you write your query letter. The greatest opening line to a query is: "I've just received a six-figure offer for my latest novel *I'm Going To Be Rich* from Moneybags Press, Inc. and I'm seeking representation." You could add another sentence about how you've reviewed the work of several agents and you've selected this lucky recipient to negotiate your deal, but honestly, that's not necessary. You had the agent hooked at "six-figure offer." A writer can have no better qualities in an agent's mind that an already sold novel seeking someone to receive the accompanying and hefty commission check. Granted, if you've received a three-figure offer, don't bother writing. For four- and five-figure offers, you should provide a few additional sentences of your exact circumstances, but let's face it: If you've already sold your novel, you have no problems—or at least no problems that any beginning writer wouldn't be happy to trade you for.

The second easiest way to keep an agent reading your query letter is to mention meeting them last week and how much you enjoyed that delicious dinner you shared (meaning: you paid for). Of course, this only works if you actually met them and took them to dinner. But this is also the place where you'd mention if anyone had recommended you contact them. For example, one of the surest ways to garner serious consideration for your query letter is to have one of the agent's top existing clients put in a good word on your behalf. Most agents don't have a ton of faith in their writers being able to spot other good writers, but it's a recommendation nonetheless. Also, it comes from a client they care about. If asked, they want to be able to respond intelligently about why they asked to see your sample chapters or why they (regretfully) had to turn you away. That's a huge advantage when it comes to getting your entire query letter read and considered.

In the extremely likely scenario you have no famous writer contacts to recommend you and you haven't already sold your novel (and therefore have an immediate desire to pay out a guaranteed commission fee), start with whatever is most likely to hook your agent's interest.

If you're a published writer, start with that. For example, if you've sold eight stories to several major market magazines or anthologies, agents will respect that. It means someone out there has already selected and paid for your work as a writer. On the other hand, if you're a self-published writer, don't mention that unless you've been wildly successful. The latter is unlikely if you're seeking an agent. The exception falls under the first scenario above. Also don't brag about any publications by non-paying or low-paying markets. Like anyone who works for a living, agents want to make money. Knowing you sold a piece for $10 to a church weekly run by your Aunt Flo isn't going to impress anyone. Mention any publications if you have any, but only lead with experience that will help you sell your novel.

For example, if you're writing a political suspense novel and you served as President Obama's Executive Clerk for three years, you have immediate credibility as a writer who knows inside information other writers don't. The same goes if you're a retired police officer writing a police procedural or a NASA engineer writing a novel about space colonization. Granted, being too much of an expert can backfire. Most people who live the life can't write about the life but often try. Still, if the one-sentence summary of your novel reveals your understanding of drama and character, having real-life credentials can set you apart from an equally good query writer who doesn't have those credentials.

Now, for everyone else. You know, the writers who aren't already wildly successful or uniquely qualified. In other words, normal beginning writers, or as I like to call them, future best-selling authors. If you fall into this category, you need to sell novels based on how interesting (and marketable) you can make your novel sound. That means you better have written a great novel and you better be able to capture the essence of that greatness in a couple sentences. If that's the case, don't draw attention to your lack of expertise or experience. Let your novel do the talking (and selling).

If you fall into this most common category, start your query letter with a one-sentence summary. This summary sentence should stand on its own and generate an impression of your book that gives people a reason to buy and read your novel.

One-Sentence Summary

All published writers should have a one-sentence summary handy for each of their books. It's an important and powerful marketing technique that's covered in detail as part of our section on "Marketing." For now, I'll give you the basics that apply specifically to query letters. Your one-sentence summary should provide the following information:

- Your novel's genre
- Your main character
- Your overall story
- The struggle

This information isn't told directly. You reveal this information through your summary sentence. For example, whatever character you mention is your main character. The genre is revealed by the story and the struggle.

Notice that I've said nothing about needing to reveal your theme. "My novel's about a boy's struggle to discover his inner adult." Okay, maybe that would catch someone's attention. Most themes are more typical and therefore won't help sell anything: Coming of age, love triumphs all, evil doesn't pay, only good vampires sparkle—whatever.

I also didn't mention anything about accuracy. While your one-sentence summary should capture the spirit of your story and the struggle, of necessity it will be incomplete. That means that if your second, more minor storyline is much more interesting than your main storyline, you talk about it instead. After all, story's in the eye of the beholder. Take *Gone with the Wind* as an example:

- A southern woman struggles to find love during and after the devastation of the Civil War
- An entrepreneurial renegade battles against the traditional, male-dominated businesses who control the economic climate in Atlanta after the Civil War
- Following the North's successful war of independence for

southern slaves, a manipulative southern belle teases and traps multiple husbands on her way to economic security and eventual tragedy

- A resourceful and desperate mother's bid to retain her childhood home reveals the glory of the Old South as told by people who were there

All of these summaries are accurate at some level. Decide on your novel's best target audience and tailor your first sentence toward them.

The best way to get a grip on one-sentence summaries is by reading (and writing) one-sentence summaries. Here are a few examples:

- Trapped on an island, eight strangers are murdered one by one as the survivors struggle to discover whom among them is the killer. (Agatha Christie's *And Then There Were None*)
- A young Hobbit battles evil foes on his treacherous journey to rid the world of a ring so powerful it could destroy all good in Middle Earth. (J. R. R. Tolkien's *The Lord of the Rings*)
- A young orphan boy discovers he's a wizard and must use his new-found powers to stop the evil tyrant who murdered his parents. (J. K. Rowling's *Harry Potter and the Philosopher's Stone*)
- A Harvard symbologist battles an ancient and deadly religious sect to decode complicated clues that lead to the powerful truth about Jesus Christ. (Dan Brown's *The Da Vinci Code*)
- A regretful pedophile struggles to control and isolate his twelve-year-old stepdaughter who both loathes him and relishes the power her sexual favors cast over him. (Vladimir Nabokov's *Lolita*)

First of all, if you want to be a best-selling novelist but haven't read any of these novels (or series of novels), you should get busy and do so. Depending on what source you reference, these novels have sold between 50 million and 150 million copies each. As an aspiring writer, you should understand why they were so successful.

As you examine the above examples, you should be able to identify the novel's genre, main character(s), and overall story and struggle for each. In no cases is anything told directly, not even genre. If the agent can't tell what the genre is from your one-sentence summary, you probably haven't written it correctly.

After a similar fashion, only specify setting if it matters. It could be argued that it isn't necessary for Agatha Christie's *And Then There Were None*, but in my opinion, specifying the strangers were trapped on an island heightens the suspense and answers many questions. Well worth the four words that information costs.

Notice that all the examples above are less than 30 words long. The majority are less than 25. A good target length is 25 words or less. For most novels, you can't capture an interesting impression in less than 15 words, but if you can make it happen, go for it.

> A spelling spider saves a friendly pig from slaughter (E. B. White's Charlotte's Web)

For myself, this nine-word summary gives an impression of the novel, but it doesn't capture the wonder or generate interest as well as a somewhat more wordy summary could.

Remember, you're not trying to tell what your book's about in the shortest way possible; you're trying to sell your novel using the fewest words needed. There's a difference.

For your own summary, weigh every word. Your sentence should read well. If it takes 32 words to make that happen, don't sweat the extra words. No one else will.

For a Few Sentences More

Feel free to expand on your opening sentence. If you wrote about yourself and your unique ability to capture the novel, feel free to add more credentials. If you provided a one-sentence summary of your novel, add a few more sentences to increase interest. The main caution I give is to use these sentences well. They're not filler. They're a few sentences more that you allow yourself as a way to sell what you've written. Take *The Lord of the Rings* example from above.

> A young Hobbit battles evil foes on his treacherous journey to rid the world of a ring so powerful it could destroy all good in Middle Earth.

What's a Hobbit? What's Middle Earth? Rings don't have power in the real world, so this novel is clearly fantasy. But what kind? High fantasy? Epic fantasy? One possible way to complete your opening paragraph would be with the following sentences:

> A tale of traditional fantasy based on Nordic mythology, the rich world of Middle Earth boasts Hobbits, elves, dwarves, trolls, orcs, goblins, and men as well as scores of magical creatures such as dragons, monstrous spiders, giant eagles, and more. Driven by the timeless struggle of good vs. evil, giant armies clash while a lone Hobbit risks his soul and everything he loves in a desperate bid to restore order to a world dangling precariously on the brink of destruction.

These additional sentences give the agent valuable information. They paint a portrait of a detailed world with plenty of potential as the setting for a lengthy (and profitable) series. They solidify this novel's genre as epic fantasy and provide a reasonable impression of character conflict. What they don't do is provide much information about the story beyond the most basic of basics. Remember, your query letter is a marketing tool. You're not trying to tell the agent what your novel's about; you're trying to sell your novel. Intrigue them. Spark enough interest that they request sample chapters and/or an outline.

The same holds true if your opening sentence focused on you. Only expand it if you have more credentials that increase the agent's interest. If not, it's time to move on to the novel.

Body of the Letter

How you started the letter will determine how you continue the letter. If your first paragraph focused on something other than your novel, your second will focus on your novel's plot, characters, and story. If you focused on the novel to start the letter, focus now on yourself and why you'll be a client they want to have.

When the agent finishes reading your letter, it's true that they should believe they know what your book is about. The beauty of a query letter is that you tweak and adjust and rewrite your letter until it hums. It needs to flow as naturally as possible, but it should pack a powerful informational and emotional punch. You want the agent (and eventually the editors and the readers) to think that this sounds like a great novel.

Granted, the main criteria that determines whether someone wants to read a particular book is often personal taste. You can't worry about that. The book is already written. Your job is to make it sound as interesting as possible without worrying about whether a single reader likes that type of novel. As far as your agent goes, if you did your research before starting your search, you should have identified agents that represent the type of novel you've written. Given that, your job is then to show that this particular novel is marketable. The only reliable way to do that is to tell them what your novel's about in an interesting way.

Get In and Get Out

Your letter now has information about your book and about yourself. In most cases, that's all you have to offer. Offer to send them your completed manuscript and thank them for their consideration. Every agent I've ever encountered valued brevity in a query letter. This is not the time to be chatty. They may well give you a call to ask questions about your novel and evaluate your engaging personality, but don't try to capture that in a query letter.

Remember, agents almost never agree to represent a writer from a query letter alone. (The exception would most often be the query letter that starts with, "I've just received a six-figure offer for my latest novel....") The query letter should tell them just enough to pique their interest and no more. After all, the more you say, the more chance you have to reveal something that would make them decide they don't want to represent you.

Get It Down

Often the best way to write a query letter is to write an initial version that is longer than the final version. Concentrate on making it interesting. Include everything you'd like to tell the agent. Tell them all about your novel. Brag up how you discovered yourself as a writer when you were trapped in the ceiling above your grade school during a fire drill. Then trim, trim, compress, sharpen, and trim. Make it short without losing anything important.

An Agent, an Editor, a Candlestick Maker

Note that all of the advice I've given for writing a query letter to an agent applies to writing a query letter to a book editor with the exception that you're asking for publication consideration instead of representation. The same basic principles would apply if you wanted to submit a short story to a closed market. In all cases you're writing a commercial for yourself.

My First Agent

I was fortunate enough early in my career to snag a professional New York agent with the query letter that appears on the next page. This is a good demonstration of the edict: "Do as I say, not as I do." I don't include this query letter as a good example (although it may give you hope that any query letter you write can't be any worse). In particular, the body of query letter is much too long and complicated. To no one's surprise but mine, the novel mentioned herein never sold.

So why was the agent interested? Getting a straight answer out of most agents about such a subject is well nigh impossible, but my own guess is that my credentials were the selling point. I was a published short story author, which proved to the agent that I could write at some minimum level of competence. I was a full member of the Science Fiction Writers of America (now Science Fiction & Fantasy Writers of America), which meant I'd had at least three professional sales. One of my published stories had been singled out for favorable review by a professional reviewer. It was enough that this agent wanted to see some sample chapters and a synopsis.

A synopsis! How do you write that? We'll cover that in the next section.

G. R. Sixbury
2100 Lonely Lane
Emerald City, OZ 66699
<<Today's Date>>

<<Agent Name>>
<<Agent Address>>
<<Agent City, State, Zip>>

Dear <<Agent First Name>>:

I am seeking representation for my fantasy novel, *Misthaven*. I am a published author and belong to SFWA.

My novel is set on Misthaven (a world of my creation). The story revolves around four powerful characters: Mykon, Jep, Vel, and Bramon (an off-worlder). Mykon and Jep are half-brothers, grandsons and heirs to King Gabel of Westplains. When Mykon kills his grandfather using an ancient potion, he accidentally creates a plague that ravages the planet. Fearing their people will perish, leaders from the six lands of Misthaven band together. Jep convinces them their only solution is to capture Mykon and force him to give them the cure. They do not know that Mykon has not yet found an antidote to the disease or that Jep is interested more in revenge. Vel, matriarchal leader of the Delrabo, married Mykon the winter after he killed King Gabel and warns him of Jep's plan. Bramon, a graduate student from University Station, is sent to the primitive world of Misthaven to join a small anthropological study team, but his shuttle crashes and he is captured by the group of leaders traveling north to find Mykon. Vel falls in love with Bramon and is torn by her secret marriage to Mykon and Bramon's desire to stay with the lead group as they travel North to Mykon's stronghold.

Misthaven is not a novel of elves, gnomes, or dragons. Rather, its fantasy element is provided by Giftusers. These special individuals have trained for years to enhance their natural mental abilities. Using these gifts, they can lift objects, change an object's shape, see objects at a molecular level, teleport themselves over small distances, or read someone's mind. Each Giftuser has only one of the above abilities. Traditionally, they are the leaders of their homelands. Jep and Vel are Giftusers. Mykon is an *Ekarlan* (a scientist). For generations, many Giftusers have feared the *Ekarlans*, realizing the devices these scientists create could become as powerful as their mental gifts. Because Bramon is captured near his wrecked shuttle, he is also labeled an *Ekarlan*.

My best-known story, "Circles", was published in *Four Moons of Darkover* in November, 1988. I have enclosed a review of this anthology.

Upon request, I will send you all or any part of the manuscript for *Misthaven*. Thank you for your time and your consideration.

Sincerely,

G. R. Sixbury

A Sellable Synopsis

So an agent's interested. That's great. But instead of (or in addition to) your entire manuscript, they want to see a synopsis of your novel. Now what?

For your sake, you should have written the synopsis before sending off your first query letter. While it's theoretically possible to write a great synopsis in a single evening, synopses are a lot like query letters. Each word should be crafted for maximum effect. Whereas your query letter was a 30-second ad for your novel, your synopsis is more of an infomercial. Your audience is interested. They want to know more, a lot more. Now's your chance to show off all the cool bells and whistles of this new-fangled novel thing you've created. But make no mistake. It's still an advertisement for your novel.

Just to make it a bit more confusing, the agent (or editor) might ask for an outline of your novel. Nearly all of the time, when they say outline, they mean synopsis. So what's a synopsis?

What It Is; What It Ain't

I feel like I'm repeating myself, because I am, but it can't be stressed enough. When it comes to writing a synopsis, most authors go astray because they don't understand what a synopsis is. It's a commercial for your book. Nothing more. Nothing less. The synopsis must sell the novel, it doesn't need to be accurate. Sure, you're trying to give a relatively truthful impression of your book. If you've written a novel about monkey-eating space aliens, don't write a synopsis about giant desert-dwelling worm babies whose byproducts power the universe. But don't let your synopsis be tied down by your novel, either. A synopsis must stand on its own as a unique and compelling version of the story you're telling. It should seem larger than life, and everything in it more important than it actually is. The synopsis is a mere shadow of the book, so exaggerate the synopsis to give it depth.

Go all out to sell your story. Distort the synopsis as much as needed to make it read smoothly and read fast. All (and I stress the word *all*) that you're trying to do with a synopsis is convince the reader that your book is great and wonderful. Best book ever!

Overview

In simplest terms, a synopsis is a two to twenty page summary of your book that covers the basic plot, possibly the theme, and typically reveals the ending. The synopsis should flow well, must be interesting, and should be a quick, easy read. A synopsis is as brief as possible to convey the information needed, but should not be choppy or confusing. It should reveal the main thrust of your story, the setting, the motivation of the characters, the scope of the novel, and provide some idea of the novel's overall structure.

Feel Your Way

A synopsis should flow as smoothly as possible. Don't reveal any jagged edges that could catch a reader's attention and stop them in their tracks. In a perfect synopsis, there is no chance for the reader to quit reading. It flows so well and reads so quickly the reader is done before they realize it. As such, get rid of any details that cloud the plot. Also, feel free to bend the plot into whatever shape makes it the most interesting. The people who are reading your synopsis aren't going to go back and compare your synopsis to the finished manuscript and scold you for any differences. They're reading the synopsis simply as a time saver. If it took the same amount of time to read your novel as it took to read your synopsis, they'd read your novel instead. It's the novel they're buying, not the synopsis.

Length

Writers spout a variety of truths regarding synopses. In all honesty, a good synopsis is one that sells. Nothing more than that. As such, it needs to be as long as it takes in order to sell the associated novel it represents. I've had editors and agents tell me they never want to read a synopsis more than five pages long. I've had others insist that a good synopsis is often 20 pages long. The real answer is that **everyone prefers something different.** There is no firm guideline. In my own research related to synopses, most professional authors I've talked with tend to hover around the 6 - 10 page mark (single-spaced). If you're looking for a hard and fast rule about length, you won't find an accurate one. If you want a general guideline, I'd recommend 5 - 15 pages (single spaced). Note that many long-published authors will provide much shorter synopses and might recommend you do the same. The problem is that editors and agents trust experienced, selling authors more than they do beginning writers. A Stephen King written synopsis will sell because it's Stephen King. You don't have that luxury.

Tense

Often synopses are done in present tense. Think about someone you know who is an entertaining verbal storyteller. Often they use present tense. "I'm going to the zoo and I see this giraffe. He's standing right in the middle of the freeway, his tongue reaching up and licking one of those new, green cars that's trapped on the overpass, stuck in traffic. The giraffe thinks it's some kind of leafy tree, see?" Present tense is a faster, more immediate telling of a story than past tense. While most people don't prefer present tense for a novel length manuscript, it tends to work well for synopses. However, if your synopsis reads better to you in past tense, do it that way. There are no hard and fast rules.

Spacing

My page lengths in the "Length" section are based on single-spaced pages, but it doesn't mean synopses must be single-spaced. Manuscripts are double-spaced so that an editor or a copy editor can mark up a printed version of the manuscript. Synopses are not for publication. As such, they aren't edited. This gives an author the freedom to single-space the synopsis, which produces a more a finished book appearance. In the old days, it also saved on postage.

Dare Not the Chapter Follow

Under no normal circumstance should a synopsis slavishly follow a chapter-by-chapter approach. Using a chapter-by-chapter synopsis is probably the best way to write a synopsis that will **never** sell your novel. If you find a source that recommends a chapter by chapter synopsis, I would ignore everything that source says about synopses. The only time to use a chapter-by-chapter synopsis is when you are specifically asked to do so by an agent. Sometimes agents say outline when they mean synopsis, so clarifying is both prudent and advisable. If the agent really is requesting a true chapter by chapter outline, I would question the validity of the agent.

Synopses are Recyclable

The same synopsis is generally appropriate for both agents and editors. You are trying to sell the novel to both of them. You aren't trying to tell either of them what the book is actually about or how it's actually put together. Barring some inside information about the preferences of a particular agent or a particular editor, the sales synopsis will be the same for both.

It Bears Repeating

The sole purpose of your synopsis is to sell your novel. It is a marketing tool. Car dealers sell cars. Clerks in a clothing stores sell clothes. Writers sell books. The difference is that most car dealers don't manufacture the cars they sell, but they did in the earliest days of car manufacturing. In a perfect world, writers could simply write books. When we finished, we could post an ad on Craigslist or eBay and when an editor or an agent wanted a book, they would look us up and order one. It doesn't work that way. Instead, writers have to wear multiple hats. First, we must write the novels we want to sell. Then we must sell them. When we go the traditional publishing route, we have to sell the same novel multiple times to different types of audiences: First to an agent, second to an editor, and third to the general public. At least writers are selling a product they can believe in, because if you don't believe in your own product, you need to start by first creating a product you do believe in. And if you do believe in the product, why wouldn't you want to sell it? That's the best part about a writer's sales job: You're supplying something agents, editors, and readers need and want, which means you're helping them.

Synopses are Tools

Few hard and fast rules exist regarding synopses. They were invented as a time-saver. Agents and editors sometimes need new clients and new novels to sell, but they don't have time to read every book they need to consider in order to find the ones they need. Synopses provide a shortcut to reading the whole work. In rare circumstances, agents and editors sometimes get all the information they need in order to make an acceptance decision based on the synopsis alone. Usually, the purpose of the synopsis is to justify the time needed to read the entire book.

Nuts and Bolts

A synopsis is nearly always pure narration (with the exception of a line or two of dialogue or a very short partial scene). This means you're allowed to state things directly if it makes sense to do so. "Sandy is the heroine. Teri is the villain." Your main emphasis should focus on relational conflicts, not problems. You're pitting character against character.

Beginning

Most synopses start in one of three ways: 1) An overall one-paragraph summary of the novel followed by the full synopsis summary, 2) The extended novel summary starting at the beginning and going to the end, and 3) A "jacket blurb" paragraph, then the novel summary. With all three techniques, you should take care to summarize the material contained in the sample chapters, so that any synopsis reader can tell how the sample chapters fit within the novel. At the same time, avoid including a disproportionate share of your first chapter in the synopsis (what many editors call "First Chapter Syndrome"). Jump right into the story and keep the story moving all the way to the end.

Middle

Condense chapters down to a paragraph, a few sentences, or even half a line. Stress what's most dramatic about your novel and let explanations slide as much as possible. Most editors/agents don't care about the reasons why something works. An old joke starts with, "What does the rocket ship in your novel run on?" Answer: "Fuel." Said another way, reduce complexity as much as possible. Keep the basic idea and trim the rest. If you say your group of adventurers jumps into a worm hole and re-emerges on the other side of the galaxy, agents/editors assume you will make this convincing in your novel. You can't make it convincing in your synopsis, so don't try. If some technical or explanatory detail can't be avoided, sum it up in a sentence, if possible. If necessary, include a whole paragraph. If you find yourself needing more background than that, rewrite the story contained in the synopsis so that you don't need that much explanation.

Your characters' motivations and actions should be clear in a synopsis. Even if you think it's a good idea to confuse your reader in the novel regarding whether they should root for or against a character, don't do it the synopsis. You also don't want any confusion about the characters' actions. It should be clear what the characters did, when they did it, and why. This goes for villains as well as heroes.

Since lengthy explanations and subtlety don't work well in a synopsis, be wary of situations that make it sound as if your character is saved when the cavalry comes charging over the hill or is saved in some sudden and unexpected way, even if this is what really happens. While the long version of these events often work, they too often sound like *deus ex machina* in a synopsis.

If you have any unexplained or seemingly irrelevant events happen in your sample chapters, make sure that these are covered by your synopsis. For example, if you have a main character leave in chapter two, have a line in your synopsis like, "Main Heroine Two goes back to Tennessee to live with her ailing mother but she will return in Chapter Fourteen." In essence, you're assuring them you know what you're doing; you've heard of Chekhov's Gun.[13]

Ending

I've talked to dozens of editors who have emphasized that you **must** reveal your novel's ending in the synopsis. I've talked to a few others who've asked, "Who wants to know the ending of a mystery novel before they've read it?" Which advice you follow is your choice. One point in favor of not revealing your ending, especially for a good whodunit novel, is that your goal is to have the editor/agent read your entire manuscript. If the editor/agent loves everything else about your novel but you don't reveal the ending, I think most editors/agents will still request the manuscript. But what about if they like everything else but don't *love* it? This is one of those areas where there is no correct answer. Use your best judgment.

_____

13. The principle of Chekhov's Gun basically says that if you have a loaded gun in the first act of your story, that gun better get fired (or play some other major part) before you reach the end of your story.

Example Structure

One possible way to structure your synopsis starts with the single paragraph summary technique where you capture the entire novel. Follow that with the extended summary that comprises the rest of the novel. One way to summarize the novel is to show:

1) **Story:** The circumstances of characters and how those circumstances and character motivations create a great story.

2) **Relationships and Conflict:** Establish relationships of characters and show how those relationships create conflict.

3) **Change:** Show how events change relationships and what changes have occurred in the characters circumstances and relationships.

Throughout the rest of the synopsis, use transitions that introduce each of the next series of events by telling what those events do for the story.

Characters

Keep the number of characters mentioned by name (and places mentioned by name) as small as possible without causing confusion or requiring explanation. Introduce them with a line or two at most. When possible, let the characters' plot actions reveal their motivations.

The first time each character's name appears, capitalize it and identify your main viewpoint character(s) by placing (POV) behind their name. Weave the introduction of characters into the narration. Do not have a separate character sheet (or in general separate explanation sheets of any kind). Many editors hate this. Having said this, if you need either to tell your story, use them.

In general, it's impossible to capture intriguing characters in your synopsis. Instead of trying to recreate those characters in your synopsis, you use the characters to tell your story in the most interesting and dramatic way possible.

Big Action/Dramatic Scenes

The big moments—those parts of your novel that provide the reason most readers read and that keep them coming back for more—are nearly impossible to capture in a synopsis. Don't try. More than one editor has told me that for a big battle scene, they would prefer a single sentence such as "And then the climactic battle takes place." The same goes for a pivotal sex scene or a giant revelation. If you make it clear to the editor that you know what you're doing by stating with confidence what you're going to do, most editors take that as a sign of maturity and control and give you credit to pull off whatever scene you've just promised.

Extras

I always like to mix a bit of description and a snippet or two of dialogue into the synopsis narration just to break up the never-ending narration. You should try to give your synopsis some style without distracting from your story. In general, editors don't buy concepts; they buy story lines. Make sure you have a good story, and then make it sound as interesting and entertaining (and therefore marketable) as you can.

Book Proposal vs. Synopsis

Sometimes agents or editors ask for a book proposal instead of a synopsis and sample chapters. Normally one is just a shortcut for the other. Often a book proposal will include some kind of information about the writer, similar to what you might have put in your query letter. Obviously a novel proposal from an accomplished short story writer who's won multiple awards will carry more weight than a proposal from a complete unknown. Some beginning writers complain about this kind of favoritism, but it's just good business sense. Not only is it safer (at least one other professional has deemed this writer's work worthy of pay), but the awards indicate that some group somewhere thought the writer's work was worthy of recognition. Don't sweat it if they ask for a proposal. Just give them your synopsis, your sample chapters, and provide a cover letter that tells a little bit about yourself (and brags the novel up in some way).

Sample Chapters

While not part of the synopsis, sample chapters are usually paired with your synopsis to create the bulk of any book proposal. For sample chapters, always send the beginning of the novel (traditionally the first three chapters). Your target for length should be 10,000 – 15,000 words. Obviously you want to cut off the sample chapters at a point of high drama. Just as with any reader, you want to give your synopsis reader a desire to keep reading.

That's All There Is

A synopsis in is much like a short story, similar in form (not in content or style!) to what a grandmother might tell her grandchildren at bedtime. Translated it comes out as: this is the situation, this is the hero, this is the villain, and this is what they do.

Remember, you are telling a story to an editor with the intention that they will like your story so much, they will want to read it in its "unabridged" form.

Feel free to break any of the "rules" I've given above, provided you keep the synopsis clear, concise, and interesting. The only result you're seeking is for the agent/editor to want to read your novel. If that happens, the synopsis is a success.

After Your Novel Sells

You found an agent (or you didn't), your novel was sent to an editor at a major publishing company, and now the editor's contacted you with an offer. What now?

This is the situation you've been working toward since you first thought about writing a novel (whether you know it or not). But it's not the end. Instead it's the part that most authors don't care for: the business end of writing. Never fear. This minefield isn't nearly as hard to navigate as it might seem. But make no mistake: It is a minefield. Let me mark out a path for you so you don't blow your chance at fame and fortune with your first step.

The Contract

In a perfect world, once you received an offer to buy your book, your work would be done. This isn't true. Your first task is to make sure you don't give up the farm in exchange for seeing your novel on a bookstore shelf.

First, understand that most agents are lousy contract negotiators (for first novels). Typically the money isn't good, you don't have a track record, and all they see is 15% commission as a return on their investment of time and faith in an unproven writer.

Read your contract carefully. My first contract said specifically that I would write the novel, submit the novel, and if they didn't like it, they didn't have to pay. That seems reasonable. But it also said that regardless whether they paid me, they had full rights to use any and all of my work. What!? This means that, as written, I could write the novel and they could use it without paying me a dime. What's important here is that this contract was reviewed and okayed by my agent before I ever saw it. How did she miss this? Your guess is as good as mine, but I will always believe that she had other things on her mind and just didn't bother to read the contract all that carefully. No skin off her nose. (Actually, it would have been. If I didn't get paid, she wouldn't have been paid, either.)

And contracts aren't easy to read. They are conflicted (on purpose perhaps?). Typically provisions aren't organized in any reasonable way and sometimes clauses are contradictory. Read your contract carefully and make sure you understand every part of it. If you have any doubt, take the contract to a literary lawyer (a lawyer who specializes in matters related to the publishing industry). Most agents advise their clients in good faith, but the typical agent is not skilled at negotiating legal documents and doesn't understand the complex and legally binding clauses any better than you do.

So what are you looking for when you read the contract?

First, what rights are they buying?

If they're buying all rights, don't accept the contract as is. Make a counter offer to sell First American Serial Rights only. In particular, you don't want to give up on any income related to audible books, Braille, international, and above all, film options. Understand that if a publisher buys all rights, they buy all rights. You don't want to end up like Harland David Sanders (better known as Colonel Sanders), who was so excited about selling his restaurant franchise that he sold too many rights. Late in life, after earning only a fraction of the profits as Heublein, Inc. (the company he sold his company to), he wanted to start over. Only then did he discover that not only had he sold his chicken recipe, he had also sold his name. He was forced to open a restaurant under his wife's name (Claudia Sanders). Even with that change, Heublein sued the old Colonel and he was forced to sell the new restaurant.

If your publisher balks and insists on buying all rights, at the very least get an expiration date. Typically you can negotiate for a return of rights if the novel ever goes out of print or if sales dip below a certain number. Often your agent can be of use on such matters. Agents know that selling rights later means another paycheck for them.

The exception to negotiating regarding all rights is when you do a media tie-in novel or something similar. If you're writing in someone else's world, they will (and should) retain all rights to anything you produce. They invented the darned thing after all. In that case, you're doing what's known as work-for-hire. This is no different than a plumber being paid to come and fix your sink. You have work to do, you do it, you're paid for that work, and that's all you're entitled to. For a media tie-in novel, this all rights agreement makes sense.

For nearly everything else, it's a fool's proposition.

After the Contract

Once the contract is signed, you are legally bound to abide by whatever it says. That means that if you weren't finished with the novel when it sold, the publishing house requested specific changes as a condition of purchase, or you've agreed to a seven-book series, you're obligated to deliver.

For example, I sold my first novel the year after losing both my mother and father within an 8-month span. Still reeling from my sudden status as an adult orphan and loaded down with family and work commitments, I somehow managed to sell this particular novel based on a synopsis alone. The publishing company gave me a generous six months to write, edit, and polish my novel. I had already agreed to be the head coach for my son's little league team and could not back out of it. Like all writers, these time stealers (called real life and being human) made the six-months goal an optimistic one. I agreed to this deadline in part because I didn't have much choice if I wanted to be published and because the publisher had sent me an example of the type of novel they were looking for that was only 70,000 words long. Surely I could finish a 70,000 word novel in six months. Unfortunately my contract specified that I would write a 100,000 word novel. I believed the example rather than the contract. My mistake.

As soon as I discovered my 30,000 word error in judgment, I adjusted my schedule accordingly. As you can imagine, finishing 100,000 words in six months given my other responsibilities was no easy task. Also, my writing future depended upon the quality of what I produced. On the other hand, several of my author friends would laugh at such a ridiculously long deadline for a single novel only 100,000 words long. It's all perspective.

When I was a couple months from the deadline, I realized having another 60 days to work on the novel would go a long way toward making it a much better novel. I forwarded this fact to my editor in an appeal for just a bit more time. He responded that I had signed a contract that called for 100,000 word novel that would be finished on time and that they would love. Anything else would be a violation of my contract, which would then make it null and void.

Okay then.

I finished the novel on time. Then the editor sat on it for eight months before he bothered to read it.

Don't get me wrong. This was his right. The contract spelled out my responsibilities. I give this example to make it clear that common sense and logic are not necessarily related to a publishing contract. If you agreed to an obligation in your contract, you will be expected to fulfill that obligation regardless of health concerns, family emergencies, or sudden death. Granted, if you're dead, there's not a lot they can do to you. But based on my experience with large traditional publishing houses, you'll still be expected to fulfill your contract.

In addition to specific contract obligations, you may be expected to provide input for a back cover blurb, tag lines, a marketing synopsis, etc. You will sometimes be asked to fill out a new author questionnaire or solicit recommendations for your novel from other authors (hopefully best-selling authors that just happen to be your best buds). You may be asked for a head shot for publicity photos and you might be expected to set up signings, schedule interviews, craft news releases, and in all other ways do as much marketing as you can.

These obligations aren't always spelled out in your contract, but in general, they're in your best interest. They're aimed at selling your novel, and for many reasons, you want to sell your novel. One reason is that your performance on your first novel greatly affects whether you'll ever sell anything under your own name again. Many of the pseudonyms in the publishing industry came about because an author's latest novel didn't earn enough money and publishing houses refused to consider any other work from that author. If you don't sell well under your own name, guess whose name you won't be selling under anymore?

There are also some practical obligations you must fulfill. Typically your novel will be dissected by a copy editor. Copy editors are a specialized form of editor. Their main task is to assure your novel is grammatically correct, formatted correctly, stylistically reliable, and has no consistency problems. For example, if a side character's name was Teddy in Chapter Two and you only refer to that character as Theodore in the last couple chapters of the book, you will be asked to make this consistent. Another consistency problem might be that your character answered the phone or the door without mention of any ring or knock, or that the hero's house faced south in Chapter One but east in Chapter Seven.

The important thing to know about copy editors is that you're not obliged to take their suggested changes. Copy editors are people, too. You might have an illiterate, homeless, unbalanced individual talking in ungrammatical gibberish, which the copy editor might correct to the Queen's English. Pay attention to their suggestions, but don't forget that you're the writer. This is your novel. Keep it the way you wrote it when there's a reason for doing so.

It's possible the editor may have changes of her own. If so, the same guidelines apply as with a copy editor. The difference is that you consider the editor's suggestions with extra care and you should be prepared to defend (argue for) your position on any suggestions you reject.

Marketing

Your publishing house might ask you to schedule book signings, interviews, and other marketing opportunities.

Provided you even have access to any physical bookstores, I suggest keeping book signings to a minimum. They take a great deal of time/energy and produce negligible results.

This will be covered more in the main section on marketing, but I would suggest you concentrate your marketing efforts on techniques that provide the most bang for the buck. While I'd never hesitate to sell your novel one-on-one to someone you happen to meet, you're not going to garner many readers this way.

The best way to increase the sales for your novel is through mass media. That means television, radio, newspaper, and internet. The underlying principle is that you want one marketing effort to reach as many readers as possible.

Beyond that, for a traditionally published novel, you're main technique for creating sales is to write and publish awesome books at a phenomenal rate and allow your readership to grow by word-of-mouth.

Keep Writing

The most important task for any writer after selling their first novel is to keep writing. Don't allow yourself to get distracted by any publicity or manuscript correction you might be required to do. It can be extremely difficult to keep writing when your novel is sitting at the publishing house but is a year or two away from publication. Most writers are nervous about how their novel will be received. Waiting can be agony. One solution to this problem is to quit relying on a publishing technique as outdated as the typewriter and move into the twenty-first century. The best way to do that is through self-publishing.

There is too much. Let me sum up

Traditional Publishing is the tried and true method of getting rich and famous that's been followed by most writers throughout recorded history. There's an excellent chance that traditional publishing in some form will still be around for centuries to come. If you're committed to the traditional publishing model, you must do all in your power to rise above the competition. That means playing industry rules that have remained relatively unchanged for decades.

- Traditional publishing is still the most reliable route to widespread fame and fortune, although your odds of winning the lottery aren't that much worse than becoming a best-selling author by selling your first novel.
- You should write, finish, and polish your novel before trying to sell it.
- Traditional Publishing is best suited for people who 1) are already famous, 2) can't produce the multiple novels per year self-publishing demands for success, or 3) are unwilling to learn or do the tasks taken care of by traditional publishers, such as cover blurbs, copy editing, cover art, and typesetting.
- Unless you want to wait years for your novel to be accepted (or rejected), you either need to know an editor personally or get yourself an agent (or get win-the-lottery lucky).
- Research agents carefully and query ones most likely to represent your work.
- A query letter is a business letter that represents you and your book in its best light and whose sole purpose is to interest the agent and convince them to request a synopsis.
- If a query letter is a 30-second ad for your novel, your synopsis is equivalent to an infomercial for your book.
- A book proposal is a combination of your cover letter, your synopsis, and sample chapters.
- Never surrender all rights to anything unless those rights weren't yours to begin with (such as with a media tie-in novel or a work-for-hire situation).

- Before signing any contract, make sure you understand, accept, and are prepared to satisfy any terms specified by the contract.
- Any marketing efforts you make on behalf of your novel should concentrate on mass media outlets where you can reach the most readers with the least time and effort.
- After selling your novel, your main goal should be to keep writing.

Chapter Eight:
Getting Published
(Self-Published)

Stigma, Schmigma

For most of history, self-published meant lousy. That's because if you wrote a quality book that people wanted to read, traditional publishers would buy it. Eventually. If you kept sending it out year after year and you kept writing. And if traditional publishers didn't buy it, good reasons existed for that book never seeing print. For the best of the self-published books in those days, publishers weren't interested just because the audience for the book was too small. Or the publishers thought the audience was too small. Credit the worst of the self-published books from those days for creating the stigma against self-published books that was common and expected until just recently.

Before looking at the (mostly) glorious revolution in publishing, let's be clear. Traditional publishing has never been perfect. If professional editors never made mistakes in their quest for bestsellers, they wouldn't have rejected Agatha Christie for the first five years of her writing career. A dozen of them certainly wouldn't have rejected J.K. Rowling. Between these two women, they've sold an estimated three **billion** dollars in novels. Without a doubt, forcing new writers to storm the castle that is traditional publishing killed off the writing careers for most the writers who tried. For the majority of those writers, those were mercy killings. But a great many wonderful writers were felled in the massacre along with the schleps. But overall, I believe the system still worked. Until about forty years ago.

A Bit of History

Traditional publishing suffered a major blow in the late 70's even though they didn't recognize it at the time. With the invention of the personal computer, suddenly anybody could write a book. As one of the last dinosaurs who wrote, edited, and polished his first novel longhand before creating a mistake-free typewritten copy, I can tell you that the amount of work and frustration called for by such a tedious process weeded out a great many people before they got started. What this meant is that finished novel manuscripts weren't streaming into the publishing houses in smothering numbers, at least not compared to later. With a bit of help from assistants, editors and agents could keep up. Once personal computers and word processing programs became common, the deluge quickly grew out of control. Form rejection letters became common. More assistants were needed. But with television stealing readers and publishing costs on the rise, less money was available.

So many factors contributed to the problems facing traditional publishing at the end of the twentieth century that it's impossible to blame any one factor. I could write a book on this subject alone. To be brief, as distribution companies became larger and regionalized and then nationalized as far as their buying agents, pockets of readers were ignored. At the same time, living on an editorial assistant's salary in New York became excessively painful for anyone who didn't have another source of wealth or income. That mostly limited the pool of editorial assistants to a select group of youngsters with a particular financial, educational, and geographical background that bore little resemblance to readers in the rest of the country. Out in the real world, readers became increasingly frustrated by the ever smaller selection of fiction from writers who they wanted to read. As a result, they quit reading completely or restricted their book buying to known commodities. The best-known authors got more money per advance, sold more novels than ever before, and represented more and more of each company's bottom line. As the publishing houses slotted less money for new writers or established writers with steady but unspectacular sales, patience for these writers grew short. Readers who liked these writers were out of luck. Selection and quality suffered. Publishing companies failed and were gobbled up by larger companies. Quality and selection suffered further.

While forcing writers to be accepted by major publishing houses kept the number of new authors down, it did little to improve the entertainment value of the novels that were published. I'm not trying to be critical. Editors are people, too. They have likes and dislikes. Unfortunately, with such a small group of people whose opinions mattered, it's inevitable that their likes and dislikes won't always match up with the reading public at large. Certainly the quality of writing (the prose) was better under the traditional model—some self-published novels read as if they were written by an illiterate six-year-old—but shock of shocks to those traditional editors, normal readers don't seem to care nearly as much about prose as they do story and characters (and price).

Which brings us to the publishing world of the early twenty-first century. While I have no doubt that most of the New York publishing industry would disagree with me, I would contend that the success of self-publishing was preordained the moment a distribution method became available for self-published novels because the needs of readers were not being met by the traditional model.

Enter Amazon, CreateSpace (and others). While a ton of books that (in my opinion) should never see the light of day are being published in record numbers, the flip side is that those same books are available to people who do appreciate them. Instead of our selection being controlled by a handful of publishing professionals who decide what everyone likes to read, suddenly the marketplace can decide for itself.

Welcome to the twenty-first century.

And Now for Something Completely Different

As of mid-2016, the world of publishing was well on its way through a major upheaval. If data from Amazon[14] is examined, what we see are years of falling market share for the big traditional publishing houses and huge growth in market share from independently published (read self-published) books. The small presses, which of necessity have always been more sensitive to their readers, have a market share that seems to be holding steady or even climbing.

What's more important to understand is that for authors who are making their living (earning $25,000+/year) and who are just getting started (meaning their first book debuted three or less years ago), most of them published their own books. To clarify further, there are more than twice as many new authors making their living publishing independently as there are authors being published by the big, traditional houses, by small and medium sized presses, and by Amazon

---

14. Why pay attention to Amazon? Because **85%** of all non-traditionally published U.S. book sales *in any format* happen on Amazon.com. Even with traditionally published U.S. book sales in any format, 50% happen on Amazon.com.

itself… combined! If you're a new author making his living, chances are better than 2 to 1 you're publishing your own work.[15]

What this means is that anyone who criticizes self-published novels as being no-good or low quality or not worth their consideration should be pitied. They may be right, but it's a bit like a carriage maker screaming at the passing automobiles. Readers have spoken clearly with their hard-earned dollars. Most of them don't really care whether you're published by New York, by Alma, Arkansas, by Amazon, or by your own good judgment.

If you write it (and publish it), they will come, dollars in hand.

What, Me Worry?

In simplest terms, if you feel like you can handle the demands of publishing your own hard work, there is no reason at this time not to do so. If anyone criticizes your finished work that's selling like crazy, you can pat them on the head and thank them for their opinion. And then write and publish another book while they're still waiting to hear back from their publisher or their agent.

---

15. You may ask how I arrived at these numbers or about their validity. I would answer that it doesn't matter. By the time you read this, they've changed. If you want the latest and greatest, the numbers are out there and can be found. I predict you'll find something similar to what's given here unless you're reading this many years after it was written.

You're the Boss

One of the great things about being the boss is not having to answer to anyone else. One of the worst things is not being able to blame anyone else when things go wrong. Confidence is one of the best attributes any writer (or any boss) can have. As a publisher of your own work, what you're looking for is a healthy dose of what I call critical confidence. For me, embodying critical confidence means periodically and methodically examining everything you're doing for validity and effectiveness, then charging ahead to the best of your ability.

To be an effective boss, you need data. Once you have that data, you should be decisive, committed, and confident. You must also motivate your employees. For self-published writers, this means motivating yourself.

Becoming a great boss isn't easy or trivial, but many of the skills can be learned.

Do you have the skills and the desire to be self-published? Under what circumstances should you self-publish rather than seeking a traditional publisher?

Pros and Cons of Self-Publishing

Below I've broken out the advantages and disadvantages of self-publishing. Use the list below to determine whether your best course of action is to try to publish your novel through the traditional model or whether you would be better served publishing your book yourself.

<u>Advantages</u>

- Better royalties, typically earning twice as much on printed novels and nearly three times as much on electronic
- Complete control over what you publish, how you write it, what cover it has, how you market it, when it's released, how long it stays on the market, etc.
- Guarantee what you write will be published if you believe it's good enough to be published (a huge motivator)
- Ability to publish books that would otherwise be

unpublishable because of limited expected audience or controversial content

<u>Disadvantages</u>

- Responsibility for all parts of the publishing process, requiring competence, initiative, and effort in many areas beyond writing
- High level of productivity required for best results
- No professional approval required, allowing you to publish some embarrassingly awful books
- Minimal or non-existent presence in physical bookstores as well as school and public libraries
- Less visibility on electronic book sites than what is enjoyed by traditionally published work
- No guaranteed pay
- Full liability for anything you put in print

<u>Analysis</u>

For me, the greatest advantage self-publishing provides is that it's a guarantee of publication. This sounds trivial, but knowing your work will be published when you finish it gives you an incentive to finish the work that you just can't obtain when any doubt lingers about whether you're wasting your time.

Why Not Both?

A common sense approach would suggest trying to publish your novel the traditional route first. If and only if that fails, self-publish the novel. In my opinion, that's not the way to go. For one thing, it will take you years to determine your novel's not likely to see print via the traditional route. Think how many novels you could have self-published in the meantime. To be clear, I'm not saying that if you go the traditional route and fail you shouldn't consider self-publishing your work. I'm saying that failing shouldn't be part of your Plan A.

Most writers can be divided into two groups. Those who should self-publish and those who should try to for publication via the traditional route. What's the difference? I've given you the pros and cons, but it's not that simple. Publishing, whether traditional or self, is a minefield, but not just any minefield. The giant stone of time is rolling down the hill of ever-diminishing energy, and it's ready to ready to squash you flat if you stop to consider any path too long. I know tons of writers who say such inane things as, "You need to take your time writing a novel because your brain needs time to process the infinite possibilities your imagination can create." Baloney. That's like saying the only way to tear down a house is to wait until it falls down on its own. Sure, it's a heck of a lot less work, but if you're willing to pick up a sledge hammer and start pounding away, you can reach your goal a lot more quickly.

Making everything more complicated is the sheer mountain of self-doubt that's more than willing to convince you that you can't do what it takes to make your career as a writer a reality.

Why not just try both? The same reason you don't drive from one town to another by just heading in roughly the right direction and guessing which way to go at every fork in the road. Sure, that path might be more interesting and might allow you to discover parts of the country you wouldn't see otherwise, but that way takes an amazing amount of time and your time is limited more than you think.

Does It Even Matter?

The answer regarding which publishing route is best for you starts with what you need from your writing. If all you're looking for is an interesting hobby where you might write for forty years and have nothing published beyond a handful of short stories and a novel or two, choose whatever path seems the most comfortable to you. If you're not willing to trade a good chunk of your life to see your work in print, don't. Meander along whatever path allows you to be the most productive, because when you're a non-productive writer, being more productive is really all that matters. You can't publish if you don't write.

Tons of writers only have incentive to write if they're writing what they want to write without regard to the market. If you're one of these writers, it also doesn't matter which route you take. Your chances of success in that case will be a combination of dumb luck, skill, and talent. You can be wildly successful under either publishing model. If you happen to enjoy writing the type of novels everybody wants to read, you're going to do well. If you write novels nobody wants to read (regardless of how well they're written), you're going to struggle. You might as well struggle under whatever model gives you the most incentive to write.

So the choice of which model to pursue only matters if you're productive and you're willing to write to market to some degree. If that's the case, there's still a difference, but seeing it is difficult, because it's all shades of gray. To help you make the right choice, we need to dig deeper.

Writer for Hire

Many successful writers will tell you that you should only write what you want to write. While it's true you need passion for what you're writing, absolutes like this aren't particularly useful. If you like writing novels about grizzly bears, whether you write about a grizzly bear set in Montana or a grizzly bear set in Wyoming may not matter that much to you, but it might make a huge difference in how that novel sells. If you follow the write whatever you want edict, you won't consider the market when choosing your bear's home state. Some writers have a mental block against exactly this type of market consideration. Some editors do, too, which may explain why the novels they buy don't sell that well. The folks in this elitist artistic camp are welcome to their opinions, but if they did any market research, they'd discover you can't predict what type of original novel readers will like, but you can determine what readers are buying now. If I tell you there's a current need for military mysteries where the main protagonist is a wounded veteran, could you write a novel fitting those requirements? If you don't think you could, pick another dozen specific examples in genres you like better and ask yourself the same question. If the answer is always no, I'd recommend you stick with the traditional publishing model, because you're a high-risk publisher. Sure, you might be successful, but I wouldn't want to invest in your publishing company. And when you're a self-published writer, that's exactly what you are: You're a one-person publishing company.

The difference between you and the typical publishing company is that you have a stable limited to exactly one writer. While most publishing houses have the luxury of considering thousands of novels and publishing only the ones that fit their marketing model, you're publishing every single novel this dreck writer (meaning you) puts out. Don't get me wrong. I'm not insulting your writing skills, but if your self-publishing company puts out ten novels that don't sell, you're not going to have the highest opinion of this lone writer, either. It's a numbers game. If you only have one shot at success (meaning one writer, you), don't you want that shot to be the best it can be?

If you're serious about your writing success, the decision as to whether to go the self-publishing route or go the traditional route comes down to one determining factor. Are you willing to listen to the market? Can you do the research to determine what novels are likely to sell and then set about producing novels that have the best chance of success you can give them? If not, stick with the traditional publishing model. If you're writing the greatest novels the twenty-first century will ever see, chances are good you'll be "discovered", published, and wildly successful. Granted, even after publication on the traditional route, you'll still need to write to market to have the best chance at keeping that success going. Don't believe me? Talk to a few best-selling authors who are so disgustingly sick of their own series that it takes all of their will power to finish the next book. If they hate it that much, why do it? Because it pays the bills. Whether you go the traditional route or the self-publishing route, if you're successful, you're going to have huge incentives at some point to write what you don't feel like writing. Why? Because you're relying on it to sell and sell well.

Step 1: Decide What to Write

Perhaps you're thinking, hold it! I already have my novel finished, how can this be Step 1? If so, you're probably right: This isn't the first self-publishing step for the novel you just finished. But it should be the first self-publishing step for every book you write from here on out. Before writing a single word, decide what type of novel (you can write) that is likely to sell the best and write that one.

Publisher As Writer

If you were Chief Editor and CEO of the largest publishing house in the world, you would have total control of which novels your company published. So which novels would you choose to publish? Would you simply pick the ones you liked best? Possibly. But what if I could wave my magic wand and guarantee that you'd like all of them exactly the same. Now which novels do you choose? Stick the titles of the novels on the wall and throw darts at them? Consult a fortune teller? Weigh the manuscripts and pick the heaviest one?

You might cry foul at this point and claim there's no way you could like all of them exactly the same, but in a self-publishing company, that's the case. As a writer who self-publishes her work, each novel you finish is the same. You're going to publish it. That decision is made, so the amount you like each of those novels never comes into play. If the quality of or preference for the novels never comes into play but you're still trying to be as successful as possible, there's only one logical way to decide which novel to publish: You choose the novel that you think will sell the best given the current market.

The main difference between my make-believe, wand-filled scenario and what you actually experience as a self-published author is that you make the decision on which novel to publish before you've written the novel.

Writing to Market Is Writing to Sell

I can already hear the dissenters screaming from the back of the room: "You can't write to market!" And if you're talking about the traditional publishing world, that's reasonably good advice. The only write-to-market exceptions in the traditional world are established authors writing more of the same stuff they've been selling, which they've already shown has good market value and which they alone can write (because, hey, it's their stuff). That's not what these dissenters are talking about (and not what I'm talking about either). We're talking about writing a similar-feeling novel to one that's currently all the rage.

If a novel comes out featuring a talking grizzly bear who's actually an alien from planet Spandex and it sells like mad, the tried and true advice is that you (as a new writer) can't take advantage of the sudden demand for novels featuring talking animals that are really aliens. This is true, but what no one likes to admit is that this kind of piggy-backing happens constantly in the entertainment world and has for far longer than anyone can remember.

Think it's coincidence that Rob Roy and Braveheart both came out in the same year (1995)? Just how many big-budget movies based on historical Scottish folk heroes do you suppose come out each year? Think it's just chance that True Blood came out one year and The Vampire Diaries was released the next? Even going way back and overseas, you have the bizarre example of *Mr. Peabody and the Mermaid* and *Miranda*, both British comedic mermaid pictures released within months of each other. I mean, come on. *Mermaids!?* What are the odds?

These are films, you claim. With novels, it's different. I would agree, but only because traditionally published novels take so long to produce. It's still not unusual for a manuscript to take a year or more after it's finished to appear on the shelf of your local bookstore. It's hard to write to market when the market has changed three times before your first attempt comes out.

This can't be stressed enough. In the old days, if you identified a new, popular type of novel, you would be right in thinking that readers likely would be wanting more novels similar to that one. You and every other writer. And quite a few of those other writers would have been a lot more well-known that you were. And when you finished your talking-animal-that's-really-an-alien story and sent it to an editor, guess who was going to be sick of reading that type of novel?

Precisely. The very editor who you hoped would buy your novel. He already had fourteen similar novels under contract with some of those other writers. The last thing he wanted was another talking animal book. "Why can't authors create something original?" he would cry out in frustration. Okay, maybe not literally. But this is the source of the information all those dissenters are relying on. Simply put, it's outdated.

That's because we all have computers (Kindles/smartphones/e-readers). In the old days, readers who wanted a book similar to the talking-animal-who's-really-an-alien one they just read went to the science fiction section and quickly discovered nothing similar at all. Now those same readers can go online and quickly track down every available novel that features a talking animal who's really an alien. Voila! Seven (or seventy) similar novels to choose from. Of course they'll buy at least one. Maybe even yours.

Readers have always enjoyed buying new novels that were somewhat similar to ones they've enjoyed before. The difference is that our modern world provides readers with the tools they need to find those similar novels with ease. And it provides you, the writer—or I should say, the publisher—with the tools to discover which types of novels are selling well. Those are the ones you want to publish.

How to Choose

Note that I said that readers want more of the similar, not the same. Readers aren't looking for an exact rehash of a favorite novel. They're looking for something that has a similar feel. They're hoping to find a new novel that they enjoy as much as the last novel they read from their favorite author. If you examine the proclivity of many readers as a group, you'll discover that their tastes fall into recognizable patterns. A great many different recognizable patterns, but patterns all the same. Some people call these tropes. Others call them genres. Some folks combine tropes and genres to make some kind of a literary Cartesian coordinate system. I will stick with the terms genre and subgenre.

The genres that come to my mind first are romance, suspense, mystery, fantasy, science fiction, religious, horror, western, and action. From there, the subgenres are too numerous to mention. If we pick one at random, such as mystery, we might end up with sub-genres below it like crime, serial killer, heist, kidnapping, murder, noir, organized crime, and vigilante justice.

Why are genres important? Because it's often how a reader finds your novel (or how that novel gets recommended to him). If you just finished a novel that could be classified as a serial killer, mystery novel, you might like another serial killer mystery novel. How does this help you, the writer? It allows you to choose a very specific genre that's not so inundated by novels that a new novel will almost certainly get lost in the shuffle while also letting you choose a genre that has the number of potential readers you're looking for.

For example, Amazon sells a lot of romance novels. A LOT. Does that mean you should write a romance novel? No. What it means is that if you were already interested (and passionate about) writing a romance novel, you should consider tweaking that romance novel so that it fits in a desirable subgenre of romance, a subgenre where authors exist who are selling novels similar to what you were already thinking about writing.

There's a great deal of numerical voodoo you can do to determine exactly what genre you should target. I don't provide details here because the precise method that works now probably won't work in the future. What's important is the general methodology, which would have worked in the past as well as today.

That methodology is simply to find novels from new authors that are selling well that are a type of novel you would be willing and able to write. Preferably you would restrict your search to first novels from new writers. The reasoning is that new writers have no following and no existing readers, which means their new novel sold on its own merits. Granted, it could be that they've written the novel of the century and captured magic in a bottle. Contrary to the thinking of those in the writing-is-artistical-magic crowd, that's the exception rather than the rule. Most new novels that are successful are good novels that fit into a genre that a significant number of readers like. Granted, the novel should be as good as you can make it to have any chance, but this is true regardless of type or publishing model.

Series, Seriously

If you can write a series of novels rather than a stand-alone novel, your chance of being read and making a living at your writing are considerably higher than if you do stand-alone novels. Why is this? Are stand-alone novels better?

No. Series are more profitable over time than equal quality stand-alone novels because It's simple math.

Let's look at the situation where you've written four novels: the first two novels in your *Money Is Good* series and two stand-alone novels called Written First and Written Second. (Granted, we should probably fire our title creator, but it's easier to follow this way.) You release *Money Is Good, Volume 1* and *Written First* at the same time. For this example, I'll allow *Written First* to be a better novel than the first book in your series (best case scenario in support of stand-alones). The readers respond and *Written First* makes more money. But what happens when you release the next two novels? When *Money Is Good, Volume 2* is released, you not only sell copies of this novel but you also sell copies of Volume 1. Plus, when sales for the second novel in your series starts to slow, you can run discount specials on the first volume in your series to get readers to try it, which provides sales for the second novel in your series that you couldn't have realized any other way. When you release *Written Second,* you get few (if any) additional sales for either your series or *Written First.*

What this means is that each subsequent novel you release in a series makes money for itself and money for every novel in the series up to that point. When you release a stand-alone novel it makes money for itself. That's it. Granted, a few readers will notice who wrote the novel they just read and go looking for other novels they've written, but practical sales numbers show this is way less common than most writers believe (and way less common than common sense would suggest).

Provided you keep the quality of the novels in your series above a minimum threshold set by your readers, this multiplying sales effect is compounded for each subsequent novel released in your series. By the time you're up to seven or eight novels in the series, your stand-alone novels don't have a chance.

Does this mean you should never write stand-alone novels? Not at all. But if you want your publishing company to start out life as a success, releasing only series novels in the beginning ups your chances considerably.

You Still Matter

So I've recommended the type of novel you should write. Find a type that sells and write that as the first in a many book series. But don't forget to consider your own abilities and tastes. If you attempt to write a novel you don't want to write, in that way madness lies. And much frustration. Not to mention failure.

Yes, you want to write to market, but you want to write something that's close to what you would have written anyway. Just as the best lies are based on truth, the best novels you can produce are based on your own tastes, feelings, talents, and inclinations. Trust your instincts. Especially when those instincts tell you to write a novel that fits the market.

Step 2: Keep Your Output High

The most important advice I can give any writer is to write. Write as much and as often as you can. Of the two hard and fast rules I have, the first is to write. This is never more important than when you're the sole writer in your own publishing company. Let's face it, the number of authors in your stable of writers is pathetic. You can't be successful if you have no product to sell. But it goes beyond that.

Did You Write Something?

We live in a Attention Deficit Disorder society. We binge-watch entire series of television shows. Technology changes faster than pioneer settlers changed their underwear. If you take years to produce your next novel, your entire career is going to start over with the release of each new novel.

On the other hand, if you produce several novels a year, momentum builds with the release of each novel. You get more recommendations from the online search engines, you make more money because you release more novels, you get more readers because you have more chances to gain those readers, and you take giant steps toward being a professional writer instead of a wannabe writer. More important, you develop the reputation among readers as a writer who can be counted on to deliver new material, which makes you worth following and worth reading.

Sure, it's always possible your first novel might be wildly successful. If it's that good, people will wait for your second. But why make them? Unless you're one of those sparkly vampires in real life, your days are numbered. Sure, you can fool yourself into thinking that rewriting your novel fifty times will make it better than writing it just once. You may even be right, but for most writers it's not true. A novel that's been rehashed fifty times will read like it's been rehashed fifty times.

Unless you're already writing *5,000 Words Per Hour,* you can im-prove the speed at which you write. Do this and you will write better, write faster, and finish more books. For one way to do this, see the section later in this book on "Writing Quickly While Writing Well."

Don't Rewrite

Novels aren't like wine. They don't automatically get better with time. Two difficulties exist in knowing how much you need to rewrite: 1) You can't trust your own judgment, and 2) You can't trust anyone else's judgment, either. All you can do is to write it as well as you can, get it edited **once** by someone who seems to know what she's doing, and move on.

This don't-rewrite advice is scorned by a large segment of the professional writing community, and with good reason. There are some truly awful self-published novels coming out these days. They contain more grammar mistakes than a failed English test. But they're out there and available for purchase. That novel you're writing and rewriting and polishing isn't. What's more, that incompetent writer just put out another five novels while you were agonizing over whether you had the almost right word or the right word.

Don't get me wrong. Writing well is important. What's hard for most writers to accept is that getting their prose just right only impresses a tiny number of readers (many of whom are other writers). But here's the thing. Writers don't buy as many books as avid readers. And the readers, for the most part, don't care. They read for stories and characters, not prose.

So, wise and powerful Oz, are you saying I should publish my first draft? Absolutely not. Especially when you're just starting out. Write the novel to the best of your ability. After a brief cool-off period to give yourself some objective distance, rework the novel, polish the resulting manuscript, and then get that finished novel edited, line-edited, and copy edited by professionals who are trained to do so. Yes, that means you'll be paying them, so choose your editors well.

The key with self-publishing is that you're not looking for perfection. You're looking for good. With traditional publishing, you didn't have a choice. You couldn't risk having an editor fail to read (and purchase) your novel because it had a punctuation mistake in your opening paragraph.

Step 3: Pay for What You Need

Finishing your book gets you a good share of the way down the road toward self-publication, but you're far from finished. In addition to creating a professional manuscript, you'll also want to have the following set up before you release the first title from your new publishing company:

- Have your book edited and copy edited
- Generate a professional cover that looks great full-size and as a thumbnail
- Format your book for publication in e-book format (and if desired, as a printed novel)
- Produce a marketing plan and marketing materials
- Create and publish a web site

The first question you need to answer regarding these items is whether you'll do them yourself or whether you'll contract others to do them. On the side of doing these yourself, you'll pay less, you'll have full control over the outcome, and you need to come up with the key information for each regardless who does them. On the negative side, you're unlikely to do as good a job on any of these as an expert would, all of them will take time away from your writing, and you have a greater chance of doing something really stupid.

For me, the greatest determining factor in whether you do these is money. If you simply can't come up with the money to pay someone to do these tasks, you don't have much choice. But if you have the money, I urge you to consider farming out as many of these as possible. Even at small publishing houses with a single editor on staff, the editor typically doesn't create the covers, the web site, or format the book. If you want to run your own publishing house, even with you being the only author, it's a good idea to pay attention to what other professionals in your line of work are doing.

Editing and Copy Editing

I mentioned in the last section that you should have your novel edited, line edited, and copy edited. This is good advice for your first two to three novels. Unless you already have these skills at a professional level, it's likely you'd benefit from some professional advice. The problem is finding good professional advice. Before you begin looking, you first need to know what you're looking for.

Developmental Editor

A developmental editor (sometimes called a content editor) is who most of the population imagines when they conjure up a mental image of an editor. These are the folks who recommend changes to your novel. At this point, you're looking for all the advice you can get, whether it be with story, characters, motivations, pacing, or use of language. Having said that, you shouldn't be hiring a developmental editor to fix your novel. *You* should fix your own novel before you send the novel to the editor. What you're looking for from the editor is to improve what you already have and catch any mistakes you might have made. Plus it's a second opinion from someone who knows nothing about the novel other than what's on the page. This fresh set of eyes can be invaluable.

Having said that, you (and you alone) know what's best for your novel. Don't allow a developmental editor to move your novel in a direction that you never intended. To be a good writer, you must know what type of novel you're trying to write and what you're trying to achieve in each scene and in each chapter. If you get advice from an editor that doesn't make sense within that framework, you must ignore the advice, no matter how good that advice might seem on the surface.

That doesn't mean you ignore your editor. You should have taken care to find the right editor before hiring them, so consider what they've said carefully before you reject it.

If this sounds complicated, it's because it is. One of the hardest skills a new writer can learn is when to ignore advice and when to follow it. I'd love to give you some handy rule that would allow you to know if someone's advice is good or bad. All I can say is that you should try to hire editors who are writers themselves and who've written a novel you can read and respect.

After getting input from your editors, you'll likely be rewriting sections of the novel, which is just one more reason not to spend the extra time swinging for the fence of perfect prose before the edit. Few things are harder for a writer than throwing out several pages that took hours and hours to get "just right." But there's a huge difference between perfect and good. Your prose should be as grammatically correct and as strong as you can make it in a first pass. Don't sweat every word, but don't blunder your way along. You want your editor to be concentrating on your story and characters, not the hundreds of grammar mistakes and plethora of typos.

Line Editor

Only after you've received feedback from your developmental editor and altered the novel in response to that feedback should you hire a line editor. Line editors do what their title implies: They go through your manuscript line by line and attempt to improve the language. Their goal is not to change what you've said but to help you say it better. They compress prose, improve verbs, correct language usage, and improve dialogue. A good line editor is worth their weight in gold, but many line editors perform their function by rote. They remove all your adverbs and most of your adjectives, all references to time, and all use of the verb "to be." When you're starting out, it's useful to employ a line editor to get a sense of how your writing can be improved, but if you agree with the style a line editor creates, you can learn to clean up and improve your prose just as easily as most line editors can.

Copy Editor

After you have received some editorial advice and have utilized the changes that made sense, polish the result. Make it as good as you can. Only then should you send it off to a copy editor. Why not let the copy editor find your mistakes? Because writers should have the skills necessary to copy edit their own work. If you don't polish your manuscript and make it the best you can before sending it to the copy editor, you'll never know if you would have caught the errors the copy editor finds. Plus the more mistakes you force your copy editor to fix, the more likely they will miss some of the corrections they should make. It's much easier to spot any given mistake in a clean page of prose than it is to catch the same mistake when it's mixed in with seventy-four others. What you're looking for from a good copy edit is another pair of skilled eyes that can catch your grammar and punctuation mistakes, spelling and diction errors, and inconsistency slip-ups.

<u>Hiring the Right Editors</u>

Take your time finding the right people to edit your manuscript. Good editors are hard to find. For your developmental editor especially, try to find someone who works with the same type of book you've written. Each genre has its own tropes and requirements. A good romance editor might be a lousy science-fiction editor (and vice-versa). Try to get recommendations from other authors and ask questions. Shop and compare. The internet makes all of this far easier than it was before the World Wide Web existed, but the process is far from foolproof. Above all, try to be the best you can be at all of these skills before you seek professional help. A good writer should also have the skills needed to be a good editor, line-editor, and copy editor.

Cover Generation

Unless you're a professional artist with excellent marketing instincts, you'll probably want to hire someone to do your cover. There are plenty of artists who specialize in creating covers for novels. Find several and compare. Good book covers still sell novels. You want your cover to be the best it can be. The problem is that nobody can agree what "good" is. There are only a couple universal truths.

- Your cover should look good as a thumbnail graphic
- Your title and your name should be easy to read

Beyond that, everything's open to debate. Typically your colors shouldn't clash, but sometimes people do that for effect. Browse books that are a similar type to yours. These are the novels your readers are buying. What do those covers look like? Figure out the look you want, then hire someone who can create that look for you.

Formatting

Getting your book into a form that will look great across all e-book readers and will look great in print is a daunting task. There are entire books not to mention author service sites devoted to the subject. For novels, there is an easier way. Google "Kindle Simple Formatting Guide"[16] and "Format for CreateSpace" and follow the guidelines given.

What!? Why would I simply tell you to follow Kindle's and CreateSpace's advice? Because at this point in time, selling on Amazon is the only model that makes sense for a self-publishing operation that's designed to make money. (Kindle is the e-book format of choice for Amazon and CreateSpace is the print format of choice for Amazon.)

But why limit yourself to Amazon? Because even if you combine the sales from every other outlet channel an independent, self-publishing author can access, those sales will pale in comparison to what you can make on Amazon. Instead of wasting your precious resources trying to satisfy all the formats available, charge ahead with Amazon and call it good. Still not convinced? Here are some reasons to go exclusively with Amazon:

- Only one e-book and one print format to worry about
- As of May, 2016, about 85% of all independently published book sales *in any format* in the U.S. happen on Amazon
- If you're productive and you write good novels, Amazon does a lot of your marketing for you
- One source for all of your royalty information, saving time both monitoring sales and gathering sales information for tax purposes

If you decide to market your novel everywhere, there are several author services available that will format your novels. As with any services you hire, do your research and hire quality professionals.

Marketing

The most important marketing concept to embrace as a self-published author is that of brand. Your goal is to have readers recognize your name and buy your novels because of that name. For all your novels, your name should be prominently displayed and easily readable on

---

16. Why not just provide a link here? The answer is that links change. Google searches will still return a proper link fifty years from now, provided Google (or a Google equivalent) is still around and we still find information this way.

the cover. The same goes for your series. They should recognize the name of the series and should be able to tell which book in the series a particular novel is from the cover alone.

To increase your series branding, you should use similar covers, the same font, and the same color scheme across all books in the series. (Not the same colors, but the same style. Books that are part of a series should look like they belong together.) This similarity across novel covers provides a professional and recognizable look that readers identify and respect.

To further increase your brand, you should consider hiring a publicist to put together a marketing plan for you. While this isn't necessary, it saves time and allows you to access expertise that would be unavailable otherwise. What's important is that if you self-publish a novel, you need to get the word out. After all, if people never hear of your novel, they can't buy it. Having said that, if you have the time and inclination to do your own marketing, do so. No one's going to care about your novel as much as you do. Even if you hire a publicist, you can't just write them a check and leave them to their own resources. Remember, you're the boss. Act like it.

Web Site

Some authors will claim that you don't need a separate web site these days. You can just use services provided by Facebook, Twitter, and other online social sites. I disagree. Not only do you have full control over your web site, you can also use it to build up your email list of folks who are interested in your books. This email list is invaluable. It represents both a list of your fans and a way to communicate with them. For any author starting out, the most valuable asset you can have is a solid base of fans who like what you write. Let's face it: Most people won't like what you write. That's no reflection on you. Different people have different tastes. What your email list gives you is an unsurpassed way to target marketing on your next novel to a group of people who have liked something you wrote in the past.

There is too much. Let me sum up

Self-publishing is not for everyone, but if you're a normal writer starting out today, self-publishing is your most reliable way to make a living if you're a highly productive writer who produces quality material written to market, and who isn't afraid of a little marketing work.

- Anyone who criticizes self-published novels simply because they are self-published is living in the past; feel free to ignore them.
- Self-published authors earn better royalties, have more control over both content and marketing, and are guaranteed publication.
- Choose your publishing method before you write your novel rather than using self-publishing as a backup plan.
- If you're a non-productive writer, being more productive is all that matters, so choose the publishing method that provides you the most incentive to write.
- As a publisher with only one writer in your stable, writing to market makes good business sense.
- If you're writing novels, series generate more revenue than stand-alone novels of the same quality.
- The single greatest factor that will determine whether you succeed as a self-published author is how fast you can write well.
- If you can afford it, pay experts to edit your manuscript, produce your cover art, format your manuscript, market your novel, and generate your web site.

Chapter Nine:
Series

Money, Money, Money

Money equals readers.

Whether you're the most free-spirited, giving person the world has ever known or the most materialistically greedy grinch since Ebenezer Scrooge, being a successful writer still comes down to money. Even if you give away everything you write, your popularity will be less than it would if people paid for your work. This is because a lot of people make money off writers: Publishers, film and TV producers, toy makers, fast food chains, clothing manufacturers, poster printers, marketers, and many more. These folks aren't going to promote a series of books that doesn't make them money.

In general, the more money you make as a writer, the more readers you have for the books you produce. This isn't always true, but desiring to make money from your writing is not as selfish as it appears to be. You want to give your readers a chance to enjoy your stories, don't you? The very nature of fiction is entertainment, which provides amusement and joy to people the world over. That's a pretty noble purpose when you think about it, regardless how much money you make doing it.

For the average writer, the most reliable way to make money is by writing a series. That's why I've dedicated part of this book to the subject. Whether you love series or hate them, they remain the most reliable form of income you can generate.

Why is that so? What makes novels in a series better than stand-alone novels?

In "Step 1: Decide What to Write", I outlined the financial logic behind why series make more money. It boils down to this: Subsequent books in a series help to sell earlier books in the series whereas stand-alone novels don't reliably lead to sales of your other work (no matter how contrary this is to common sense). But it goes beyond that.

At its base, readers have preferences. The type and setting of a novel is a bit like wine regions. If I go into a store looking for a bottle of wine, the easiest way for me to find one I like is to stick with regions I know and like. Readers are no different. It's also a matter of simple practicality.

Imagine you're a film producer. You're looking for a new story idea. You're a series bigot, so you buy only stand-alone novels to turn into movies. The producer down the road only buys the rights to series. Guess what happens. If you are both equally talented, the movie producer down the road becomes rich, famous, and powerful while you make one bad decision and go broke. That's because it's a lot cheaper to raise money in Hollywood for a proven commodity than it is to raise money for a story you believe in.

The same is even more true for television series based on books. If your stand-alone novel was deep enough to drive an entire television series, it was more than deep enough for you to create a great series of novels instead of just one. That's the reason it so rarely happens. Most TV series based on the written word are based on a series of novels rather than just one book. Don't believe me? Check out the most popular series on TV that came from a novel (or from a series of novels) and see which happens most often.

That doesn't mean that stand-alone novels don't have their place. If you want to write only stand-alone novels, feel free to do. You're fighting a bit of an uphill battle, but if your stand-alone novels are ten times better than any series book you'd ever put out, you're making the right choice. If that's the case, skip the rest of this part of the book. On the other hand, if you're like most of us and need to write series in order to pay the bills, the following sections will provide good information on how to do that.

Be a Serial Thinker

One of the reasons I've pushed series so much in this book compared to stand-alone books is because too many series were never meant to be series at all. Unfortunately it's not as easy as many writers think to turn a great stand-alone novel into a great series of novels. Overlap certainly exists—most great characters do just fine whether their lives consist of a single novel or span hundreds of novels—but almost without exception, series are better if they were originally conceived as a series rather than being tacked on after the first novel sold well.

By definition, conceiving a series before writing the first book means you plan your series to some extent before you start writing. While I'm sure there have been many successful authors who didn't plan anything in advance, most good series were created before a single chapter was ever written.

To Grow or Not To Grow

One of the great fallacies in most modern writing circles is that your characters must fundamentally change throughout the course of a novel. I don't believe this. For every series I ever gave up reading, I quit mostly because the main character had changed. I liked the original character. That's why I bought and read books two through eighty-five. But in that eighty-sixth book, I realized that the character who I loved so much had been growing distant for a while now. He just wasn't the same character I fell in love with. It was time to end the relationship.

I'm not saying that your main character shouldn't change at all, but never forget that your readers like your main character. That's one of the reasons they're reading your novels. If you change that character, you risk losing those readers. With a stand-alone novel, this is less important. If the novel was enjoyable and thought-provoking, readers are less likely to harbor any regrets about the changes the hero experiences. But if you write a series of novels where the main character is constantly changing, you're bound to stumble eventually upon a combination your readers don't like. At that point, they quit buying your books. Game over.

When you do allow your main character to grow, your goal is to improve what readers don't like and keep what readers do.

For example, in the Janet Evanovich series featuring Stephanie Plum, one of the biggest reader complaints you see in reviews is that Stephanie remains an inexperienced idiot. She often succeeds through assistance from others or through sheer dumb luck. It's clear a lot of readers believe Stephanie would be a better character if she grew in intelligence and competence from novel to novel. Since she's constantly gaining experience, it violates the laws of common sense for her to remain so inept after several novels have gone by. In comparison, Harry Potter is a much more accomplished wizard by the end of the seventh novel than he was at the beginning of the first. The gradual increase in skill he gains from novel to novel is normal and expected for most characters.

At the opposite end of the spectrum lies the problem of improving your main character too much. For many readers, nothing gets older faster than a character who already had fantastic capabilities in the first novel and rises rapidly until they have godlike capabilities in subsequent novels. Two problems with this exist: 1) You have nowhere left to improve and 2) The character goes beyond someone readers can relate to.

When you create the main characters for your series, either leave them room to improve or don't have them improve much.

Readers don't love your characters for their perfections alone but also for their flaws. For every step you allow your character to move forward, consider having them take a step back in some other area.

A good technique for creating a series character that grows in a way your readers like is to create two versions of your character. The first is your character as he appears in your first novel. The second is your character as he will become by your last novel. While the exhausting ordeal of writing the series may change your original intent, having both versions of your character in mind not only gives you a target at which to aim but also provides an existing version of that character to test for adequacy. You want your character in his final form to be passionate, active, capable, interesting, and believable.

The most frequent problems I see with characters who grow are that they lose their passion, they fail to be interesting (often because they've lost their entire sense of humor), and they're no longer believable because they've become too incredible for credibility.

Your best bet, as you grow your character, is to leave their essential core unchanged. Sure, they've been altered by what's happened to them (your story), but at heart they're the same person your reader first fell in love with.

The easiest way to do this is to give your character a strong set of core values and a ton of depth. While you should always know volumes more about your characters than what ends up in your books, the amount of knowledge you need for a main character from a series is much higher than what you need for the main character from a stand-alone novel. Give them room to grow that doesn't involve changing who they are.

Exception to the Rule

Some series have different characters (even different main characters) in every book. For these novels, it's not the characters that drive the series forward, but the story. For those series, none of these comments related to character growth are relevant. For novels from this kind of series, characters are equivalent to those found in a stand-alone series.

It's All Relative

While your characters don't change in fundamental ways, relationships between characters are constantly changing. Typically it will be an ebb and flow where the relationships end up back close to where they started, but some progression will inevitably take place. This is particularly true with any romantic connections between your characters. If two characters fall in love, have sex, or even have a fundamental disagreement, their relationship is never quite the same again.

Often relationships between characters are as important to a reader's enjoyment of a series as are the characters themselves. If that trio of characters who became lifelong friends in book one are still around in book seventeen, most readers want their relationship to be intact (although a bit altered). When they triumph over the big bad together, the reader's enjoyment is magnified.

Take Me to your Leader

The main character in a series is the driving force behind that series. Create a lousy main character and your series is doomed before it starts.

You're looking for a character who cares deeply about the people around her and who cares deeply about solving the problems you throw at her. You're going to throw problems at her book after book after book. She needs that depth of passion to keep going when the going gets tough.

She should be a doer, not a complainer. That means a problem solver, preferably a non-conformist problem solver. There are plenty of people who follow the rules. In Oz, we have a name for those people: Boring! You're not looking for someone who breaks the rules for her own gain, but for the good of others. Individuals are more important than groups here. Her friends, her family, her dog, her cat, and her pet hamster are vital to her sense of self. She'll sacrifice a lot for the people who matter, although she'll always be trying to sacrifice herself first. "Kill me instead," is a good mantra for her to follow.

Fortunately she's not going to die as a result. That's because she's capable of great things. She may not seem like it on the surface, but that depth of character you've given her brings her through when others fail. She will excel in some areas and lag in others, but she will use her strengths to conquer the evils of the world. Often, she will not come through unscathed, but she will always come through.

Finally, she will be larger than life. You're looking for someone who has iconic qualities. She needs to be a symbol that others can recognize, identify with, and long to be.

Or you can just make her really funny. Humor conquers all, as Janet Evanovich has proven. That's because humor is interesting. Humor is fun. If your main character is so interesting she's irresistible, you can break any rules and ignore any advice I give you. Most writers aren't capable of creating a character who's that interesting without a little help.

The Big Question

Three main kinds of series exist: 1) Those that have an overall story arc that continues from book to book, 2) those that have major story elements that carry over from book to book, have a significant impact on the plot, and have no end in sight, and 3) those with books that stand alone but have a world (setting) and characters that carry over from novel to novel.

The most famous example of the first kind (building story) is the Harry Potter series. While each novel has its own story with its own conclusion, all novels build to an overall story conclusion. A well known example of the second kind (meandering carryover) is the Harry Bosch series by Michael Connelly. Events that happen to Harry in one novel impact Harry in the next one. The most famous recent example of the third kind (mostly independent novels) is by Dan Brown. The Robert Langdon novels certainly have carryover from novel to novel, but they don't share one building story arc that will be resolved by the last novel in the series.

The first and second kinds of series are by far the most common. Readers like series because they share similar elements. In general, the less elements shared between novels in a series, the less readers enjoy the series. Most readers like the inside jokes and interesting tidbits that are gleaned only for readers who have read previous novels in the series. It's a not universal. Some readers want to pick up any book in a series and be able to enjoy it regardless whether they've read any of the other books in the series. Some authors bore their loyal readers to tears by trying to make this easier through the repetition of facts any reader of the series already knows. For example, each of the subsequent Harry Potter books becomes increasingly painful in the early chapters as readers are tortured by repetition of information we already know. Eventually J. K. Rowling gives this up as a bad job, but only after several novels.

When designing a series, one of the first decisions you should make regards which of the three types of series your series is going to be. If you choose the second or third types where you have limited carryover from novel to novel, you can get away with having a lot less series story arc. If you plan to do the first type of series where you're really telling one long story in multiple installments, the importance of planning and having an overall story plot is increased.

While character depth in a series is important, story depth is equally important. (You can get away with mediocre characters if your story is strong enough.) Since you're writing a series of novels rather than one novel, everything is expanded. The techniques you use to plot a single novel are the same techniques you use to plot a series of novels, except in maxiature. (Yes, I know maxiature isn't a word, but it should be.) You're looking to build the tension and raise the stakes until everything hangs in the balance (and is resolved) in the final book.

Creating a Series Story Arc

The best way to create a story arc that can support a many novel series, in my opinion, is to create as many story threads as you can weave together—and then weave them together. This sounds easier than it is, and it doesn't sound all that easy. What I'm talking about here is an attempt to link everything together into a greater whole.

How do you do this? Patience, determination, talent, and a hell of a lot of work. I know no one wants to hear that, but while your overall story might come to you while riding a train from Manchester to London, it doesn't come alive until you've filled it out with as many threads as you can master.

The only reliable way I know to do this is by figuring out your main story arc and then working backwards from the end.

For example, your hero might need to be the best sharpshooter in the world by the last scene of the last book in the series. Starting with that fact, you spiderweb your way out. Your main character needs an overwhelming reason to become such a good shot. Maybe he had a chance to save his wife from the villain in novel three, but he missed the shot, and he swears that will never happen again. Perhaps he goes broke and in desperation he opens a gun club where he gives shooting lessons. A young arrogant punk embarrasses him in a shooting competition. Rather than trying to get revenge or cause the young kid problems, he has the kid give him shooting lessons. So now we need to give our hero reasons to go broke and to be humble enough that he's willing to take lessons from someone half his age. Maybe he decides to make the young kid a partner in his gun club. Maybe the young kid dies and he decides to seek revenge.

The key is that you start with what you need and grow your story organically. While I prefer to work from end to beginning, some writers do better working from beginning to end. Either way, you mix and match and move possibilities around until you start seeing connections. This is where the talent comes into play. That ability to see the dramatic in the every day is something that can be improved upon but not created from nothing.

It's interesting to note that this tapestry can be weaved by starting with story and allowing it to define the characters, starting with characters and allowing them to define the story, or, what happens most often, starting with both story and characters and allowing them to define each other. You can even start with your world and use the circumstances of the situation to determine the characters and story you need.

Always there must be character motivations that arise from the natural circumstances of the original events. The forces at work should be as powerful as you can make them, and they must oppose each other.

In the most basic and time-honored stories, these forces are good vs. evil. They oppose each other because they can't coexist. Order vs. chaos. Freedom vs. regulation. These types of polar opposites make excellent land masses upon which to build your story civilizations. In most stories, such polar opposites begin in focus. Black vs. white. Right vs. wrong. As the novels progress, the situation grows more complicated. Readers learn the evil side isn't all evil and the good side isn't all good. There are legitimate reasons for both sides, but in the end, if you want to have a series that survives the ages, the easiest way to do it is to make it easy for the reader to root for one side over the other. When the final triumph comes, it's a total triumph rather than a triumph with reservations.

Your World

The process of world-building is like writing: There are nearly as many methods for creating fictional worlds as there are writers who create them. A few common guidelines exist:

- Always know much more about your world than you've told your reader
- Create opposing worldviews
- Don't overcomplicate your world, especially in the first few novels
- Know the history and possibly the future of your world as well as the here and now
- Create opportunities for humor

Often humor comes from characters, but those characters need a world to live in.

For most novels, culture is a vital part of any worldbuilding you do. All cultures have a reason for their existence and reasons why they are the way they are (and your reason can't be "Because I need them for my story"). Cultures aren't uniform. You're looking for beef stew here rather than chicken broth.

Sometimes You Need a Plumber

Understand how infrastructure works. This is more obvious in a magical or science-fiction world, but it's true for real worlds as well. If your main character is a detective who's constantly solving crimes, why is the detective stuck at the same position? Why haven't the higher-ups promoted him to captain or at least lieutenant? Your answer may lie in the traits your character exhibits, such as a complete disregard for authority, but it can also exist in the world itself. Maybe all that matters is seniority rather than performance.

A vital part of worldbuilding is going beyond what you need and understanding what repercussions those needs create.

Learn How to Piss Someone Off

To drive a series forward, you want cultures that have fundamentally different views and beliefs. That means you need to know why those cultures vary so greatly. What factors shaped the cultures and why do the people of those cultures care so much about keeping their culture intact? Allow those differences to have repercussions. After all, if one side got it completely right, why wouldn't every side adopt the same world view? Note that "because they're evil!" is not an acceptable answer to that question.

Keep It Simple Smeagol

The simpler initial view of your world given, the easier it is to create a dramatic story that takes place in that world. Especially in a series where the depth of a world can be explored over the course of many novels. Limiting the world view in the first few novels allows a reader to gain familiarity organically rather than having it thrust upon them.

Don't Forget to Laugh

Because the emotional stakes in a series tend to rise over time, many authors forget how important humor can be to a reader's enjoyment of a novel. For most humans, the more stress they encounter, the greater their need for laughter. The reason humor is difficult to maintain in a series often stems directly from the author. As more storylines weave together in a never-ending crescendo, it's easy for an author to become overwhelmed. Often, the first part of the series to suffer is the humor. Making sure to keep humor in a series not only benefits the reader but often it benefits the writer, too.

There is too much. Let me sum up

If you're a writer for long, you will probably want to write at least one series at some point in your career. Many successful writers spend their entire careers on a single series.

- All else being equal, books in a series will make more money (and be read by more readers) than standalone books that are not part of a series.
- Novels that are designed to be part of a series from the start are typically better than those based on a standalone novel that was turned into a series.
- The main characters in a series are not expected to change as much as many characters do in standalone novels. Changing the main characters in a series too much often results in lost readers.
- The main heroes in a series are often iconic characters who tend to be larger than life.
- To create a great story arc for a series, weave many storylines tightly together.
- To build a great world for your series, create a deep and detailed world with a rich history and future. Don't over-complicate the world, but have opposing factions that can drive your plots forward.
- Never forget how important humor is to a series. Especially in a series, it's easy for drama to overshadow humor.

Chapter Ten:
Marketing

Not My Job

I wish someone else had written this book and I had read it before Tor published my first novel. Even though I'd been in the business long enough to know that traditional publishers barely lift a finger to promote a novel by a new author and that most of the marketing was up to me, I didn't know how to market my novel. Even so, I didn't stand on the sideline doing nothing. I managed to snag articles in several newspapers, did four book signings, and one radio interview. I created a web site devoted to the release of the novel. I created marketing materials and distributed them in any place that made any sense at all.

And it meant nothing.

The reason was simple. It just wasn't enough. I didn't understand that marketing my novel required nearly as much effort and time as writing it. More important, doing 90% of the marketing required to sell a novel isn't much different than doing 10%. Until you reach a critical threshold of readers that allows your novel to start selling itself, you really have no chance.

Fortunately, in today's world, marketing is easier than ever before. It still takes times, but using the techniques covered on the following pages, it's possible to effectively market a first novel and make a real impact on sales.

"Wait!" you scream. "That's why I sold my novel to traditional publishers in the first place—so that I wouldn't need to do all this marketing stuff!"

Forgive me while I shake my head and tsk-tsk sadly.

When it comes to marketing, it doesn't matter whether your book is being published by one of the big five out of New York or whether you're publishing it yourself. Unless you received a six-figure advance, the amount of marketing you will receive will do nothing to sell your book. Even if this isn't the case, do you really want to take that chance? You wrote your novel so that people could read it. They can't read it if they don't know it exists.

The good news is that the techniques you use to market your novel are pretty much the same regardless of how the book is published.

The main differences relate to what you're allowed to use for your reader magnets (covered in a moment) and the amount of control you exert over your cover and blurb.

If you want to be a successful writer, you better learn to be a successful marketer.

The Fine Print

Many of the techniques I cover are directed at writers who are just starting out. It's easy to market your work when you have a large body of work to market and a loyal following of devoted readers. What I'm more concerned with in this chapter is marketing your first novel or your first couple of novels. Having said that, plenty of the techniques covered here will serve you well throughout your writing career. Adjust my advice as needed to fit your current situation.

Brand I Am

People love brands they can trust. In our modern world, buying decisions are more complicated than ever before. If you can find a brand that delivers, your buying decision becomes easy: Just look for that brand.

For writers, this concept of brand is not limited simply to name alone. Sure, if you're an avid reader who loves Stephen King or Dean Koontz, you buy a novel simply because it's written by one of those writers. But what about J. K. Rowling? She has plenty of brand clout, too, but her personal author brand pales in comparison to the Harry Potter brand. When I talk to people about their favorite novels, I hear plenty of readers say they love Harry Potter. Few say they love J. K. Rowling. It's not that they don't love J. K. Rowling—they do—but when they think of her, they think of Harry Potter first.

As authors, when we talk about branding, we have two considerations. If you're a writer of stand-alone novels, you're marketing your own name. If you write series, you're marketing both the series name and your own name. After all, you'll probably finish that series someday and you'd love your readers to join you on your next great adventure.

What you want are satisfied readers who trust your brand. Violate that trust and you risk losing that reader forever.

Pseudonyms as Imprints

Most readers like certain kinds (genres) of novels more than others. That's why traditional publishers invented the imprint. Imprints allowed readers to easily distinguish between different types of books. You don't want the fans of your hard-boiled police procedural series making the mistake of picking up the young adult romance novel you just released expecting to find a police procedural. Some writers think this situation is fine—it's another book sold—but sell a book and lose a reader forever is not a good tradeoff.

Under normal circumstances, as a lone author, you have no control over imprints (whether you're self-published or whether you sold your novel through traditional channels). What you do control is the name you put on a book you wrote. That's where pseudonyms come into play. Having pen names for each of the different types of novels you write keeps you from disappointing readers who are expecting Jane Austin and get Jane Casey.

Using pseudonyms to distinguish between novels written in different genres isn't necessary, but it is a time-honored technique used by writers for decades. Research shows that midlist and below writers receive few crossover buys between the various genres they write. While releasing all of your novels under your own name has a certain appeal, it's hard to justify from a marketing standpoint if you write novels in widely differing genres.

The key question in determining whether pseudonyms are appropriate is asking whether most of your current readers would like your new novel. If not, branding that new novel differently with a pseudonym is a no-brainer.

Talk Once, Sell Many Times

I know hundreds of writers who think a great marketing plan consists of doing signings, composing a blog, interacting with people on social media, and otherwise building their readers one at a time. The problem with this concept is that it's not efficient. For every hour you commit to marketing, you have one less hour to write. While every devoted and admiring reader is precious, there is a better way to gain those readers.

The bulk of your marketing time and dollars should focus on doing the marketing once and having the chance at many readers in return. Part of this is getting the word out to places and people who are likely to spread the word further still. Here are a few examples of this work once, get many readers philosophy:

- Television, radio, and newspaper interviews
- Book reviews
- Advertising
- Web Site and s
- Newsletter

All of these techniques involve very different skills. As such, we should probably take them one at a time and see what we can make of them.

Television, Radio, and Newspaper Interviews

Entry into any of these outlets is typically an uphill battle. Lots of people have something to sell. What you must have is something to offer as well as something to sell. While successful self-promotion through the media is a topic worthy of a book unto itself (or perhaps a series of books), a few general pieces of advice are handy:

1) Learn how to write a press release. An easy way to do this is to google "how to write a press release." It's a learned skill, which means it's a skill *you* can *learn.*

2) Figure out a way to leverage any knowledge or background material that went into your novel. Likely targets are science, history, and geography. This is one advantage provided by writing about real places rather than made-up towns and cities.

3) Learn how to give a good interview and remember that while your eventual goal is the promotion of your novel, your immediate task with everything you say is to be entertaining.

Don't get discouraged if your first attempts to land an interview fail. Also, no interview is too small, especially when you're starting out. That interview for the local paper gives you valuable practice for later in life when you're being interviewed for an audience of millions. If you don't prepare for it to happen, it never will.

Book Reviews

The person reviewing your book is more important than the review itself. Does that person have a following? If so, what kind of following? You want reviews from people who mainly read novels like the one you wrote. If their focus is narrow, the chance of their review being viewed by others who would want to buy your book goes up. So, if you want the "right" people to review your book, start by looking at who reviewed recently-released books that are similar to yours and send your book to those people for review.

Beyond that, try not to pay too much attention to reviews of your book. Whether a particular reader liked or didn't like your novel is irrelevant. The only helpful information you can gain is why a reader felt the way they did. Were they the wrong type of reader? If so, then their negative (or positive) review says more about them than it does your work. Learn from your reviews and move on. It's guaranteed people exist who will hate your book no matter how good the book is. If you have no negative reviews, you simply haven't found those people yet.

Advertising

It'd be great if I could tell you exactly what you need to do to advertise your novel effectively. Unfortunately, every book is different just as every writer is different. As with reviews, you want to target your advertising toward people who have a good chance to like your novel. Advertising across the board is so ineffective that it's useless.

Opportunities for advertising your novel change almost daily. To decide if an advertising opportunity is right for you, evaluate it on the following criteria:

1) How well does it target the readers you want versus readers in general?
2) How much does it cost per response?
3) How well can you measure your success?

In a perfect world, your advertising will reach only the readers you're interested in reaching, will cost a fraction of what you make per sale, and will provide every useful metric you can imagine. In reality, one or more of these areas will be less than you would prefer, but they provide a useful measuring stick for effectiveness.

Web Site and Author Pages

Having your own web site is important, because it's the only internet based web site over which you have complete control. Ultimate power has its uses. Plus the cost of having your own web site is minimal for a professional author. If the revenue from your writing doesn't provide enough funds to support your own web site, then you're still in the wanna-be writer, hobby phase of your career. There's nothing wrong with that, but you have to invest in yourself at some point. Creating your own web site is as good a place to start as any.

Many services provide free pages for authors to use for promoting their work. Some common examples are the author page on Amazon, a celebrity Facebook page, and the author page on Goodreads. Many others exist. While it can be time-consuming to get all of these set up with relevant and intriguing information including the image of your smiling mug, the update rate of these pages can be minimal. Some helpful guidelines:

1) All public displays should be as professional and as well thought out as you have time to make them.
2) Update these pages regularly, but don't overwhelm your followers.

Along with web pages spreading the good word, feel free to utilize Twitter and any other electronic communication service that allows you to reach your readers. The warning I give here is that using a service like Twitter for self-promotion alone is like working at a restaurant for 8 hours every day because you're hungry. Sure, you're surrounded by food, but it takes you forever to get anything to eat. Said another way, feel free to use these frequent update services if you're already using them. If not, they're probably not worth the time they'll steal from your writing.

Newsletter

For most authors, your newsletter should be nothing more than a quick chat with your readers to announce something *related to your work* that they would find relevant. You can certainly do more than this, but the length and frequency of your newsletter relates directly to how useful and entertaining your readers find your newsletters to be. I know writers who can hit their readers with a newsletter every day. The readers eat it up because the writer is such a dynamic personality or shares such fascinating information that the readers simply can't get enough. For other writers, each time they send out a newsletter, they risk losing readers. Know your strengths and your weaknesses. Lean on your newsletter accordingly.

Besides deciding what to put in your newsletter and deciding how often to send it, you need to know who to send it to. The answer to this question is quite simple, even if making it happen can be time-consuming and difficult. Only send your newsletter to people who are likely to enjoy whatever book you're telling them about. This means that you don't want everyone on the planet reading your news-letter. Newsletters (and the lists of readers those newsletters are sent to) provide an invaluable resource for each new book you release. No advertising in existence beats telling people who are interested in a product that such a product is available and telling them where they can get one of their very own.

The reasons you want to restrict the readers on your list only to those who would be interested in what you have to sell them is because this allows you to evaluate the success or failure of any announcement. Plus, it gives you a loyal band of followers who pro-vide information you simply can't get anywhere else. Thinking of ending your series at book 10? Let your newsletter readers know and see what kind of reaction you get. Thinking of writing a new series that might interest these readers? Drop a line about your new possible project and see what the response is.

<u>Reader Magnets</u>

The Catch-22 of newsletters is that getting people to sign up for one works best after those people are already fans of your writing. So how do you start out? For writing nonfiction, it's pretty easy. Make snippets of information available related to your subject with the promise of more complete and detailed information available in newsletter form. Then when your nonfiction book is released, you already have a following of people who are naturally interested in your book. But what about fiction? How do you attract readers before you have any readers?

In simple terms, you have to have already written something. I know some writers who have done this by releasing short stories set in their series world. Same characters. Same genre. Attractive to the same type of readers who would enjoy their novel. At the end of each short story, you put in a link that takes readers to a page where they can sign up for your newsletter. As an alternative, you can publish your first novel and put a link in the back of it. Granted, this doesn't help you sell your first novel, but it does start the email list building process that should benefit later books in the series. Many writers offer their readers something for free if they sign up for their newsletter, but when you're just starting out, be wary of giving away everything you've written to date. If your novel is good enough, your readers will want to know when the next novel in the series is being released. If your novel isn't good enough, you've already lost the battle, so offering trinkets in exchange for their email addresses doesn't provide you with much.

The great thing about reader magnets is that they work whether your novels are self-published or published by the big boys. Note that your giveaway freebees (if you use them) will of necessity be something you create and have total control over.

What about a Blog?

Some authors write more in their blogs than they do their books. For nonfiction authors, blogs can be an effective marketing tool. For fiction writers, blogs provide uncertain benefits at best. It's not hard to imagine a group of readers who love a writer's blog but don't care much for his fiction; yet, they still buy his books out of loyalty. It may seem like any reader is a good reader to have, but in our modern world, this is definitely not true.

Blogs work best for fiction writers when a nonfiction subject overlaps nicely with fiction interests. For example, many hard science-fiction authors are interested in space exploration. If you're a sf author who blogs about the latest space missions and rocket technology being developed, chances are good that a significant block of your readers would be interested in your latest space opera novel. If you're a romance writer who blogs about ways to improve your marital relationship, chances are good many of your blog readers are the same readers buying your novels.

Two main problems keep blogs from being an effective marketing tool when you're first starting out: 1) Time spent getting people to follow your blog could be spent getting people to buy your books, and 2) Blogs are a clumsy and inaccurate tool for reaching your fiction readers. A newsletter directed at readers who want to know when your next book is coming out is much more effective and much less time consuming. Just as with social media such as Twitter and Pinterest, if you're already writing a blog, keep writing it. If you're not writing one yet, there are better ways to spend your marketing time.

Feeding the Amazonian Beast

It continues to amaze me when I meet U.S. or British writers who scoff at the importance of Amazon to their writing careers. They talk about other distributors such as Barnes & Noble, Kobo, Apple's iBooks, Google Play, Stanza, and others, as if they matter for a writer starting out. For nearly all new fiction writers, these other distributors literally represent a drop in your revenue stream.

Without question, the largest electronic bookstore in the world is Amazon Kindle. The second largest is Kindle Unlimited. The exact percentage of market share Amazon controls is changing all the time, but if you don't go exclusively with Amazon, you aren't allowed to be part of the Kindle Unlimited program. That means you just set fire to a distribution deal with the second largest bookseller in the world.

There are other reasons to go exclusively with Amazon that go beyond how many novels you can sell:

- One market to target
- One distribution channel to sync
- Higher royalties from Amazon
- Access to an audience you won't reach any other way (readers who only read free books via Kindle Unlimited)
- Amazon's marketing machine

The first and last items appear similar, but we will see they are not.

Rather than going through these items one by one, I can summarize them quite simply. As of 2017, the easiest way for a new writer to make the most money from their novels is by selling those novels exclusively through Amazon.

Granted, if you have a traditional publishing deal it's unlikely you'll have any say in where your novels are sold—another reason to go the indie route—but even if your novels are distributed through many channels, Amazon still matters a great deal.

Not Just Any Reader

Let's say I give you 100 pears and tell you to sell them in the next two hours. For every pear you sell, you'll get $1. If you sell them all, I'll give you a bonus of $1,000. To make your job more interesting,

I lead you to a pair of doors. Behind the first door is a group of 500 random people I grabbed off the street. Behind the second door I've assembled a group of 200 pear lovers who haven't eaten today and have money in their pockets. After I load you up with the pears, I let you choose which door to go through. How many of you would choose the room with the random group? How many would choose the room filled with pear lovers?

Most writers choose the random group. Why? That group contains more people. Here's the problem: Since they were chosen randomly, we know very little about that group. We can assume some will be hungry, some will like pears, and some will have enough money to buy a pear, but how many will be hungry, like pears, and have money? Probably not enough. Also, each time you try to sell a pear and fail, you won't know why. Maybe they weren't hungry. Maybe they just didn't like the look of your pears. Maybe you shouldn't be trying to sell ice to Eskimos.

For the pear lovers, we know they have the interest and the means to buy your pears. If they don't buy, it's pretty clear the problem isn't with them.

But here's where it gets interesting.

What if I tell you that if you manage to sell half your pears to the pear lovers, I'll immediately bring an additional 500 pear lovers into the room and give you an additional two hours to sell the pears? The more pears you sell, the more hungry pear lovers I'll push into your room and the more time I'll give you.

Now how many of you would choose to sell to the random group?

What if I told you a couple dozen other people were going to be selling all kinds of fruit in each room at the same time you're trying to sell your pears? That room filled with pear lovers is looking pretty good now, isn't it?

This may seem like a silly example, but it's not all that different that what actually happens on Amazon. The difference is that Amazon doesn't decide what kind of people to bring into the room based on what you're selling. Instead, they look at what people are buying and use that knowledge to select the next group of people (if any) to bring into the room.

No More Pears

Amazon is the DM (data master) of the book buying world. They've spent over 20 years figuring out how to sell books online. What they discovered early is that data is the key to success. The biggest problem faced by every avid reader is finding the next novel they want to read. Amazon knows that recommending the right books to the right readers means they will sell more books. This doesn't make Amazon the big bad. Far from it. It makes readers happier and allows authors to sell more books. Granted, both Amazon (and the authors they recommend) will make a lot more money, but that's why people go into business: to make money. The difficulty for Amazon is identifying books their readers would like to read.

It's no surprise then that readers who have the narrowest focuses are the easiest to please. If the only books a reader buys are military science fiction, you wouldn't recommend they try a historical romance. On the other hand, if a reader intermittently buys romances, mysteries, self-help nonfiction, fantasies, biographies, police procedurals, and mainstream award-winning books, how do you recommend that perfect next novel? You don't know—and neither does Amazon.

Which brings us to your newly released novel. If you sell, for example, 50 copies of that novel, Amazon's data crunching machines examine the buyers who purchased those copies. If 46 are readers who mostly buy military science-fiction novels, Amazon concludes that you must have written a military science-fiction novel. That's when those vast stores of data come in handy. Amazon knows that of those 46 readers, half also bought three other military science-fiction novels. In this simple example, any idiot could readily identify a likely group of readers who might like your novel: It's the set of readers who purchased those other three novels but haven't yet bought yours.

For many reasons, Amazon doesn't immediately hawk your book to this group of readers. Instead they let a select group of those readers know about your new novel. If a significant portion of those readers check out your book and decide to buy it, all those electrons at Amazon start to get excited. The emails and notifications start to fly. More potential readers flock to your book's page on Amazon. If those readers like what they see and keep buying, Amazon rightly decides to ride the wave. Suddenly you go from selling 50 novels to 5,000. The next thing you know, Amazon's mighty marketing machine is driving readers to your page in a way that's impossible to buy or replicate.

What's best about this approach is that everybody wins. Readers discover a new author who they want to read, the writer finds readers who want to buy their book, and Amazon sells more books. As an added bonus, this system is incredibly difficult to game. Even if you went out and created 50 user accounts and had those accounts buy books you thought were similar to yours, the initial, tentative marketing push by Amazon on your behalf would only succeed if readers who checked out your novel actually bought it. On the other hand, if your cover or your summary isn't up to snuff, not enough of those readers would think your novel looked all that interesting. They wouldn't buy the book. Amazon would then halt the marketing push before it really started. Don't forget, not only will those buyers be influenced by your cover and your blurb, they'll also be influenced by the reviews that start streaming in. If half the readers who buy your novel hate it, you aren't going to sell many more copies.

The system only works when everybody wins.

Death by Amazon

At this point, most folks out there start pointing out the obvious flaw in this marketing system. "Ya, but what about when Amazon changes their marketing model?"

I can't say this will never happen. Someday Amazon will almost certainly become too big for its britches. Executives there will make that stupid and greedy decision to take advantage of the authors who've helped them to unprecedented success, but that decision won't come easily.

It's not that Amazon is pure of heart. They're in the business of selling books (among many other things). To do so, they need to keep their readers happy. They might reduce the profit margins for authors. They might favor the books they publish themselves over every other publisher.

Here's what won't change: If you write a great novel that a readily identifiable group of people enjoy reading, Amazon will drive those readers to your page. To do anything else would reduce the number of books they sell for no good reason.

The big traditional publishing houses have already allowed their hubris to drive the best and brightest of the new authors from their ranks. Readers followed. If Amazon repeats those mistakes, another company will step in to fill the void. It's not that the traditional publishing houses were stupid or intentionally harsh. They were maximizing their profits based on the business logic of the day. That business logic changed, and they were slow to adapt, but they're getting there.

A Helping Hand

When it comes to marketing in an Amazon driven world, the best technique you can use to sell your new novel, regardless whether it's traditionally published or indie, is to identify a loyal group of readers who like the type of novel you've written and will want to buy that novel as soon as it's released.

This is the hard part.

Sure, after you have tons of success, this is easy. At that point, readers are seeking you out. But what about when you're first getting started? How do you find those readers then?

The truth is, it can be hard and typically involves a decent amount of effort. The techniques needed for success are a book unto themselves. I talked about Reader Magnets in the Newsletter section, but finding that loyal group of readers, especially for your first novel, involves much more than that. If possible, you need to use every marketing technique I cover here plus a few more I haven't thought of. Or you just need to master one of them exceptionally well. Or you just need to get lucky. No, I'm not confused. It's just that there's no easy one-size-fits-all answer. What works great for one writer may not work for others.

The best single piece of advice I can provide here is to do some prep work before you launch your novel. Try to come up with as many readers as you can however you can. Continue the process immediately after the novel launches. Remember, you want to mainly attract folks who typically buy books on Amazon similar to the one you're selling. The absolute best and more powerful marketing you can get is to have someone else (Amazon in this case) do the marketing for you. The sooner you can get them to take over the job, the better you will do. The easiest way to do that is to sell books right from the start and keep selling books, especially when those books are sold to a group of readers with similar tastes.

There is too much. Let me sum up

Marketing is important to all writers at every stage of their careers. No matter how successful you are, you can increase your success through marketing, if you do it well.

- Similar techniques can be used to market a novel regardless whether it is traditionally or self published.
- The main branding control all authors maintain is the author name they attach to their novels. The easiest way to help your readers distinguish between the different types (genres) of books you write is by using a pseudonym unique to each.
- The most efficient type of marketing an author can do always involves reaching the greatest number of potential readers for each marketing action taken. For example, being interviewed for any public media format is always more effective than doing a book-signing.
- Use as many types of marketing as you can to get the word out to your readers, including doing interviews and press releases, having a web page, sending a newsletter to readers of your previous work, encouraging book reviews, and employing advertising targeted toward likely readers.
- Beware communicating repeatedly through any social medium (such as your personal Twitter account, your personal Facebook page, Pinterest, your blog, etc.) that reaches a general group of readers rather than a select group likely to buy books similar to the one you're selling.
- Selling exclusively through Amazon is currently the most reliable way for a new writer to make money while building a loyal group of readers.
- Not all readers are created equal.
- When you release a novel, do everything in your power to sell that novel to readers who like books similar to the one you just released. If you're successful, chances are good that Amazon will take over the marketing for you. As a result, you'll sell more books than you could through nearly any other means.

The most effective marketing you can ever do is generating more material to market. That means writing fast, which only works if you're also writing well.

Chapter Eleven: Writing Quickly While Writing Well

Why bother?

Joseph Heller (who wrote *Catch-22*) only produced seven published novels during a four-decade career. Harper Lee (author of *To Kill a Mockingbird*) only finished one novel[17] in her lifetime. If you want to become wealthy, famous, and win awards, here are two examples of authors who took their time writing. Or did they? If Wikipedia can be believed, Harper Lee completed To Kill a Mockingbird in two and a half years. Not exactly speedy, but for someone who wrote only one novel total, that's flat out flying.

So why write quickly? Is it even a worthy goal?

To be blunt, if you want to be a successful writer in today's world, you might have little choice. Miss a deadline and you risk losing your contract. Fail to finish novels quickly, and readers who loved the first novel in your self-published series will look elsewhere for their next fiction fix. As an example of success from my past, I sold a novel based on nothing more than my synopsis and a spotless reputation. That was July and I had to deliver the final draft, ready for press, in December. The entire manuscript was written in less than five months while I was working long hours and acting as head coach for my son's little league football team. That novel became my *first* published novel. The techniques I used to produce a novel so quickly are covered in the following pages.

Beyond all else, understand this: Writing quickly is a waste of time if the finished product is not as good as you can make it in the time you have to work on it. If the only way you can write a decent novel is by taking eight years per novel, then take eight years. However, make sure you've tried the other way before you stake your immutable claim to turtle-dom. Most writers I know who say they can't write quickly have never given it an honest try. Yes, they sat down one afternoon, tried to write ten pages of sterling prose, failed, and declared it was impossible for them to ever finish more than a page per day. Writing quickly is not just a choice, but also a learned skill.

---

17. *Go Set a Watchman* doesn't count. Reliable sources claim that novel is nothing more an early draft of *To Kill a Mockingbird*. Multiple other sources claim it was published without Harper Lee's competent consent.

My experience also disagrees with the common wisdom that says taking more time produces higher quality work. Most talented writers I know produce *better* work when they write their first drafts quickly. Granted, they're ofttimes too daft to recognize their brilliance, spend weeks mucking up what they've written, and end up with something more complicated but less compelling as a result. There's a difference between writing quickly out of laziness and writing slowly because you believe you can't produce works of art unless you sweat blood over each word.

Almost every successful writer I know claims that 90% of what other people write is crap. Granted, they're blinded by their own gifts for producing timeless masterpieces so they think this 90% rule doesn't apply to them. Statistics say otherwise. If you're a slow, thoughtful, meticulous writer, maybe you can improve that percentage a bit, but there are no guarantees. Typically the more product you finish, the better your chances will be to create something truly worthwhile.

Beyond the 90% rule, which is probably 90% wrong anyway, most writers improve the more they write. That means they produce more finished pages in less time. It also means they can immerse themselves in their story more easily and more deeply than they can when they write slowly. That allows them to build momentum.

Momentum Rules!

The most important requirement for writing quickly while writing well is momentum. First you must create momentum. Then you must jealously guard it for the fragile flame it is. Without momentum, even the most determined writer can falter. With enough momentum, even the least dedicated writer can churn out hundreds of pages.

In "Chatper One: First, a Word...," we covered the basic ideas related to creating and building momentum. Writers should have passion for writing. They should write regularly, which is easier if they have a schedule and have solid and achievable goals. To create more time for writing, they should be willing to make sacrifices. Being a writer requires commitment.

What we've covered in less detail is what happens after you start writing. At least at first, chances are that no one will respect your writing time, ***not even you***. The first step to writing quickly and writing well is believing you're a writer and taking your writing seriously, because your precious momentum will be constantly under attack. Friends and family will assault the walls you've erected to protect your time. Your own self-doubts will encourage your commitment to waver. Personal illness will steal days or even weeks. Major life events will hurl flaming arrows into your carefully crafted sanctuary of production and threaten to burn it to the ground.

The best way to stop these attacks is to understand and accept one simple concept: ***Anything that interferes with your momentum is dangerous.***

The key word in the above sentence is *anything*. If you want to write fast and write well, you must avoid anything that slows down your writing. Pay attention to yourself. Notice and correct any areas of your life that interfere with your writing. If you stay up late at night and don't write well the next day, don't stay up late at night. If you allow others to read your writing and their comments cause you to doubt your abilities, don't allow others to read your writing. Commitment, remember?

At the same time, pay attention to and foster anything that promotes your writing. If your writing gets faster the less clothes you wear, then strip to your skivvies and get to work. If you work best in a crowd, then set up your laptop at your local Starbucks. I'd advise you not to mix these two methods, but you get the drift.

Detecting attacks against your momentum is easy provided you remain brutally honest with yourself. Once detected, devise creative solutions that keep your momentum intact. When other solutions fail, elevate the importance of your writing.

Be especially wary of factors within the writing itself that detract from your progress. Research, character backgrounds, polishing of your prose, and interesting and vibrant dialogue are all needed in your final draft, but these take time and effort. Attempt them on the fly, but don't let your attention to detail steal your precious momentum. If you stop writing, the quality of your writing is ZERO. Do all you can to keep your production going.

The Kernel

Now that you understand the importance of momentum, how do you get started? How do you take your first step down the yellow brick road that leads to being a writer who writes fast and who writes well?

For this discussion, you must have an idea for the novel or story you're trying to write. If you don't have an idea, you're not ready to write. Re-read the "Ideas-R-Us" section. Better yet, go out and live. Take chances. Explore your inner self. Spend time with people. Listen to them speak, study their body language, pay attention to motivations, actions, and reactions. Fly over the rainbow and back again.

If you have the potential to be a writer, *you will have ideas* about what to write. Expand any idea that follows you around and won't leave you alone. Allow the ideas to grow that fascinate you by jotting down notes, doing research, talking to people about your ideas—do whatever gets your creative juices flowing. Write pages and pages if they're handy and want out of your brain. Continue this process for days, weeks, months, or years. When an idea separates itself from the pack and demands you use it to write a novel *now*, it's time to get started. Once you start, give this single novel all you've got until you either finish the resulting novel or until you can go no further despite your best effort. If this first idea turns into a red herring, try another idea. But if you want to write fast and write well, never go into a project halfway.

A Time to Sow

Many writers recommend you boil your novel down to a single sentence before you write your first word. Or you write an outline. Or you do complete character backgrounds for every character. Or you start on page one and keep typing until you reach *The End*. These concepts certainly work for some writers. If they work for you, by all means use them. But I don't believe they work for most people if those people are trying to write fast and write well.

How are you supposed to summarize your novel in a single sentence if you have yet to write a single page? What if your novel turns out to be about something else? The same applies to writing an outline. How do you know what's going to happen two thirds of the way through your novel if you haven't written it yet? And what if that main character gets upstaged by one of your minor characters? Then you've wasted tons of time on the minor character you thought was your lead and you're sadly lacking in background material for your main character.

For me, creating a novel is like giving birth. No ladies, I'm not insulting the sacred plumbing that's used to squeeze a bowling ball through an opening three sizes too small. This form of birth refers to the chaotic, unpredictable process that fashions a living, breathing whole from inert and disparate pieces. This is creation at its most Frankensteinian roots.

While I don't believe that creation typically comes from rigid methods of construction, I do believe you need a critical mass of material from which to grow your novel. You should have an overall impression for where your novel's headed and what your novel will be about. You've already made your initial contributions to this mass in the form of the thoughts and other bits of fluff you've recorded during your idea gestation process. Now concentrate on that idea and record everything that comes to mind.

When I say everything, I mean everything. Each time you sit down to work on your novel, try to record as many thoughts as possible. These thoughts should concern the people who will live in your novel (characters), the places those people live (settings), the actions they need to take (motivations), and the obstacles they will face (plot), plus whatever else seems relevant. Feel free to write snippets of scenes but don't worry about finishing anything. Keep this process as free-form as possible so that you're at your creative best, but don't indulge yourself by creating reams of material you know will never be used. If you want to be a writer, chances are you've read tons of novels. Those experiences have sharpened your instincts. Listen to them.

Auguste Rodin—when asked how he managed to create such magnificent sculptures—answered, "I choose a block of marble and chop off whatever I don't need." As a writer, the block of marble from which you create your story exists only inside your brain. Before you can mold it into a finished work of art, you need to extract it from your gray matter quarry. Growing this initial kernel is the first step in that process.

A Time to Weed

As your creative energy ebbs and wanes, take the opportunity to organize your ideas. Traditionally, this organization will take the form of character backgrounds, story ideas, scene snippets and ideas, scraps of dialogue, and other miscellaneous topics. Organize your material in whatever way makes sense to you. Use any information or structure that will help you write your novel. What you're creating is for your eyes only so be completely honest and open.

As you organize your thoughts, try to create distinct nuggets that can be moved as need be. Use separate files, page breaks, white space, or any and all of the above. In the dark ages before computers, many writers performed this function using index cards. The problem with index cards (besides your ability to spill coffee on them) is they're all a specific size. The pieces you're seeking to create should be able to grow and shrink. Complete scenes or even entire chapters might form some of these nuggets. Others might be a single sentence or just a phrase. To guard against spilling virtual coffee on them, make sure you backup everything as you go along! You haven't written much prose yet, but ideas and thoughts are often harder to recreate than finished prose.

While organizing, use whatever creative energy you generate to add to your material. If you're moving bits of fluff about and you get the idea for a scene, write it down, but don't allow anything to interfere with your momentum. If you start a scene and find yourself worrying about grammar or prose or character names, either quit worrying about those items or abort the process, jot a couple notes down concerning what you would have written, and then carry on with what you were doing.

A Time to Reap

When you've built up a sufficient kernel of material, it's time to harvest what you have. How much is enough? There's no set amount.

For some folks, writing that single sentence I mentioned a page ago is all it takes. The rest is stored in their heads. For others, they might need a thousand pages of incomprehensible gibberish before they have enough raw material to grow a novel. The goal in building your kernel is for you to have a basic understanding of what your novel will be about. You're allowed to change your mind later, but changing your mind will slow you down. The closer you can come before you begin your initial attempt, the more quickly you'll finish.

Once you have enough material, it's time to write what I call your *novel summary*. For me, a novel summary is a snapshot of the novel that exists inside your head. The goal is to get your story down so you can hold it up to the light and take a look at it.

To create your summary, you write down the story you want to tell. Start at the beginning, tell your story through to the end, and then stop. And oh, by the way, do it as quickly as possible. Pretend you've come back in time after finishing your bestselling novel and you're telling your present self the story you wrote. You need to finish telling the story before your time window closes and you get sucked back into the future.

In a perfect world, you'd write your novel summary in a single sitting. This may sound daunting, but your novel summary is supposed to be a snapshot. It's an outpouring of energy into an idea for a novel. You're trying to capture the story as it currently exists inside your head. To do that, you can't take weeks to capture it, because it will change and grow during that time. Wait to write the novel summary until you've allowed your ideas to build to the breaking point. If possible, devote at least one uninterrupted day to the task.

In J. K. Rowling's case, she reputedly had the idea for her series of Harry Potter novels on a long train ride. What many people don't know is that she is said to have written two other novels before this and that she started writing her first novel in first grade. Many people work for years to become an overnight success. The point is that the idea came to her at a time when she had the time and energy to record it in some detail. The ideas rushed out of her and she produced a novel summary (or in her case, several novel summaries). The old cliché about striking when the iron is hot is definitely true in this case. One of the keys to writing quickly is to generate ideas when you have the energy to do so, and focus on topics that feed this energy in a way that keeps the creative juices flowing. If you want to write quickly, build momentum every chance you have to do so.

Reap What?

Most folks want more details about this novel summary. How long should it be? What form should it have? Are there scenes? Characters? Settings?

As with most of this process, your novel summary should contain whatever will help you write your finished novel. With that said, for most folks, the best novel summary is a straightforward narrative that tells your story in its simplest form. It's usually five to fifteen single-spaced pages in length but will work if it's shorter or longer. It contains only the most basic of facts, but it should contain your main story elements. Remember, a story usually involves a likable character who has a goal she's trying to achieve. What you do in the novel summary is tell the story of her attempts to achieve that goal. You cover the important events that happen along that journey. Your summary will be incomplete, but it should provide that snapshot we needed.

When your novel summary is finished, don't let anyone read it! Novel summaries are not for reading. If someone were to read a typical summary, it would provide a good idea about what the novel would be about, but allowing someone else to read your novel summary will anchor it to the real world and will make the story harder to change when the need arises. If by chance you're writing a novel summary and you're attempting to sell your novel based solely on that summary (a synopsis), then I assume you've written successful novels and synopses before and have the experience to know what you're doing. In that case, why are you reading this book? Get back to writing!

The Novel Sketch

With your novel summary in hand, you're nearly ready to get started. It may seem like we're taking a long time to write the first page of our novel, but it's just because I've tried to explain the why's and wherefore's as we've went along. In simple terms, you jot down notes about your novel until the urge to write it becomes overwhelming. When you're ready, spend a day or two writing one long narration that encapsulates the entire novel. Depending on how completely ideas form in your head, you may have done everything up to this point in one long afternoon (just as J. K. Rowling is said to have done when she came up with the idea for her seven-book *Harry Potter* series).

Sketch It

With their mass of raw ideas, most writers start by carving out a rough draft of their novel that can be read and critiqued by other people. If you want to write quickly while writing well, I recommend you avoid starting with a rough draft (or first draft, as some people call it). Sketch the novel instead.

Creating a novel sketch in the shortest time you can allows you to be more consistent, honest, motivated, and focused than you could be by methodically writing a first draft.

First, you want to capture the novel before it gets away. Just like a brilliant artist witnessing a magnificent sunset, you're quickly recording as many details of the vision as possible before the light disappears. Most people can't keep an entire novel in their head, at least not for long. Your sketch captures the initial vision of the novel before it fades or changes. Capturing your original vision is vital. If that vision of the novel changes, you risk getting locked into an infinite loop where you can never reach the end of your novel because your vision of the novel keeps mutating over time, forcing you to restart over and over in a vain attempt to create a novel that's consistent in tone, theme, and style from beginning to end.

Second, no matter how brutal, honest, and dedicated to quality a writer is, the more time a writer spends on a scene, the harder that scene is to cut or change. By writing your novel sketch as quickly as you can, it guarantees you have minimal attachment to any particular scene. You may still find it difficult to cut a given scene—maybe it's the first scene you envisioned when you came up with your idea for this novel—but if you spent three total hours writing it, you'll find it a lot easier to cut than you would if you had invested thirty hours in rewriting, editing, and polishing that same scene.

Third, completing your novel sketch quickly builds and protects momentum. We've already covered the importance of momentum in general, but it's especially important during the creation of your novel sketch. If your normal writing goal is writing six hours a week, you should attempt to write eight. If you think you can put in nine or ten hours, try for an even dozen. As with all of your writing, the more time you can put in, the better, but time is of the essence during this initial creative process. Your precious momentum is often under full assault and the only way you can keep the outside world and your own self-doubts at bay is to immerse yourself as fully as you can in your writing.

Finally, creating a novel sketch provides a crude shape that reveals your entire novel. Once you have that shape, you have your block of marble. Chipping away at it will refine the sculpture beneath, but having that crude shape provides a vital impression of the whole. Writing a novel is a daunting task to most people, but if you've already carved out the basic shape of the novel, you no longer need to concentrate on writing the novel as a whole. Instead you can concentrate on a given chapter or even a given scene. Your novel sketch gives you the power to focus.

Go!

What do I mean when I say you should start by capturing your novel in the shortest time you can? How long am I talking about? A couple weeks would be great. Don't laugh. Each Labor Day weekend since 1977, multitudes of wanna-be writers do better than that. They finish a novel in three days. Seventy-two hours to be exact. They start writing at midnight Friday night and finish by midnight Monday night.[18] And don't think these are picture books only ten pages long. Most successful contestants produce over a hundred pages of manuscript in one weekend! Even if you do little beyond eat, sleep, and write, this is a couple manuscript pages an hour. When you write your novel sketch, ***your minimum acceptable goal should be to produce at least two manuscript pages (five hundred words) per hour.*** While you may not have the time or energy to run the marathon of writing your entire novel sketch in a single weekend, the pace is what matters. If you finish at least two pages per hour every time you sit down to write—and sometimes more—you'll complete a typical novel sketch in less than three months. Granted, if you're writing *War and Peace*, it might take you as long as nine months, but that minimum two pages per hour (hopefully more!) pace should be maintained throughout.

On the other hand, you might be stressing over this seemingly impossible goal of two pages per hour. If so, take heart. Nobody starts out writing fast while writing well. If you write more slowly, two pages per hour is a worthwhile initial goal. A lot of experienced writers I know would scoff at a measly two pages per hour. "If I wrote that slowly, I'd never get anything done!" But unless you're writing 5,000 words an hour (20 manuscript pages), you have room for improvement.

So how do you produce two pages per hour if you don't think you can? The answer to this question provides a solution to your stress. Most people get stressed when they think of writing two pages per hour because they're thinking of two edited and polished pages. Two pages that they plan on other people reading. Your novel sketch is never meant to be read by anyone but you. That's why it's called a sketch.

Since no one will read your novel sketch, no one will judge you for what you've done. Writing the novel sketch should be a freeing experience. The quality of your prose doesn't matter. Grammar is irrelevant. Spelling is unimportant. Research is completely missing. Settings have only as much detail as you can create on the fly. Almost

---

18. As of this writing you could find details about this at http://www.3day-novel.com/.

none of the *chores* of writing have any meaning! And what if you like creating settings? What if you live for research? That's okay, too. A certain amount of delusions can be useful for a writer. But the goal in writing fast is to complete the writing. Research on your own time.

Since no one else will judge your sketch (because they will never read it), you must also resist the temptation to judge it. Remember, you're trying to capture an impression of the novel on paper. To do it right, you must let go of your concerns and your prejudices. Focus on the fact that you're finally writing the novel you've always wanted to write. Have confidence! Anything that isn't right in this initial sketch will be fixed in the rough draft.

Concentrate on story, characters, and feelings. Try to get to know your characters. Give your subconscious free reign to capture the characters as real people. Allow your imagination to come up with plot twists and turns. Don't worry about whether everything works perfectly. Ideas are more important than details. As long as what you're doing is interesting, that's enough for now. Most of all, try to capture the emotions of the moments in your novel. Don't be afraid of overwriting. Emotions are typically harder to add than to cut. You can scale back any overuse of melodrama during your first draft.

This process may sound similar to the one you used for the novel summary, but they're actually quite different beasts. The novel summary is typically a narration. It lacks significant structure, scenes, and dialogue. It should represent the story in its simplest form. In contrast your novel sketch should represent your finished novel in structure and content. You'll have scenes, dialogue, descriptions, sentences, paragraphs, and chapters. All of these will be painted with rough quick strokes, but all of the elements should be there.

Your novel sketch is typically half to two-thirds the length of your finished novel.[19] The expectation is that you'll add most of the missing pages when you write your first draft. Typically you will add

---

19. Notice that a hundred page novel sketch typically can't contain the complexity you'd need for a successful novel in most of today's genres. While I credit those folks who run the marathon of writing and finish a novel in a weekend, there honestly isn't enough time to finish a "real" novel sketch that quickly for any but the shortest novels.

entire scenes that you didn't know you needed until the sketch was finished. You may also add new story arcs. Remaining pages will fill in missing details, create fuller settings, and allow you to increase the eloquence of your prose.

But what if you're having problems getting started? What if you've been unable to hit that two pages per hour goal? What's most likely keeping you paralyzed is that you're comparing your novel sketch to finished novels. Just like that artist sketching a sunset, his lightly drawn lines will never be hung next to and compared with finished oil paintings. Remember, quality's unimportant when writing your novel sketch. Ideas and feelings are what matter.

If you're still having trouble, borrow someone's excitable three-year-old (unless you have one of your own). Ask him what he's been doing and then listen to him. He won't worry about grammar, punctuation, or diction. He'll just tell his story in its simplest form, because he wants to communicate something that's meaningful to him. That's all you're trying to do with your novel sketch. Capture what's meaningful to *you*. I guarantee you can do it better than that three-year-old.

If you're confident you can write and you're not judging your writing but you're still having difficulties putting words on paper, then perhaps your idea isn't the right idea for your novel. I'm not talking about having problems for a single day—we all have bad days—but having problems over an extended period of time. Assuming that real life isn't interfering in ways you can't overcome, either you're pursuing the wrong idea or you're subconscious is tripping over a plot complication that it just can't seem to get over. Assume you can write the scene you're working on and move past it. Don't get trapped in the quicksand that a single scene can set for you. Your job with the novel sketch is to get the general shape of the novel down as quickly as possible. If anything slows you down, skip it.

Stop!

When you reach the end of your novel, stop. Don't immediately go back and re-read it. Don't start editing scenes. If you've created a successful sketch, you've just poured out as much energy and captured as many ideas as you could muster. You should feel a bit drained. If you don't, good for you, but even in that circumstance, it's time to take a breather.

This time off isn't just to re-charge your batteries. It's a cool-down period that's designed to allow your brain to reset. How long you stay away depends on you. You don't want to stay away so long that your passion for the project and your momentum start to wane. At the same time, you want to stay away long enough that you can bring fresh eyes to what you've just written. For most people, the time to stay away is somewhere between three and ten days. Take advantage of this time off to let your family know you're still alive, get work done around your house or apartment, try to get caught up at your day job, or even take an actual vacation. Try to keep busy in ways that take you away from the novel.

Admire Your Brilliance

After your break, set aside enough time to read your novel in one sitting. Most U.S. adults read at rates between 100 and 200 words per minute. Even assuming that you, the writer, read somewhat faster than this, you'll probably still need to set aside an entire day for this purpose.

As you read the novel, try to immerse yourself in the story. Whatever you do, don't edit the prose, check the spelling, correct the grammar, or perform any other editorial functions. If you notice story elements that are missing or need to be fixed, jot down a quick note. For myself, I like to use a digital voice recorder for this purpose. Since I never dictate my stories, taking notes in this way prevents my succumbing to the temptation to edit. While I still might read with a pen in reach, I try not to use it for more than circling a section and jotting a sentence or two beside it.

Whatever you do while reading your sketch, don't judge it! Artists know a masterpiece can't be created with one sweep of their brush: why beginning[20] writers continue to believe they can write finished

---

20. Some experienced writers can churn out finished prose at an amazing rate, but I wouldn't advise attempting this level of performance until you have at least a million published words under your belt.

prose on their first attempt is beyond me. When you write, you're shaping a story into words. Just like any work of art, you can't judge it until it's finished.

Your goal in reading your novel sketch is to understand the novel you're about to write. If you've created a successful novel sketch, you should be able to "see" the story that's trapped inside the stone. By recording your impression of that story in the form of a novel sketch, you now have a mechanism for getting your thoughts around the entire novel at one time. You may find that your novel sketch is better than what you imagined it to be while you were writing it. If you've managed to create good story elements and good characters, you're on your way to finishing a great novel.

Fill In the Holes

While your novel may indeed be brilliant at its core, chances are good you're missing vital pieces. Now that you know what your novel *is*, it's time to start the transformation into what your novel *should be*.

Story

The first item on the agenda is to ask yourself if you've told a good story. If your novel summary doesn't contain a good story, why not? What are you missing? A worthwhile goal? Obstacles to achieving that goal? A climactic scene where it looks like all is lost but where the hero prevails? If you don't have a good story, now's the time to fix it. More than that, ask yourself why you didn't write a good story. What story were you trying to tell and why didn't the telling work? What impelled you to write this story? If you lost the kernel of your intended story in the telling and the result is not what you wanted, decide how to get back to the story you originally wanted to tell.

Characters

Examine your characters with a critical eye. Are they believable? Are they motivated? Are they acting to the best of their abilities? Are they interesting? Do their motivations and actions make sense? Do they remain consistent at their core throughout the novel? Add missing background information for your main characters and extend that information whenever possible. You should know your main characters as well as you know your family. For minor characters, you should know more than what you could find out from a typical dating service. For tertiary characters, it's acceptable to resort to stereotypes, although the more you know about your character, the more real they become. Record as much as you have time and interest to record.

Plot

You've recorded your story. Now you need to determine the best way to tell your story. As you examine your novel sketch, determine the optimal order of events so the story's emotional intensity builds to a crescendo. Try to identify the critical moments in your story and determine how those moments can be enhanced. Correct the emotional integrity of your characters by making certain their emotional states match the actions they take. If you've forced your characters to act in ways contrary to their natures to satisfy your story or plot requirements, then change the setting or the situation so that their actions are more natural.

Research

Writers get to play God. We create entire worlds. We give birth to characters and cause others to die. We can even resurrect the dead. All powerful? Yes. But with that power comes the expectation of omnipotence. If you make a factual mistake in your book, you risk losing your reader. Anything that you didn't know while you were writing the novel you now need to know. If it can be known, you need to know it. If it can't be known, you need to make an intelligent and believable extrapolation from what can be known. The good news is that by writing your novel sketch, you efficiently discovered what you need to know. With specific goals in mind, your research time is a fraction of what it would have been had you performed widespread and generic research before you started your sketch. At the same time, if your initial set of research uncovers additional areas of research, do that now. If any research you do causes changes to your novel, you want to make those changes now. It's vital that your research is finished before you start your first draft. Too many writers fall behind in their page goals because they're doing research and become distracted by it. You have the opportunity to avoid that by completing all your research now and your novel sketch has given you the power to do that.

Factual Foundation

All stories depend on the reader knowing background information about the setting and the characters. This information forms the factual foundation on which the novel is built. Integrating that information into your novel in a seamless and interesting way is one of the most important skills a writer can have. Probability says that much of the information you presented during your novel sketch is incomplete and poorly placed. With the finished sketch in hand, you should be able to identify what the reader needs to know and when the reader needs to know it. Beyond that, you need to invent interesting, believable, and natural ways to present this information to the reader. If that requires adding characters, scenes, or plot complications, now is the time to add those elements. Give information to the reader when the reader wants to know it rather than when it's easy for you to present it.

Foreshadowing

As discussed in "Foreshadowing," some events demand preparation so the reader doesn't throw your book against the wall in frustration. Now that you've read the novel, you should be able to identify any crucial moments that need that preparation.

Inside Jobs

Trade outside jobs for inside jobs by searching for solutions from within for obstacles you've created. Sometimes writers force a solution into existence when a perfectly good solution is already available in the fictional world they've created. Be especially attentive to plot spurs that exist to solve a single problem. If you're bringing in characters, settings, or complications that serve only one purpose, try to find ways to merge the plot spur into your novel. At all times seek out the most natural solution to any problem.

All the Rest

There are dozens more areas to check than what I've listed above. If you use the techniques described in this chapter, the time between when you finish your novel sketch and when you start on your first draft is when your novel is actually created. Anything that isn't right, you now decide how to make right. For most people, this process of reshaping their novel is a tremendous amount of tedious, detailed work. The people who fail when trying to write fast while writing well usually fail because they can't shut off the editor in their brains during the novel sketch—or they fail here. They want to write without thinking about it overmuch. Some go so far as to claim the process of analyzing their work in such detail robs them of their creativity. Others love this part of the process. They recognize that spending a couple weeks reworking their novel now will save them many months and several rewrites later while also producing a better novel.

Finish the Sketch

The process of reading your novel sketch in one setting, analyzing it, and deciding how to fix any discrepancies, deficiencies, and detractions from your original vision is an integral part of your novel sketch. Only when the sketch is combined with its analysis and the resulting notes does it provide an accurate representation of the novel about to be written.

To give the novel its intended shape, use your notes to write a chapter by chapter summary, create a traditional outline, or re-work your original novel summary. Your goal is to record enough organized information so that you can completely understand your intentions concerning any given section of your novel, even if months or years pass before you work on that section of your book. For myself, I get the best results by creating a document with a separate section of notes for each chapter. My goal is to record an accurate snapshot of what each chapter should be, including reasons why that chapter exists and what it accomplishes. For some of my better chapters, I might only have a page or two of notes. For other chapters, I might have more pages of notes than what will exist in the finished chapter.

When you have your chapter by chapter summary, your outline, your novel, or whatever form works best for you, you have completed your novel sketch. Now you're ready to use that novel sketch to create your first draft. And to be clear, from this point on, *whenever I refer to a novel sketch, I mean the sketch, the analysis, the resulting notes, and your chapter by chapter outlined summary.*

The First Draft

Using your novel sketch as a guide, you're now ready to write your novel. For lack of a better term, I call what you're about to write a first draft, but unlike most first drafts, this version of your novel should be good enough that it could go directly to the printer. Not that you'd want it to—it wouldn't represent your *best* work—but if you're a talented writer, it should be as good as or better than much of what's found on the shelves at your corner bookstore.

Your novel sketch allowed you to discover what your novel would be. Your first draft *is* your novel. To write the first draft, you typically start with your first chapter and write the subsequent chapters in order until you reach THE END. Since beginnings are so important, don't be surprised if your first chapters take longer than the chapters that follow, but your objective should be to get into a comfortable and maintainable rhythm. To help you stay focused, I've jotted down some advice.

Pace Yourself

Writing a novel sketch is like running a 100 meter dash. Writing a first draft is more like running a marathon. The key to writing a good first draft is creating a pace you can sustain over the long haul. Your first draft may lack a bit of polish, but it should be the highest quality product you can create.

To keep your writing on track, implement the techniques I discussed in "Passionate Pounding". Beyond daily goals in pages or hours, you should also set chapter goals. Estimate the number of pages you'll need for each chapter using your novel sketch and set appropriate goals. Having realistic chapter goals also means you can set a goal for completing your first draft. These goals are meant to help you stay on track and finish your novel as quickly as possible. If you get behind, write more each week until you catch up. If you get ahead of your goals, do a happy dance but keep going. You never know what life might throw at you, so it's always nice to have a cushion.

Flexible Rigidity

Skyscrapers seem solid, but they're not. They sway in high winds. If they didn't sway, they'd collapse during the first good wind storm. If they swayed too much, their steel skeletons would twist and shear and they'd still collapse. You need a similar amount of flexible rigidity in your adherence to your novel sketch. If you divert too much from your original vision, you risk your entire novel sketch collapsing like one of those twisting skyscrapers. If you doggedly adhere to your novel sketch, you ignore valid ideas that would improve your novel.

A good rule of thumb is to be more accepting of changes to your novel sketch that affect only the current chapter. If you rework a single chapter until you get exactly what you're looking for, the result will take longer than getting it right the first time, but if the extra work creates a better novel, it's worth the time. If you have changes that affect your novel as a whole, either resist making those changes or rewrite your novel sketch to incorporate the changes. Making changes of that magnitude alters your original vision so that you're writing a different novel. As such, you need a different novel sketch. The tricky changes are the ones that affect multiple chapters in your novel but don't require you to restructure the novel as a whole.

I've watched too many talented authors fail to finish a novel because they changed their minds about what they wanted to write halfway through. The novel sketch is designed to prevent this, but some people can't resist incorporating ongoing personal growth into their novels. The only solution for people who suffer this affliction is to write much more quickly. For example, instead of finishing their first draft in two years, they need to finish it in six months (or much less!).

The Best It Can Be

When you were writing the novel sketch, your goal was to capture your vision of the novel as quickly as possible. When you write your first draft, your goal is to write a great novel. Don't settle for anything less. Before you consider a chapter finished, you should have produced a clean manuscript. All story elements should be in place. Every part of the manuscript should be as good as you can make it.

Most of this book is aimed at helping you create a great novel, so refer to the appropriate sections for advice.

As I said at the beginning of this section, your first draft should be good enough to go directly to the printer. It's especially important that you allow no one else to see your manuscript until you've created what you consider to be finished copy. Few activities are a bigger waste of time for everyone involved than obtaining feedback on a manuscript that you know isn't up to par. If a reader's distracted by grammar mistakes, misspellings, logic errors, story holes, cardboard characters, and flat dialogue, any comments she makes are automatically invalid. No editor would ever accept a manuscript in such a state and you shouldn't ask any other reader to do so.

Getting Feedback

How much you protect a work in progress depends on your personality. For me, having someone read my novel sketch would be a bit like exposing myself in front of the ten most distinguished people I know … with the internet cam running. I can't imagine having someone read my deepest thoughts that form the raw material from which I will construct my novel.

My first draft needs no such protection. By the time I reach that stage, I've crafted something that can be touched by others. It's meant to be public in the same sense a painting on my living room wall is public. The whole world doesn't see it, but revealing it to trusted individuals is not only okay but desired. **Having a select group of intelligent and caring readers provide feedback about your first draft usually makes it a better novel.** The best readers for this purpose are often like-minded writers, but not always. Seek readers whose advice helps *you* improve *your* novel. These readers should understand your novel's genre and they should support the type of novel you're trying to write. Make your choices carefully. If you choose the wrong readers, their advice could ruin your novel.

Your novel sketch is designed to protect you from this danger. It tells you what your novel *should be*. If your readers are giving you advice that encourages you to steer a different course than the one you created in your novel sketch, ignore the advice. No matter how good their ideas are, those ideas didn't come from you. If you follow their ideas, the resulting novel won't be yours, and your unique take on a novel is always your greatest contribution to that novel.

If you can't ignore the advice because you realize you're not writing the novel you wanted to write, reclaim the novel by starting over:

1) Take notes about what you want your book to be.
2) Write a brand new novel sketch.
3) Do your own analysis of that sketch.
4) Create a new chapter by chapter guide.

Complete all these steps without communicating in any way with your original readers. Starting over is a tremendous amount of work, but if you fundamentally changed the original vision you had for your novel—whether you acknowledge it or not—you're now writing a different novel. Redoing your original work gives you the chance to claim this new novel as your own.

Ideas and suggestions that don't fundamentally change your novel are always welcome. Heck, that's why you ask folks to read your first draft. It then becomes your job as the writer to incorporate any advice you receive into your vision of the novel. Take advice whenever it makes sense to do so and ignore the rest.

Creating your first draft only after you've finished your novel sketch makes it easier to ignore advice that doesn't fit your vision of the novel. By sketching your novel first, you already understand your novel in a way no one else can. You've consciously chosen the order and method of all information presented. You know why you wrote it that way. The confidence your sketch provides is invaluable.

If you belong to a traditional writing group, it's especially important to complete your novel sketch before allowing anyone to critique your first draft. If this novel is your first, wait to join the group until you've completed your novel sketch, or—if the group allows it—spend those weeks or months participating in the group by critiquing others and learning about writing. Once you have your sketch finished, you can bring in chapters from your first draft the same as other participants do. If it's your second or later novel and the group meets at regular intervals, you should have finished your novel sketch for the current novel before they've finished critiquing your previous novel. Working on a new novel before polishing your old one gives you the distance you need to make tough choices relating to cuts and changes to your beloved work. If the group is set up such that you can't work on your next novel while they're critiquing your last novel, you can always wait to bring in material just as you did for your first novel. Just as you control all parts of your novel, you can also control when people read your work.

Correct as You Go

If you're participating in a writing group that meets regularly, feel free to incorporate simple changes into your first draft as you receive them. Simple changes are corrections involving typos, grammar mistakes, diction mistakes, and any other changes to the prose that are quick to make and require little thought. Be wary, however. If incorporating these changes causes your progress on the first draft to falter, put them aside and incorporate them after your first draft's finished. Not only will this protect your momentum, but it will also allow you to evaluate those changes in a more objective manner.

Even if you don't incorporate changes, you should take careful notes on any comments you receive. Since months or even years may pass before you work on a chapter that's been reviewed by others, make sure all the comments are precise enough to remain clear even after they've been clouded by time.

Finish the Draft

When you finally type "The End," give yourself a pat on the back. Granted, you have some changes to make before you're done, but you've written a complete novel. That's an accomplishment. And if you've followed the techniques outlined in this section, you've probably completed that novel in record time. Now it's time to send that novel off for feedback, provided you have a group of readers lined up who are waiting to read the novel in its entirety.

Before sending your manuscript off to that group, finish making any simple changes you've already received (as outlined above). There are a couple reasons why you want to make those changes before the second group sees the manuscript.

The cleaner your manuscript, the more accurate and meaningful any feedback you receive will be. Even professional readers become distracted by mistakes.

Any readers you have are doing you a favor. The least you can do is provide them with the cleanest manuscript you can create. Few actions are as thoughtless as asking a reader to waste their time correcting simple mistakes that you already know about.

Even if you don't have any readers waiting for your manuscript, finish making those simple changes. You count as a reader and the reasons above apply to you as much as any other reader.

Are We Done Yet?

Some writers love to talk about how it took them ten years to write their first novel, as if it's a badge of honor. If you took ten years to write your novel, either you didn't work on it very hard or you didn't know what you were doing. Granted, if your name is Shelby Foote and you're writing a 1.2 million word history of the Civil War, then go ahead and take a couple decades to finish the project. Otherwise your job is to get the novel finished and get it out the door.

One of the reasons a novelist takes so long to finish a novel is that he continuously rewrites it until it's such a jumbled mishmash that even his own mother won't read it. One of the ways to write quickly while writing well is to limit the number of times you rewrite your novel. I recommend you limit the number of writes/rewrites to three:
1) Sketch
2) First Draft
3) Final Draft

Granted, you'll likely need to make changes to your manuscript after the editor and the copy editor have chewed on it a while, but those changes aren't your doing. Besides, they typically come with a check and contract in hand, and who can complain about that?

To get started on your Final Draft, you'll want to follow a pattern that's similar to the one you used before writing your First Draft.

Take a Break

You've finished your first draft and sent it off to any readers who've agreed to give you a helpful critique. Now it's time for a break. This break typically lasts anywhere from a long weekend to a couple weeks. Unlike the break you took after finishing your novel sketch, this break is designed less to recharge your brain and more to give you some distance from your novel. Feel free to work on other projects during this time, including research for your next novel or even writing a short story or two.

Read your completed novel

When your break is done, it's time to read your first draft. Just as you did after finishing your novel sketch, set aside enough time to read your novel as quickly as possible, preferably in one sitting. Unlike your novel sketch, what you're reading now should be a finished novel. Granted, you plan to fix anything that needs to be fixed and polish until you can polish no more, but when you have your first draft in hand, your novel's in the can (to borrow a bit of movie-making jargon). You have some editing to do, but unless you've made a mistake, you've captured everything you meant to capture.

Feel free to read with a pen in hand. Correct any simple mistakes in spelling, grammar, or diction, but do not polish the prose. That step will come later. Your goal here is to read your novel the way an enthused fan might read it. Since your first draft should have been written cleanly enough to go directly to the printer, you shouldn't find many mistakes. If you do find a mistake now and then, jotting down a correction now will ensure the mistake is caught and corrected. The same advice applies to any notes regarding story elements, characters, plot points, or overall prose quality in a given section. The goal of these notes is not to make the corrections now but to record your thoughts concerning what those corrections should be so you can remember your intentions later.

Unlike your novel sketch, you definitely want to judge this manuscript as you read it. If your novel isn't working, now's the time to recognize its deficiencies. At the end of each chapter, record your impressions. Did you enjoy the chapter? Did you achieve the emotional reaction you were looking for? Were the chapter's critical moments as effective as they need to be? Is there enough humor? Does the dialogue need to be punched up? Is this the chapter that's going to sell the novel or get it rejected? While you can't mimic the reactions of a reader coming to the book for the first time, you should do your best to come close. Be objective. Be honest. Now's not the time to settle. Concentrate on what can be fixed and make plans to fix it.

Novel, ho!

Meld your impressions with any feedback you've received and create a unified vision of what you want your novel to be. Using whatever organizational method works for you, combine all notes concerning a given section into a single line of changes. For myself, I typically employ the same technique I used before starting on the first draft: I create a document with a separate section of notes for each chapter that needs changed. You may have entire chapters that need little to no changes or you may have twenty pages of notes for each chapter. Either way, all the reader will see is your final draft. If that final draft is great, readers will never know how many changes you made to your first draft.

You can create your final list of changes before all your manuscripts are returned from your selected group of readers. If you've done a good job with your own analysis, few of these late changes from the first readers will get added to your list anyway. Either you will have spotted the same problem and will know better how to fix it than your readers or you'll reject the suggested changes outright. There are always exceptions, which is the reason you requested feedback, but the number of changes should be few. Besides, you've already written a novel sketch and a first draft. You know what your novel should be. If you have to tweak your final list of changes even after you've completed half of them, that process shouldn't slow your progress much.

Using your notes, make all desired changes to your first draft. Try to create the highest quality prose you can for these changes, but don't polish anything until you've completed the entire set of changes.

Shiny

Most of the techniques you need to change your altered First Draft into your Final Draft are covered in the section on "Polish that Puppy." Cleaning up your prose and making it the best it can be takes about the same amount of time whether you spent ten years writing your book or you finished it in three months. That seems counterintuitive but the longer you write, the more true it will become. For most people, if they can write well slowly, they can train themselves to write well quickly.

Your Final Read-through

When you've finished the changes to your first draft and polished every page of your manuscript to the best of your abilities, your novel is complete. Now it's time for your final read-through.

This final read-through, as covered earlier, is normally done out loud. By this point, a dozen sets of eyes might have read the same page and yet you will find you still catch errors when you read the work aloud. As with all your other read-throughs, this reading should be done in the shortest time possible. That doesn't mean you should read quickly—quite the opposite—but in addition to catching typos and grammar mistakes, this final reading also provides one last chance to detect any fatal flaws that might have been missed. In theory, the novel you read aloud should be the best novel you can write, but like the typos, sometimes a fixable problem will slip through the repeated readings and make it to this stage.

A Final Note

The techniques I've outlined for writing fast while writing well don't always work. For some people, they never work. I've known writers who couldn't get past the desire to edit as they went along. Not only does this editorial compulsion slow them down, but by definition, it requires them to examine what they've written with a critical eye. If you spend every day meticulously noting your deficiencies and carefully correcting your mistakes, your odds of ever writing fast are extremely slim.

For other successful writers who fail using these techniques, they honestly don't know what they want their novel to be. They can recognize a good finished product when they create it, but their perception of what a chapter will be before it's written often or always fails to match what that chapter becomes when it's written. This problem occurs most often when a writer doesn't consciously understand how their own writing works. The ability to predict the results of their work can be learned, but until this ability is mastered, multiple rewrites are needed to create a publishable novel. This obviously slows the writing process. These writers may still be writing well, but it's unlikely they're writing quickly.

There is too much. Let me sum up

Writing quickly does not mean writing poorly. The techniques covered in this section provide one proven path to finishing a novel quickly.

- Once a base level of competence is reached, the amount of time spent on a novel does not predict the quality or popularity of a novel.
- Getting and keeping momentum is the most important factor in writing quickly while writing well.
- To write a novel quickly, you need plenty of information about that novel before you start writing. Gathering enough information is your first step.
- Write a 5-15 page summary that covers your entire novel.
- Sketch out your novel by writing your novel literally as quickly as you can. For short novels, this could be done by most writers in a long weekend.
- Identify the holes in your novel sketch and write a chapter by chapter summary that contains enough information to fill out your novel and correct any problems you have.
- Create a high quality first draft that's good enough to go straight to the printer.
- Get feedback on your first draft if you have good sources for feedback.
- Meld your impressions of your first draft with any feedback you've received and create a detailed vision of your finished novel. Implement that vision.
- Polish your prose to the best of your ability given the time you have to do so.
- Do a final read-through out loud to catch any mistakes you have remaining.

Chapter Twelve:
Productivity

Number One Rule

I've never met a writer who complained about being **too** productive. All writers want to increase (or at least maintain) their level of productivity. Most writers struggle at some point in their career to remain productive. They either slow down or stop completely. Whether you're just starting out or whether you've been writing for fifty years, there are some universal truths related to productivity that every writer should know.

All That Matters

My number one rule of writing is to write. The reason is obvious. If you don't write, nothing else matters. Not your story, your characters, your beginnings, your endings—nothing. And yet the number one reason writers are not successful is because they don't write. Or they don't write enough. The second part of my one and only rule of writing—to try to sell what you write—is just a all-encompassing way of saying that you need to produce the highest quality writing you can, you need to finish what you write, and you need to have it in a form that's easily consumed by other people. I've never met a writer who did all those things but refused to send out the manuscript, although I've heard tell those writers do exist. In its simplest form, my one and only rule on writing is atomic rather than molecular.

Write.

Since that's all that matters (if you're not doing it), why do so many writers fail to fulfill that one and absolutely vital requirement? Why do so many spend so much time with so little finished product to show for it?

Most of our discussion on productivity will center around how to be more productive with the time you have, but first, we need to make sure we're being productive at all.

The Biggest Hurdle

Everyone is influenced by their state of mind, both at their jobs and in life outside work, but a writer's success balances on a much finer psychological line than what you find in most professions. That's because we create something out of nothing. We live in a world where there is no right or wrong, where we have no supervisors to prod us along, and where self-motivation is the only kind of motivation that works. It's important to understand how your brain works because getting your brain in the right place and keeping it there is one of the most important things a writer can do.

Damn, I'm Good

One of the more important traits a writer can have is confidence. In this book's first chapter, I call it arrogance, with good reason. The biggest difference between arrogance and confidence is whether you're right. When inept people believe in themselves, they're considered arrogant. When competent people believe in themselves, they're considered confident. People like to fool themselves into thinking this isn't true, but arrogance really is in the eye of the beholder.

The problem is that it doesn't matter how much confidence you have or how little confidence you have, there will always be people who will tell you you're not good enough. In other words, there will always be people who believe you're inept. It's arrogant to believe you're right and they're wrong, but that is precisely what you need to do to succeed.

If you're more comfortable with the terms confident and self-assured, that's great. The key is that you don't lose that confidence or self-assurance regardless of the facts. If you write for five years and not enough people like what you've written to make you happy, you still need to believe in yourself or you're going to fail as a writer. And you need to believe in yourself each and every day.

The simplest definition of arrogance is believing you are better, smarter, and more important than other people. As a writer, that should be your goal. Not only do you need to believe you're right when other people say you're wrong, but you also need to put your needs above the needs of those around you, at least when you're writing. It's impossible to do that if you believe you're not as important as they are. That's why the two main keys to obtaining the confidence you need to succeed as a writer are:

1) Accepting the importance of confidence
2) Learning to be confident

Importance

Confidence is linked to so many areas of writing. If you lack confidence, it's nearly impossible to develop a distinctive style. Since you will always have people who criticize the way you write, if you lack confidence, you'll attempt to change the way you write to satisfy them. This translates to an inconsistent and unrecognizable style.

Without confidence, motivation is nearly impossible to come by. If you harbor too much doubt about your own success, the self-preservation area of your brain will do its best to talk you out of writing. "Why bother? You're wasting your time." How are you supposed to battle that without the shield of confidence to protect you?

If you lack confidence, you'll never achieve originality. If no one else has done it quite this way, why would you even consider it? Surely if it was a good idea, someone else would have already done it.

Finishing what you start is intrinsically linked to confidence. If you lack confidence, it's impossible to declare a novel finished. It's not as good as you want it to be, so obviously it's not finished. This same lack of confidence produces fear of the unknown. You don't release your work to the world, because as long as you keep it under wraps, no one can tell you what you already know—that it's not good enough. Confidence smothers these fears.

Having confidence is what allows you to keep going when results don't meet your expectations. All prolific novelists produce books that don't sell as well as they expected. All writers create work that doesn't measure up and has to be tossed or completely rewritten. Having confidence doesn't mean deluding yourself into believing what you've written is great: It means deluding yourself into believing what you're about to write will be great.

The benefits just by clicking your heels together three times. It's also not something you can accomplish overnight. Becoming confident is a gradual process achieved through daily effort.

<u>Change for the Better</u>

The first step in becoming confident is accepting that you have the power to change. This is a *Catch-22* situation because if you don't believe in yourself, then it's hard to believe you control what happens to you. No one has more power over you than you. The only power that other people can exert over you is power that you give them. If you don't give them any power, they have none.

It doesn't always seem this way because usually it's not our conscious mind that gives away our power, it's our sneaky subconscious. The good news is that the subconscious works both ways. When it gives our power away, it's acting based on habit. At some point in our past, we allowed our power to slip through our fingers and escape. The subconscious is just continuing that pattern the same way your feet will navigate a familiar hallway without conscious thought.

Our job is to retrain the habitual behavior of our subconscious such that it chooses to automatically protect our power rather than give it away.

The only way to do that is through a conscious effort. That's why self-help advice like what I'm giving here so often seems artificial and inconsequential. It's because we didn't consciously fall into our current pattern. We stumbled our way there by not paying attention to where we were going. Now we want to go somewhere different than the place we've always been. Isn't it natural that we should then need to concentrate on each step.

Gaining self-confidence is not artificial. It's intentional.

First, become aware of your negative thinking and quash it at every opportunity by blasting it aside with the power of positive thought.

This sounds unbelievably hokey, even to me, but that's because people talk about it as if it's easy. It's not. It requires dedication, force of will, and constant repetition. You're trying to transform your self-confidence from a 98-pound weakling into a hulking behemoth. That's far from trivial and it doesn't happen overnight.

One area of negative thought to attack is dwelling on past

mistakes. While it's useful to learn from past mistakes so that you don't repeat them, there's a difference between analyzing a mistake and dwelling on it. To avoid dwelling on a mistake, set yourself a time limit. Indulge yourself in examining and re-examining something until you find yourself going over the same ground a second time. The moment that happens, you know you've squeezed all the juice out of that learning experience. Put it aside. Your brain will inevitably return to it, but each time it does, immediately and forcefully kick it to the curb again.

The same technique should be used whether the mistakes are yours or someone else's. Instead of dwelling on some wrongful or thoughtless act committed against you, decide what you're going to do about it if it happens again. If the answer is nothing, then either change what you plan to do or understand that you've chosen to accept this action. If you've chosen to accept it, getting mad about it is a waste of time. Again, push it away as soon as you can.

Embrace and accept disappointment as a part of everything. Don't look for it, but don't allow it to have any control over you, either. Not to go all Yogi Berra on you, but you can't do better than your best. We want to be better than we are, so inevitably we're never able to produce something as good as we'd like it to be. This is an unchangeable fact not only for you but for every writer who has ever lived.

That's okay, because it's not your job to judge your own work. Your job is to decide if you can make it better in the time you have to work on it. If you can make it better, make it better. If you can't, call it done. You can't control anything beyond your own effort, so concentrate on what you can do and focus on ways to improve your skills and your effort. Leave the judging to someone else *after* it's published.

This takes work and effort. It's worth it. Remember, your goal is to build self-confidence. You can't do that without learning to control your thoughts, because you're trying to replace one way of thinking with a different way of thinking. It's true that you can't control what you feel, but through constant effort, you can lessen your feelings in some areas and strengthen your feelings in others.

Everything Else Is in Second Place

If you want to straighten out your brain when it comes to writing, one overriding principle clarifies most situations:

Writing Comes First

This applies not only in priority but also sequentially. We'll cover sequential order later. For this section, we're concentrating on importance.

Whenever you're faced with a decision, you will be more successful as a writer if you always choose writing above everything else.

That doesn't mean any particular decision is simple. For example, let's say your daughter has a piano recital that takes place during a time when you'd normally write. You don't enjoy recitals and you'd rather not go, but if you don't go, your daughter will be heart-broken and cry uncontrollably for days, and your wife will resent it forever and probably divorce you if you skip family activities like this too often. Given these dire results of your not going, what do you do?

You stay home and write, of course.

Just kidding. You might write. You might go to the recital. The point is that writing should be the first consideration in any situation. If your spouse and your daughter want you to go to the recital, they should be aware that they're interrupting your writing. Not because you tell them, "Hey, that's my writing time. Bugger off!" They know because you've allowed writing to pervade every aspect of your life. It's always there, always in the middle of every conversation. It comes first by default.

For any particular situation, your own personal guiding principles on how to behave in life will determine what you do, but if you want to have the best chance to succeed as a writer, first become a writer. The way to do that is to allow writing to come first.

You Can Do It All, But Only If You Do It Now

But wait! You don't want to alienate your children and spend thousands on divorce lawyers. You want to see your parents before they make that trip to the great beyond. You have a few hobbies. You have friends. You have a life, damn it!

Way back at the start of this book, we covered that being a writer means giving something up, but there is hope. If you want to do more than write, then embrace the power of organization. It's no accident that the most successful and productive people on the planet are also the most organized. Part of being organized is recognizing procrastination as the great evil of evils.

Being a highly productive writer comes with the huge cost of *earning* your time off. Every minute you spend on tasks that don't help you write or become a better writer are minutes you'll need to make up for later in order to produce the same amount of finished work. This doesn't mean that you don't ever take any time off. Far from it. Writers need plenty of down time to restore energy, to soak in new experiences, and to encounter new people. What it means is that *you need to manage your non-productive time rather than allowing it to manage you.*

The easiest and most reliable way to do that is to eliminate procrastination from your life. Not procrastination as determined by other people, but procrastination as determined by you.

If you like to spend fifteen minutes every morning quietly drinking a cup of coffee and staring at the birds fluttering about the feeder in your front yard, this is not procrastination. It's a ritual designed to prepare your creative balance and energy. If you plan to start writing at 8:30, but decide to check Facebook first, this is procrastination. Or is it? Maybe it's just the opposite. What determines whether an activity is procrastination is whether it's an unnecessary delay to the start of a planned task. If your normal routine is to check Facebook every day before you start to write and you **limit that activity to a planned length of time** (such as fifteen minutes), then it's not procrastination. It's a choice you've made. You've assigned this activity a high priority. You feel it's necessary for your mental health. You've decided this activity is so important and vital that you can delay the start of your day until it's complete.

The easiest way to do more now than you did yesterday is to not waste the time you have. One of the easiest ways to do this is to remind yourself that everything you do affects your writing. That doesn't mean that you don't do what you need to do to make your life work as a whole. It means you take care of those other aspects of your life so that you can concentrate on your writing when it's time to do so.

Physical Health = Mental Health

Physical activity is vital if you don't want to be sick or die an early death. It's also vital for your writing. If you're a writer who doesn't schedule time to get up and move in a healthy way, you might be somewhat more productive in the short run, but your lifelong productivity will almost certainly take a major hit. Exercise is especially important for writers, who are obliged to spend way too much time sitting on their behinds.

Being physically active does more than help you live longer. It also helps protect and improve your mental faculties related to memory, reasoning, and concentration. If you're physically active on a regular basis, your brain works better than it does if you're not.

And while you're up moving around, spend some time eating healthy. Every part of living takes time, which is why most writers love fast food. Nearly every busy person struggles to eat right, but like our exercise allotment, if we cheat by eating fast food to gain time, it will cost us in the end.

While keeping your body healthy benefits your mind, you need to take care of the physical organ of the mind directly. That means experiencing new situations and new people. A we age, our neural processes slow down. To protect against this, it's important that we consistently try new things. As writers, this is especially difficult, because so much of our time is already spoken for. One way to improve our efficiency is to delegate the discovery process to other people. If we have a wide circle of friends, we don't have to go looking for new experiences to try, because they will come to us. Our friends will foist activities upon us. "You've got to try this!" Granted, most of what they recommend will probably consist of new TV shows and restaurants, but new is new. If their descriptions entice you, give it a try. If not, wait for something better to come along.

Part of staying healthy is sleeping well. Nothing allows you to stay more physically and mentally sharp than getting enough sleep.

Part of sleeping well is consistency, but a larger part is pure priority. If you allow getting enough sleep to take on a huge importance in your life, you will find a way to get the sleep you need. Not by taking drugs, which is an attempt to cheat the system, but by making changes in your life that allow you to improve the length and quality of your sleep. What you're looking for are blocks of sleep that last 80 to 120 minutes.

Research now indicates that adult humans never evolved to sleep straight through the night. It's normal to wake up and stay awake for an hour or so in the middle of the night. But what you do with that hour is also important. The biggest factors in getting enough sleep are to allow yourself the time you need and listen to your body. And with all things related to writing, keep trying different techniques until you find one that works for you.

The final benefit of increased physical health isn't often realized until you lose it. When your body breaks down, it intrudes on all other aspects of your life. Declining health often results in increased medical visits, additional tasks you must perform, and reduced available energy. Nothing is more distracting from a person's focus than physical or mental pain.

So do your best without stressing over any of it. I've just told you to exercise, eat right, get plenty of sleep, spend time trying new things and meeting new people. Just when, you might ask, are you supposed to write? The answer is balance. Get your writing done first, then spend the rest of your time doing what you're supposed to do with some down time mixed in. On those days when you don't get everything done, don't beat yourself up over it.

Once Is Never Enough

As writers, we tend to set high standards for ourselves. We have goals, we have dreams, we have bill collectors that go bump in the night. Part of this is because writing is such an all-encompassing activity. Not the writing itself, necessarily, but the need to know everything about everything. We're trying to capture the drama, suspense, joy, satisfaction, and humor of real life and bottle it in a form that can be reconstituted in the brains of readers we've never met.

Productivity is important. Not only is increasing your productivity the easiest way to improve your writing, it's also the easiest way to increase sales. But there's a great danger in the lure of ever increasing productivity.

It can't be done.

Avoid the Productivity Trap

No matter how dedicated and focused you are, it's impossible to continue increasing your productivity forever. Not only will you fail to write more—you'll write less. Writing less can quickly lead to not writing at all.

Life sometimes has a nasty way of kicking you when you're down. Whether you wrote fifty pages or five hundred pages last month, few results are more frustrating to a writer than getting through this month and discovering you've only managed to do three pages.

The only reliable way I know to fight this is to look forward. While you can never write too much, it's also true that you can never write too little to make it worthwhile. There's a phrase that relates to exercise that says no matter how little you exercise, you're still doing laps around the guy sitting on the couch. The same applies to writing. If you only write one page, that's one more page than you might have written.

The hardest part of looking forward is actually doing it. So many writers say that there's nothing more to writing than getting your butt in that chair and your fingers on that keyboard. The saddest part is that they're absolutely right. In a way. Unfortunately being told to "Just Do It!" isn't all that helpful when your brain is poking holes in your psyche with the flying fickle finger of failure.

That's why it's so important to build a little momentum every day and do everything in your power to keep that momentum going. You do that by seizing every opportunity to build confidence in yourself, putting writing first while keeping your life balanced, paying attention to your health, and staying organized.

This Is Your Brain on Writing

This subject is so important to writers, even though they don't know it, that I'll probably write a book on the subject eventually. As writers, we tend to be an opinionated lot. It goes back to that whole arrogance quality that keeps us going when no one else in the world cares whether we succeed. Unfortunately, it often makes us less likely to listen to reason.

What I discuss below is based on the latest neuroscience research and is more fact than opinion. If you want to improve your productivity as a writer, especially if you've been trying to do so for years with limited success, it's useful to know what science has to say on the subject.

Master Jugglers We Are Not

This unalterable faith in our own opinions is one of the reasons writers think they can multitask even though all scientific research points to the contrary. The conscious brain does not multitask. It switches from one task to another with enough rapidity that we fool ourselves into thinking we're doing two things at once. That would be okay, except that switching between tasks comes with a mental and physical cost. It increases the stress hormone cortisol as well as adrenaline. The biggest danger of multitasking is that our brain rewards us for this bad behavior. Each time we lose focus, it becomes easier to do so in the future. Our brain likes the new and the shiny. We switch to doing something different, and our brain goes to its happy place.

Our desire to do something different does more than distract us. Even if we resist the siren song of our brain and we stay on task, if we possess knowledge that a distractor is sitting out in the ether somewhere or even in the other room, our IQ drops by as much as 10 points. As humans, it's not about having the willpower to concentrate. We can't. We're not wired that way. As writers, we suffer distractions more than most. Research shows that the same qualities that make people highly creative also make it harder for them to resist distraction.

That's why it's tempting to allow our brains to delude us into thinking we can get more done when we multitask. Even if we embrace our deluded state, we at least need to acknowledge the metabolic cost of allowing the brain to go racing between tasks like an ADD two-year-old. Our brain needs oxygenated glucose to switch between tasks, which it greedily consumes every time we change focus. Soon we're exhausted and disoriented, but delusively convinced that we got sooooo much more work done than we would have if we'd limited our focus to one task at a time.

Multitasking ruins our memories, turns our brains to mush and burns too much energy. So why do we do it? Our brain tells us it's a good idea by rewarding us chemically each time we misbehave.

It gets worse. Part of multitasking is making lots of decisions. This causes your pre-frontal cortex to get tired. Soon it says to hell with it, do whatever you want. This pricks up the ears of your pleasure centers. The next thing you know, you're goofing off instead of writing, with your brain whispering rationalizations in your ear about how it's okay and how you deserve a break.

It's true that your mileage may vary. Everybody's brain is different. Some of us can switch tasks at less cost than it takes others to do so. Also, the tasks we're doing matter. If you're cleaning house while listening to music while planning what you're going to do tomorrow, you're really only focused on one task: your plans for the next day. Because you've done your house cleaning chores so many times, a different part of your brain is taking care of them. Still another part of your brain is listening to the music. At any given time, your focus might be pulled away from its planning duties and concentrate momentarily on the music or the chores, but it's not a constant back and forth.

If you still have any doubts about your multitasking limits, get three of your friends together. Arm each with a different book. Have each begin reading at the same time from the book they're holding. Listen to all three of them at the same time (multitask). At the end of five minutes, report to them on what they read. Then repeat this experiment, except this time, only concentrate on one of them and do your best to ignore the other two. I'm betting you'll see a distinct difference in what you were able to comprehend. Not because the reader in the second experiment was easier to hear, but because you didn't attempt to multitask.

Even if we abandon multitasking as a bad job, we're still in danger from distractions. Think of distractions as forced multitasking. The attention filters that exist in all of our brains are evolved to warn us of unexpected dangers or opportunities. There's no way to shut them off completely. Yet each time we are distracted, it breaks a delicate chain that allows us to do our best work. Writing demands all of your attention because the imaginative part of your brain needs to wander in as many directions as possible while the logical, goal-oriented part of your brain is constructing sentences and paragraphs and scenes (and telling yourself not to get distracted by the beautiful day outside).

If you toss some distractions onto the fire, the mental switching that must take place to be a good writer will overload your brain. This doesn't produce an obvious external symptom. You don't drop nose-first into your keyboard, muttering, "Error! Error! Error!" until someone hits your reset button. Instead, you wear out more easily, your dialogue and your scenes become mechanical, and the intricate web of connections between characters and plot become less detailed. In theory, you could fix all of these problems later, if you catch and recognize each and every problem that slipped in under your splintered guard. Not only is that way more difficult, but also it takes additional time.

Distracted writing is bad writing. Distracted writing is inefficient writing.

I'm in the Zone, Dude

The most productive any writer can be is when they've entered what psychologists call the flow state. Most people have been lucky enough to experience this in their lives. If you've ever had a time when you were fully focused on a task and time just dropped away, you were in a flow state. Obviously it's a more productive state of being, because it's a heightened level of focus, but it's much more powerful than most people realize.

When you're in a flow state, the parts of your brain that cause you to be both less creative and less productive get shut down. In particular, the part of your prefrontal cortex that houses your self-editor gets put on hold. Instead of hearing that voice inside your head telling you that what you're writing isn't good enough or that no one will ever want to read it, you get silence. Oh, what bliss! You're in control. You're going full-speed. No wonder it's a heightened state of being. Somebody finally told that little self-editing devil to shut up!

To make matters even better, the part of your brain that generates fear gets shut down. No more worrying about whether people will like you or like what you're writing. No more worrying about whether you'll succeed. Of course you'll succeed! How could you not?

What's really wonderful about this flow state is that the normal distractions that barely lift a finger and distract us under normal circumstances now get ignored. If you reach this flow state, you are no longer tempted to look at your phone or check Facebook or get something to eat or drink or even go to the bathroom. You are in a world that consists entirely of the task you're doing.

In this state, you can produce more and produce better than you ever have before. It's like magic, except it's real. If you want to be a better writer as well as a more productive one, the importance of regularly reaching your flow state can't be overstated. Many times if you later read what you've written when you were in this zen-like mental flow state, it's hard to believe you were the one who wrote it. It's way too good.

Granted, to reach this state, you have to obtain a certain level of expertise. The more you write, the better your chance to become a good writer. The better writer you are, the better your chance of immersing yourself in the flow of what you're doing. You also need time. Just like falling asleep when you're not tired or sleepy, you need to spin your wheels for a while. Not only do you need time to get into the flow state, but you want as much time as possible once you get there. That means you take care of yourself (get a drink, go to the bathroom, get plenty of rest before you start writing) and you block off enough time to make the attempt worthwhile.

I should warn you, though. This blissful state of hyper-productivity and quality comes with one hell of a catch: If you get interrupted, it's gone. If you're in a flow state, you can often ignore distractions that would otherwise derail you, but if you fail, you lose. In our overly communicative world, that means that if you notice a single text, phone call, email, chirp, vibration, or light from your phone or other communication device, then the jig is up. Your flow state is gone. You crash and burn in the agony of defeat.

There are millions of distractions out there, just waiting for their chance to destroy one of your flow states. For God's sake, protect yourself.

Repel Them—Or Else

Everybody and everything wants a piece of your writing time. Even if you fully understand the importance of keeping your mind on your writing, the rest of the world is clueless. Worse, the rest of the world not only doesn't care but also doesn't believe it's important to care.

The truth is that we're most productive as writers when we're allowed and encouraged to write and to fully immerse ourselves in our writing. Admittedly, this is a luxury. Most successful people aren't allowed to isolate themselves from the distractions of the world as much as they would like, but most successful people find a way to do it anyway. That's because they've discovered what we, as writers, need to know:

> No one is ever likely to respect your writing time and space as much as they need to for you to be as successful as you could be.

The only way for you to protect your writing environment is for you to do it yourself. Don't give people the chance to take it away from you.

This is why a majority of successful people are early risers. It has nothing to do with what time they get up and everything to do with what time everybody else gets up. For example, a busy and successful executive likes to get in to work by 6:00 every morning while the rest of the office doesn't get in until 8:00. This gives him two hours of alone time to be highly productive, non-distracted guy. That puts him well more than two hours ahead of everybody else. Remember, their time is distracted and fragmented and therefore less productive. As a result, if our example executive works a nine hour shift with thirty minutes off for lunch (not that uncommon a possibility), he gets off at 3:30 having worked nine hours but likely accomplishing the same work most people do in thirteen or fourteen hours. Assuming this executive lives in a large city, his getting to work early and leaving early has also likely cut down on his commute time, providing him extra time each day that the rest of his office doesn't enjoy. That turns him into a much more productive, more relaxed employee than much of his competition. If the CEO of the company notices how productive this executive is and gets the bright idea to have everyone come in at 6:00, no one's productivity goes up and the executive's productivity goes down. To no one's surprise, the executive then starts coming to work at 4:00 a.m.

The unique problem that writers (and other artistic types face) is that our down time is nearly as important as our writing time. We need to de-stress, get plenty of sleep, get our life in order so that we're not distracted while trying to write, and meet new people. If you're a non-writer, this is where you point out that everybody needs to do this—and you would be right. The difference is that if you have a job as an emergency room technician, a fireman, a policeman, or an army grunt stationed overseas during a conflict, people automatically accept that you need your down time and that your job requires a high level of performance. When it comes to writers, it's the opposite. What they don't understand is that a writer is *always* working. Literally any activity we pursue can make it into our writing.

Your Own Time

As writers, part of our job is scheduling time to write. The sanctity you bestow on that time directly determines how much respect it receives from the rest of the world. If you say your writing time is 8:00-10:00 p.m. every day, then you better be writing from 8:00-10:00 p.m. every day. Granted, life events, especially planned or emergency life events, will disrupt that schedule, just as it would any work schedule, but any events that take you away from writing should be major, infrequent, and necessary.

Having a consistent schedule not only helps you protect your writing time, but it also allows your brain to prepare itself for your writing day. Most of us brush our teeth every night before we go to bed. As children, this is a difficult task to master without being reminded, but as adults, we find it easy to do. This isn't only because we're adults. It's also because it's become a habit.

Habits are incredibly powerful controls for both human and animal behavior. Healthy habits provide us comfort. They relieve our brains from making decisions. If you make your writing a habit, your own brain chemistry will help you write when otherwise you wouldn't have felt like writing. But you have to give your brain a leg up. You do that by allowing your brain to anticipate your writing time and to look forward to it.

It's not a bad idea to take the "writing should come first" mantra to its logical implication. Write in the morning shortly after you get up. Most famous and successful writers do this. The reason is simple. If you do your writing first, it's done. No matter what else you accomplish that day, your writing is taken care of. Some people call this "swallowing the frog," but that implies that writing is the worst part of your day. Even so, there's no arguing with success. On the other hand, if writing doesn't work for you in the morning, there's nothing wrong with writing at night. The key is figuring out what time works best for you and writing during that time.

Our writing time is not the only time that must be scheduled. If you want to avoid distractions, you need to take care of the non-writing-related parts of your life during the times when you're not writing. This means you need to organize and prioritize that time, too.

For example, a natural and nearly unavoidable temptation when writing to deadline is to ignore everything else until you finish the book you're working on. For any time period lasting more than a couple days, this is typically a mistake. If your other tasks in life start piling up because you're ignoring them, it won't take long for them to come crashing through your protective walls, rumbling toward you as surely as that giant boulder at the beginning of *Raiders of the Lost Ark.*

There are many ideas and techniques related to organizing your time. Find a technique or combination of techniques that work for you and use them.

Your Own Place

It's also vital that we find a comfortable place to write. Research shows that humans evolved to ignore much of what we see and hear as well as much of what we smell and feel provided it doesn't change.

If you write in the same place every day, especially if it's a place where you write and do nothing else, when you go to that place, your brain will automatically switch to writing mode. Since most of us can't afford a space that we use *only* for writing, we benefit when our space remains unchanged from day to day. This unchanging space applies to more than just our writing area. Even when we're writing, we need a drink of water or need to use the bathroom. That takes us out of our writing space and exposes us to the vagaries of the outside world.

The human brain has evolved to notice change above all else. When your spouse decides to rearrange the furniture in your house on a whim, it scrambles the neurons in your brain. Provided you have few distractions in life, this furniture rearrangement could be a benefit. It provides new stimuli to keep your brain young and active. But if you're like most of us in the modern world and you're already overwhelmed by the distractions of life, this disruption of your environment adds to the work your brain has to do.

This is true of your writing area, except more so. While not everything should look perfect in someone else's eyes—your pencils don't need to be arranged in a straight line across a clean desk—everything should look perfectly arranged *to you*.

The ability to organize your work area into an arrangement that works for you means that each day when you start work, you don't need to spend energy deciding where to sit, where to put your glass, how to adjust the tilt of your computer monitor or where to sit your lap top, or a thousand other decisions that sap us in ways too subtle for most people to notice.

Clutter is okay provided it's your clutter and is arranged according to your brain's organizational patterns. The key is for you to feel completely comfortable in your writing space and in the area that surrounds your writing space. Since we're all unique individuals, this won't happen if the space is shared unless everyone around you conforms to your wishes. It's better for everyone if the only alterations ever made to your space are your changes alone.

Attack of the Fifty-Foot Spouse

In my opinion, writers don't make good spouses. This doesn't mean there aren't exceptions, but by necessity, writers are hypersensitive to the people around them. As a result, many writers build an emotional wall surrounding themselves as a means of protection. That's why so many writers seem both touchy and emotionally distant at the same time.

As a writer, your spouse holds a special position of power to screw up your writing. Other factors such as health, work, and kids can cause plenty of havoc on their own, but spouses wield incredible power. Keep your writing strong by focusing on what's important.

If you want to be the most successful writer you can be, writing must come first. That doesn't mean you don't love your spouse, your kids, your dog, or even your mother-in-law—but many spouses take it that way. This is another reason to have a set time and place for your writing. As a young Wizard living in Oz, most of the arguments between my wife and I concerned my writing even if she didn't realize it. I didn't clean the house enough, I didn't pay enough attention to her or the kids, I didn't visit with her family enough, I didn't do enough yard work, and on and on and on. I didn't do those things because I was writing, or getting ready to write, or recovering from writing.

What's interesting is that this same wife who was perpetually dissatisfied eventually came to respect my writing time and my writing space. She still thought I should do more of the things she wanted me to do, but that's normal marriage for most people regardless of age or gender. The key is that she finally learned that when I was writing, I was working.

As a writer, here's my top 10 list of things you should share with your spouse. After all, if you don't tell your spouse what you need, how are they supposed to know?

1) When I'm writing, don't interrupt me.
2) Acknowledge that writing is a tough occupation that will take its toll mentally and physically.
3) If I ever act weird, by all means encourage me.

4) If my time to start writing arrives and I don't immediately start, that means I'm preparing my mind for writing and this is the second worst time to distract me (the first being when I'm in the flow and you come in to ask if I made that appointment for next week).

5) Sitting down to write can sometimes be the hardest thing I do all day. This doesn't mean I'm weak or that I lack willpower or that I'm not really committed to my writing. It means my inexhaustible supply of self-confidence and self-discipline is running low and that you, life, or both have probably contributed to it.

6) If I'm staring off into space, deep in thought, don't interrupt me.

7) You are a vital contributor to whatever successes or failures I experience.

8) Writing is a job, just as important as your job.

9) My mental state affects how well I write; you have the power to affect my mental state more than any other factor.

10) When I'm writing, don't interrupt me.

Okay, I admit it, I cheated with a repeat, but so many writers I know struggle throughout their careers to make friends, family, and spouses understand that when they're writing, they're working, that this deserves a second mention. The benefit of having everyone around you respect your writing time helps you to respect your writing time. Guilt is a powerful motivator. If you've made a huge fuss about being given time to write and then you're given time to write, it's hard *not* to write.

If you're married to a writer and you're reading this, you're probably saying something about how this list isn't fair. What about you? What about your needs? Hey, you're the one who married the writer. Writing is certainly not the only occupation that requires the support of an understanding spouse. It's just one of those that seldom gets it. Unless, of course, you hit the big time. It's amazing how supportive a non-supportive spouse can be when the royalty checks start rolling in.

As a writer, the best advice I can give for helping your spouse support your writing is to do a good job. I've been saying that writing needs to come first and that it's a job. If you want your spouse to respect what you do, you need to respect what you do first. And figure out how to be successful.

I know too many writers who aren't successful because they refuse to write what people want to read. They protest that they can't. It isn't true to their artistic vision or some such nonsense. It's like folks who have a master's in history, so that they can work at McDonald's. I like history, but available jobs for historians is limited to only a tiny fraction of the number of people who graduate with the degree.

This doesn't mean you write romances if you love to write hardcore military fiction. It means that you swirl your interests around until they line up with something that has good potential to make you money. Never forget that money means readers. If you're not writing to be read, then nothing I've said in this book matters. Get yourself a journal and knock yourself out.

Sometimes, even as writers, we have to live in the real world. If you want your spouse to support you're writing, then it's your job to be successful.

Prose

Writing great prose is a wonderful and heady thing. It's why so many writers spend so much time on their prose. They've heard the old saying attributed to Mark Twain about the almost right word and the right word being the difference between the lightning bug and the lightning. Which is just plain stupid. I'm not saying his idea was wrong, but his example sucks. That's not a difference between the right word and the almost right word; that's the difference between the right word and two unrelated words.

The Pareto Principle

I don't disagree that often the way we say things has more power than what we say. What's interesting for me is that I've discovered that even the best written novels (in terms of prose) have sections of prose that can at best be described as mundane, repetitive, and woefully ordinary. What these great writers knew is that stellar prose on a page by page basis has little bearing on a novel's effectiveness or success.

This doesn't mean you should be satisfied writing crap. You should always write the best you can. You should always strive to write better. Just do so within reason.

The Pareto principle leads us to realize that 80% of the effectiveness of a novel derived from fantastic prose comes from only 20% of the prose. Some sections of a novel are more important than others. For these sections, spending extra time on the prose is likely to produce a much greater effect in your reader's satisfaction than spending extra time on the prose in other sections will. For most novels, these sections are:

- The Beginning
- The End
- Moments

With few exceptions, you can pretty much slog your way through the rest of the novel and the reader won't notice one bit.

No, you disagree, I'll just make it all great and then I won't have to worry about which sections should be great and which sections aren't as important. Except you're forgetting that your time is limited.

If you spend an hour searching for the right word instead of the almost right word thousands of times per novel, you've just doubled, tripled, or quadrupled the time it takes you to write that novel. And for 80% of those searches, it didn't matter. The reader won't notice one way or the other.

You're wasting your time. Stop it. No one will know but you.

Competence Is Golden

While I don't believe you should spend an inordinate amount of time on your prose, I've met way too many readers who hate typos, obvious grammar mistakes, and bad diction to believe that bad writing doesn't matter. This fact still follows the Pareto principle outlined above, but here 20% of your mistakes are causing 80% of their irritation. Eliminate that 20% and you have a much happier reader. That's because those 20% are the ones the reader catches.

The easiest mistake for a reader to catch is a typo. What Mark Twain should have said is, "The difference between the almost right word and the right word is the difference between sit and shit." Here are my top ten prose mistakes you should do everything in your power to avoid:

- Typos
- Spelling errors
- Using its and it's inappropriately
- Bad diction, meaning wrong word usage (He excepted the promotion. Accept for the long hours, he was very happy.)
- Superfluous commas (Would you prefer milk, or cream?)
- Lack of commas where needed (This novel is dedicated to my parents, my agent and God) or (Before I knew what I was doing my father was in trouble) or (I threw him the football and he caught it in the end zone)
- Improper capitalization (Please help your uncle jack off his horse)
- Subject-verb disagreement (The two best things about life is the drinking and smoking)
- Lack of parallel structure (He jumped, he swam, and flew an airplane in order to reach the finish line before the others)

- Comma splicing (That's not a difference between right and wrong, that's a difference between good and bad)

If you don't know what's wrong with the examples in the above items, all of which are wrong, now is the time to learn basic grammar. We all make mistakes, but you should have the knowledge to recognize your mistakes and correct them.

The Eight-Year Novel

Some writers brag about how long it takes them to write a novel.

Fools.

That's like bragging how long it takes you to tie your shoes. What they're really bragging about is not knowing what they're doing.

None of us are immortal, at least not on a plane of existence that has Kindle and CreateSpace. If you only have one novel in you, I suppose it would be fine to spend your whole life writing it. But nobody knows that in advance.

That's the problem. None of us owns a reliable crystal ball and none of us are particularly good at predicting which novels will sell and which novels will tank. That eight-year novel? Perhaps it's the worst novel those writers will every write. And they spent eight years writing it!

As writers, our goals should not be producing the best novels we can, but rather the best novels we can in the time we have to work on them. If you sign a contract to deliver a novel three months from now, guess what? You get exactly three months to work on that novel. If you do your best during that time period, the novel you produce *is* the best novel you can write. Why then would any of us aspire to spend years writing a novel no one will ever read?

The answer is that we don't. We fool ourselves into believing that spending more time on the novel always creates a better novel. Typically it doesn't.

A novel's worth is most often determined by story and characters. If you insist on rewriting your novel many times, plan for it. Assume that you're going to throw away or rewrite nearly every chapter you create.

Creating great prose should be a one-time activity. Crafting the best prose possible only to toss it in the trash is a crime against nature. Instead rewrite the novel as many times as you need to get your story and your characters where they need to be. Believe in your own ability to create the level of prose you desire when the time comes.

The great benefit of write-once prose is that you will have more time to spend on your prose if you aren't wasting time on prose that never finds its way into your finished book.

This is especially true for writers who discover their story and characters only as they write the novel. For writers who work this way, nothing is a greater aid to productivity than ditching the desire for prose perfection in their interim drafts.

Polish That Puppy

In the last section, I talked a lot about not spending too much time on your prose. This doesn't mean that you shouldn't polish your prose at all. It means that you want to be efficient. Part of that efficiency comes from waiting until your final draft to polish your prose. Doing that means any paragraphs, scenes, or chapters you toss out or rewrite for reasons related to story, plot, or character will represent a minimal investment in time, at least where prose is concerned.

You'll want to develop your own list of checks that you use for the final polish of your prose. This list doesn't relate to dialogue, which should rarely sound as polished as your prose. Also, these checks aren't the common typos, spelling, and grammar mistakes I highlighted in the last section. Those are related to basic competence whereas the following list is meant to help your prose go beyond competent to professional.

The Deadly Adverb

While I'm not a believer in avoiding adverbs entirely, I do believe you should examine every adverb you find and determine whether that adverb is necessary. Sometimes you can eliminate adverbs entirely without effect. Other times you can render an adverb unnecessary without changing your original meaning simply by using a stronger verb. Some adverbs are easier to get rid of than others:

- Very
- Almost
- So
- Quite
- Then

These adverbs are needed less often than others because they typically modify other adverbs or adjectives rather than verbs. For example, you can't say, "He ran very," or "She jumped quite." The exception is "then," which often modifies verbs.

The easiest way to spot a normal adverb is to look for words that end in "ly." Most often these are adverbs but not always (silly, curly, hilly, ugly). The following adverbs are a bit harder to spot, but they should receive the same consideration for removal as their "ly" cousins.

- Always
- Never
- Often
- Only
- Seldom
- Sometimes
- Well

What I'm recommending is that you reduce the number of adverbs you use to only those that are needed. I still recommend that you ignore writers who claim adverbs are inherently evil. Only an overuse of adverbs weakens writing for most normal readers. Don't believe me? Get Kindle versions of the novels you like most and search them for adverbs. If you're an adverb hater, you might be shocked to discover how many are used by your favorite author.

General to Specific

Besides being weak, adverbs promote a tendency toward generalization. The reason many authors don't like adverbs stems from this tendency, but the danger of generality creeping into your prose comes from more than adverbs. For example, compare the following sentences:

The room was overfilled with furniture.

vs

A movie sofa and wing chair fought for dominance over his ramshackle study.

The second sentence provides a clearer and more interesting picture of the room than the first sentence does. In the first sentence, it's impossible to know what "overfilled" means. The same goes for furniture.

It's not always better to be more detailed and specific. Not only does it generally take more words, but also it may shine a spotlight where no spotlight is needed. Depending on how much emphasis you want to place on how the room looks determines how specific you would normally be. If you're always drawing attention to settings or characters that are barely relevant by providing overly specific details, most readers will soon get the sense you don't know what you're doing. They'll miss relevant details and be bored by irrelevant ones.

Stay Out of the Way

There's a difference between perceiving the world through your viewpoint character and describing the world perceived by your viewpoint character.

> Cyndi left her hotel room. James watched her walk across the parking lot and disappear between a couple of SUVs. He heard the sound of a car door as it clicked open and slammed closed.
>
> vs
>
> Cyndi left her hotel room. She walked across the parking lot and disappeared between a couple of SUVs. A car door clicked open and then slammed closed.

If James is our viewpoint character, saying he saw or heard anything distances our reader from what's happening. Of course he saw it or heard it. He's our viewpoint character. We don't need to say he saw, he heard, he smelled, or he felt. The reader knows this is what's happening, but saying so not only distances our reader from what's happening, but also it takes more words and leads to cluttered prose.

Another way your interference as author manifests itself in your prose is through abstraction. He realized, she thought, they wondered, and he decided accomplish little beyond distancing your reader from what's happening.

> He thought again about how late he was and felt a stab of panic as he watched the light change from green to amber and realized he'd never make it. He wondered if she would wait for him.
>
> vs
>
> He was so late! Panic squeezed his chest as the light changed from green to amber. He'd

never make it. Would she wait for him?

It's easy to put in these abstractions while writing our first drafts, but any that are unnecessary should be removed. As with adverbs, it's sometimes necessary to use these abstractions, but for most writers, they creep into our first drafts like weeds just waiting to be pulled.

The Little Protagonist That Could

Instead of writing that one of your characters can do something, just allow them to do it.

> He could see her head resting on the pillow.
>
> He could tell that she wanted him to leave.

Sometimes these are attempts to stay in viewpoint. If the viewpoint character describes what another character is thinking, isn't that head-hopping? It can be. The difference is what comes before the head-hopping moment.

> Pointing at the door, she stomped her foot.
> She wanted him to leave.

In these cases, saying your viewpoint character "could tell" she wanted him to leave is redundant. If the reader can guess at the thoughts of a non-viewpoint character based on that character's actions, the reader expects the viewpoint character to guess the same thoughts.

Passive Voice

In the academic world, passive voice abounds because the person or thing doing the action is often less important than the object or person acted upon. Passive voice is also preferred in these settings because it's less risky and less presumptuous. As a writer in an academic setting, if you don't specify the person doing the action, you can't get sued or called out by the person who did that action, and by not using the personal pronoun, "I," you're trying to focus on the data, not on your unfair biasing and statistical slanting of the data.

This reliance on passive voice in the world of academia often produces college-trained writers who were taught that passive voice is preferable. In fiction, it isn't. Fiction readers want action and they want to know who's performing that action.

> This novel was written by an author.
>
> vs
>
> An author wrote this novel.

Exceptions do occur. If the object is the only important part of the sentence or if the subject is non-existent in the current scene, then passive voice works in fiction, too, but it should be rare.

When writing fiction, you generally use active verbs to express subjects performing actions rather than describing actions that were performed *by* someone or something.

That's Not Passive!

The problem with the whole passive voice rule is that many professional writers and other self-proclaimed grammar experts have no clue what passive voice is, and the problem's getting worse.

> It was just after midnight.
>
> Nothing about her was unusual.
>
> Jeffrey was six years old.

These are *not* examples of passive voice. They are active. The structure of each is: Subject-Verb-Adjective. Just because the verb of a sentence is "was," that doesn't mean that sentence is using passive voice. Sometimes it's okay to say, "She was tired."

Turn, Turn, Turn

Some writers have their characters turning so often, I'm waiting for them to turn into ballerinas.

> I turned my head and studied my friend.
>
> I turned and stared.
>
> He turned to face me.

Sometimes specifying that someone turned before they did something else is necessary, but usually they're just wasted words that add no meaning. The same goes for the verb "begin."

> I began to study my friend.
>
> I began to stare.
>
> I began to walk away.

In all of these cases, there is no need to specify that the process began. Of course it began. The main use for specifying that an action began is when the action didn't finish.

> I began to climb the steps but stopped at the sound of gunfire.
>
> I began to take a deep breath but a wave smothered me.

Examine these wasted action starters and remove them whenever they're not needed.

To Be or Not To Be

I have a writer friend who carefully removes all occurrences of the verb "to be" from her writing for her final draft. She claims that using "to be" is always weak. I can't say she's entirely wrong, but the hoops she jumps through to pull out some of these "to bes" from her prose are Herculean and unnecessary.

As with so much of the advice from this section, I recommend examining each use of "to be" in your manuscript. Many times "was" acts as a flag signaling weak prose.

Conjunction Injunction

While we were all taught in English class that it's inappropriate to begin a sentence with a conjunction, fiction sometimes works better with this English teacher pet peeve. The problem stems from that relaxation of the rule leading to unnecessary conjuntionitis.

> The horse fidgeted, its nostrils flaring at the smell of blood and death. But Jack smelled something else. Tar perhaps.

vs

> The horse fidgeted, its nostrils flaring at the smell of blood and death. Jack smelled something else. Tar perhaps.

In truth, the first two sentences could have been combined with the conjunction into one sentence and nothing would have been amiss. In this particular example, I didn't do that because I tend to be a rhythm writer. A sentence ends with a full stop. It adds an extra beat between thoughts. Since the first sentence is talking about a horse and the second is talking about viewpoint character, Jack, I wanted that full stop. It *felt* better. Since I was continuing the previous thought, the "But" seemed necessary. It wasn't.

Writing Groups

I've benefited greatly from writing groups over the years. I've also had novels ruined by them. Writing groups are a bit like nitroglycerin. Handled carefully, they can help you write your novels better and faster. Take your eye off them and your writing might get blown to bits.

Take Only What You Want

The best way to keep writing groups from destroying your writing is to limit their power over you. Early in your career, you may need everything a group has to offer. As you gain more experience, you should cast off each benefit of the group until you have no reason left to go (other than to help others). Regardless, you should only allow a writing group to influence you to the point it benefits your writing. To show you what I mean, let's look at the benefits a writing group can give you:

- Increase Productivity
- Improve Prose
- Identify Story or Character Problems
- Teach Critiquing Skills
- Provide Esprit de Corps

I've listed these in the order you should typically attempt to cast them aside.

Productivity

Improving productivity is the trickiest benefit. Many authors write for decades without being able to get past this one. The reason I list it as the first item to cast aside is because all writers should cultivate their own work ethic at every opportunity. Since the number one rule of writing is to write, your dependence on an outside motivating force is just too risky. If that force is taken away, guess what happens to most writers? They fail to write. They've broken the one rule they absolutely cannot break if they want to be successful.

However, if the only way you can motivate yourself to write is by giving your writing to a group of people who've agreed to read it, by all means use what works. My advice remains: Never quit trying to rid yourself of this crutch.

A more dangerous outcome happens when your attendance at a writing group causes your productivity to decrease or disappear entirely. If this happens, leave the group and never go back until you're sure your productivity won't be harmed. This problem may not be the group's fault. It may be an interaction reaction that's particular to you. It doesn't matter why. What matters is that a writing group should never decrease your productivity. If it does and it's not some issue you can get past, find a different group or avoid writing groups completely.

Prose

It's vital to your writing career that you learn to write prose at an acceptable level of competence. Unfortunately nobody knows what that level is. Certainly writers have been wildly successful who are undeniably awful at prose.

This is why you should avoid writing groups who focus on prose as their main form of feedback. It's also why it's one of the first benefits you cast aside. Once you've reached a competent level of expertise, you should view all prose corrections with a jaundiced eye. First, you should have few prose mistakes if you're a competent writer. Second, effective prose is in the eye of the beholder. When I published my first novel, my final review reader (who has worked as a professional editor) made hundreds of changes to my prose. I dutifully followed this prose advice. The copy editor who later worked on my novel reversed the majority of those changes. Professionals tend to care a great deal about prose and tend to have strong opinions on the subject. It matters to most readers not at all (once a competent level of prose is reached).

This doesn't mean that you should ignore prose advice without giving it the consideration it deserves. It means that if it's not an oversight or a grammar mistake on your part, be wary. Your prose comprises a large part of your unique voice. Because others have a different voice, their non-grammatical corrections to your prose will typically reflect their voice, not yours. If allowed to have too much sway, a good prose revision from your best and most capable writer friend can result in a weak final product.

Story/Character Problems

When learning to write, it can be extremely difficult to know whether you're creating a novel people won't be able to put down or a novel people won't want to pick up again. Getting the informed opinion of others can be invaluable. Knowing what works and doesn't is always helpful.

What you want to avoid is allowing other authors to write your novel for you. This is not because their advice would produce a worse novel; it's because the novel produced wouldn't be yours. This has nothing to do with ownership or some esoteric benefit. If you allow a non-collaborating writer to define your story, you will never be able to tell that story as well as you could without their "help." Writers are constantly worrying about creating work that's new and different. What they don't realize is that every story has already been told. Every character has already been used. Your work becomes different only when you smother it with your own perspective.

When another writer gives you feedback on story or characters, either take that advice and mold it into something uniquely yours or reject it entirely. While the clever plot twist one of the other writers in your group provides may be way better than what you had originally intended, use it only if it maintains the balance of your story. Achieving one great scene at the sacrifice of your novel is not a worthwhile trade. The litmus test is whether it feels right. If their suggested change feels like a change you would have made eventually on your own, take it.

I recommend casting this benefit aside because you should eventually reach a point where your story and your characters are finalized before a writing group ever sees any of your work. While feedback might correct an occasional problem, the benefit gained will be mostly gone.

Critiquing Skills

Providing insights that can help another writer to improve their work is a valuable skill. It allows you to give back some of what you took from the writing community and balance the karmic scales that led to your success. It also improves your ability to analyze your own writing and the writing of others. You learn what works and why. You gain faith in your own beliefs while expanding your knowledge by seeing how others accomplish similar tasks in a different way.

This benefit disappears on its own. Eventually you'll critique enough manuscripts that you know what you're doing. The knowledge gained diminishes until the time spent isn't worth sacrificing time that you could be using on your own work.

Esprit de Corps

Writing is a lonely life. The energy you receive from time spent with other writers is invaluable. Only another writer truly understands what it's like to be a writer. Being around others who share your passion rejuvenates that passion.

I recommend casting this benefit aside only when you have another outlet for shared time with other writers. In my early days, I went to lunch once each week with another writer from my writing group. Even though we didn't critique each other's writing during those long lunches, we inevitably talked about writing. The feedback and energy I received from her was worth five times what I got from the group as a whole. The problem is that sometimes your only opportunity to socialize with other writers comes from a writing group. For whatever reason, schedules (or spouses) don't permit meeting outside of group. In my case, my wife alternated between being extremely jealous of these long lunches to complete indifference. Perhaps this is because the lunches tended to promote unfounded gossip. Eventually my wife understood that no matter how much people talked, the lunches were just my chance to talk about writing with another writer.

Writing groups can become too social. In some ways, this is a fantastic development. Your closest friends end up being the other writers in your group. It's a problem when the social aspect takes over. If you can no longer be honest with your critique or if other writers in the group quit taking the writing aspect seriously because these are friends who understand if she doesn't bring her best work to the group, then it's time to end the group.

It's difficult to maintain the delicate balance a writing group needs to thrive. When that balance tilts too far to one side or the other, it can be difficult to let go, especially when the writers in the group have become your best friends. Many factors come into play, but the most important is *dependence.* If you rely on the group, especially for your productivity, walk away when balance is lost. Writing groups are often an excellent catalyst for growth, but when you've sucked all the marrow from your writing group, they can also be an excellent catalyst for stagnation.

Dip a Toe In

I know tons of professional writers who cast aspersions toward all writing groups and state flatly that no one should ever go near a writing group. Obviously their load of nitro glycerin went off at some point. Once you've been burned, it's hard to imagine any benefit from this volatile and destructive force. How do you know whether you should run away from a group? What qualities should you look for when joining a writing group?

Where'd They Go?

First, maybe I should cover how you find a writing group. Here are the top places I would look:

- Internet
- Writing Workshops
- Professional Writing Organizations

In our modern world, the internet provides a cornucopia of possibilities. From doing a simple search on writing groups in your area to social media, if you can't figure out how to connect with other writers near where you live, you're either not trying very hard or few writers exist in your area. Note that I only count writers you can see in person. While there's nothing inherently wrong with connecting with writers in far flung places, the benefits of the writing group are watered down by relying solely on an electronic connection.

Writing workshops or retreats are a great way to meet other writers who are often at a similar point in their careers. Again, I would urge you to connect with other writers within easy driving distance.

Writing organizations can sometimes provide contact information for existing members in your area. The problem with writers discovered this way comes from the variety of writers found. Some have careers so far beyond yours that they have no interest or time for writing groups. Some once thought they'd like to be a writer, but haven't written anything for years.

<u>What to Look For</u>

Once you've discovered a writing group (or gathered a group of writers who're willing to start one), how do you decide if the group is right for you?

First, it's important that you don't overcommit. If you're joining an existing group, tell them you'd like to attend one of their meetings rather than saying you'd like to join. If you're forming your own group, make sure you either have full control of the group or that you're not the driving force behind it. If you have full control, you can kick out members who become toxic to the group. If you're just one of many, you can leave the group if they don't provide enough benefit.

Second, make sure the group is beneficial rather than harmful. I've covered reasons to walk away related to the benefits a writing group should provide. Beyond those benefits, your decision to walk away is usually based on group dynamics. If you don't like the other writers in your group, it's rarely going to be a good group long term. A more common possibility is that the group is inbred. By that I mean they share a common mindset. You don't want constant consensus in a writing group. If everyone in the group thinks adverbs and passive voice should never be used under any circumstances and that all chapters must be at least twenty pages long, you've stumbled into a scene from *1984*. The last result you want from a writing group is a confrontation from the Thought Police.

Another bad group dynamic occurs when one of the writers in the group is much more successful or just more pushy than other members of the group. Your evaluation of the group then hinges on your evaluation of that writer. If you trust their opinion, the group can work for you. I once attended a group where everyone in the group liked the short story I had brought, but the leader of the group told me it should be rewritten from scratch and outlined the ways I should do it. The other members of the group hastened to agree with their fearless leader. It was a great story, they said, but if their leader thought it should be rewritten, then, by all means, I should rewrite it. Surprised by this reversal, I asked the leader, "So you think this has little chance to sell to a professional market?" He shook his head. "It'll almost certainly sell, but just because a story sells doesn't mean it's any good." Ah. That told me all I needed to know. What he was saying was that he didn't like the story. Based on the reactions of his minions, he realized that most readers would like the story and that the story would probably sell, but he didn't like it. Therefore it wasn't any good. At the same meeting, I watched him dole out similar bad advice to several of the other writers. I never went back to the group and the unchanged story sold to the first market I submitted it to.

Finally, be wary of writing groups where most of the writing lies outside your chosen genre. I can't count the number of times I've been in a writing group where one of the literary writers gave the worst advice possible to someone writing romance or fantasy or science fiction. Each genre has its own customs and tropes. These are understood by the readers and editors within that genre. Advice from readers outside the genre, especially to explain what everyone who reads within a genre already knows, do much more harm than good. Multi-genre writing groups can be great writing groups, but weigh all feedback differently based on who's providing that feedback.

Rules Aren't All Bad

My earlier example concerning a strong personality (a leader) of a writing group doesn't mean that groups with leaders don't work well. Typically a more experienced and successful writer will have better advice than writers who are just starting out. They can often soften or correct critiques that go astray. They can resolve disputes, keep comments from becoming personal, and generally keep the group on track. One of the more important qualities such a leader can have is encouragement of dissenting opinions.

That's because rules related to writing are typically bad, but rules related to behavior within the group are often beneficial.

For example, some writers hate adverbs. They will point out every adverb they encounter and encourage you to get rid of it. Except that we know adverbs aren't bad. They're a matter of taste. The adverb haters continue to blast J. K. Rowling as a lousy writer because she uses too many adverbs. In truth, Joanne Rowling may like adverbs better than the average reader, but that's the point. Like and dislike. Passive voice and adverbs are generally signs of weak writing, but they exist in language for a reason. To prohibit them without exception is just plain silly. Yet, having a writer within the group who points out each and every one is valuable. It allows each adverb to be examined for necessity. Having someone promoting the "No adverbs or passive voice!" side of the aisle is beneficial.

Therefore, rules such as "Don't use adverbs" or "Adverbs are okay" are not useful. They're opinions and should be treated as such.

The way writers critique each other is less open to debate. That's why I recommend the following rules for all writing groups:

- Critiques should never be personal and should not be taken as such.
- Try to comment on the positive as well as the negative.
- Aim all comments at helping others improve the stories or novels they're trying to write.
- If your manuscript is receiving comments, don't interrupt or argue with the critique. If you have questions, save the questions until the critique is finished.
- Show up on time whenever possible.
- Bring your best work.
- Use examples with care.

Being told that a scene doesn't measure up is always painful, especially if you thought the scene was great or if you invested a ton of time in the scene. It happens to all of us. It should never be personal. Revenge should never enter into any critique. Each writer providing a critique should do their best to determine what the writer is trying to do with their story and tailor their comments based on that.

Never argue or explain with someone who's giving you a critique. You can't argue and explain to each reader, so anything you say is automatically irrelevant. The only time a person receiving a critique should speak during the critique is to clarify something being said.

For example, if someone says, "The character in this chapter wasn't interesting for me," you might ask, "Do you mean the hero or the villain?" If you want additional clarification about why they made the comments they did, save those questions until they've finished their entire critique.

Critiques that include examples that start with, "If I were writing this, I would...." can be useful, but should be given sparingly. Nobody wants to be told how to write their novel. What they need to know is what worked or didn't work, and why, if appropriate.

Bringing your best work means the best you could produce in the time available. What you want to avoid is bringing in a scene you know you plan to rewrite or change significantly. If you already have important changes in mind for the scene, then what use are any comments you receive? You'll be measuring those comments against the scene in your mind rather than the one on paper. That's a waste of time for you, but it's a waste of time for the writers critiquing the scene as well.

Showing up on time is just common courtesy. The most valuable resource any writer has is time. Wasting the time of people who are trying to help you is indefensible.

It's a Long, Hard Read

Be wary of writing groups that exchange material in advance and then just get together to critique that material. This method can work, but I believe writing groups work best when the writers doing the critique have less time to think about it. This is because readers (and editors) don't take a lot of time to consider whether they like a particular work. They read it and decide. First impressions are critical. Readers don't ponder a scene for days, contemplating how it could be better. But isn't better, well, better? No. Many suggestions that might make a story better days after it's been read don't make it better while it's being read. Readers who finish your work should immediately want more, not have a like for what you wrote grow on them over time.

Given that members of the writing group you're considering (or forming) reads the manuscript and immediately supplies their critiques, you still have several options for how that reading and critiquing can happen.

My personal favorite is for each writer to bring a printed (double-spaced) copy of their story/scene/chapter and allow each writer to read and critique the manuscript right there and then. They correct or suggest changes to the prose as they read and write a paragraph or two of comments at the end of the manuscript. It's true that his means you're all sitting around reading for an hour or two, but that time is hardly wasted. It's especially relevant for bits of humor. Nothing is more gratifying than to have a reader laugh out loud at something that was supposed to be funny. (It's usually not as enjoyable if they're laughing about something that wasn't supposed to be funny. Both have happened to me.) For this to work, each writer critiques a manuscript and then passes it on to the next writer when they finish it. Folks can disagree with previous comments if they have a different point-of-view. After everything has been read, the manuscripts are critiqued verbally. This allows clarification of comments without suffering significant hand cramps and allows the writer of the manuscript to seek clarification for comments or seek additional information.

Another technique I employ in my professional writing class is to have the authors read their manuscripts aloud. The students in the class then give verbal critiques. As teacher for the class, I comment last so that my comments don't influence or inhibit comments from the students. This technique works especially well if time is a factor. While listening to a piece read aloud is slower than reading it yourself, it's a shared experience. In essence, everyone's reading the manuscript at the same time. This technique has the further advantage of giving students a chance to read aloud in front of a group. This is a useful skill for all professional authors to have. On the down side, listening comprehension is a learned skill. Also, no one has the chance to catch typos, punctuation errors, or formatting problems.

I've also participated in some groups where the writer brought enough copies of their manuscript for everyone. This has the advantage that no one's comments are influenced by anyone else's, but it kills a lot of trees and makes going through all the comments more time-consuming.

Retreads Are Unreliable

Regardless what writing group format you prefer, one result is unavoidable. If you rewrite your novel (or a section of your novel) and you bring the rewrite to the same group of people who read the original material, any comments they make are questionable. No matter how skilled the writer making the comments, if the material has been seen before, that writer cannot view it with a new reader's unbiased eye. As a result, if they tell you it's boring, is it really boring? Or do they find it boring because they've read it before? If they comment that you need background on your world or your characters, is it because you need more background or because they already know what you're telling them and so are interested in hearing more?

Having the same material critiqued by the same people has limited value. They can help you catch typos and grammar mistakes, but any advice they provide about story and characters is nearly worthless except as it relates to creating a novel that can be read over and over. That's always a dangerous goal. A better goal is to create a great story populated by great characters. If you do that, readers will be able to enjoy it again and again.

The Buck Stops Here

You are always the ultimate boss. Only you know what your novel should be. Whenever dealing with feedback from any kind of reader, accept changes that help your novel become what it should be. Reject changes that create a novel different from the one you want to write. How do you know the difference? That's part of being a writer: knowing what you want. When in doubt, don't be afraid to trust your intuition. That doesn't mean you reject the advice out of hand. Some of the best advice I've ever received (and given) has been off the mark, but thinking about that advice led to the "right" answer.

Hit the Gas

We've talked about how important it is to get your brain and body right, reserve a time and place for writing, and eliminate distractions. Now it's time to punch up the productivity and start writing faster than you ever have before.

Remember, before you try any of the techniques mentioned in this section, you should have a set time and place to write that's free of distractions, you should have broken yourself of the multitasking habit, your mind and body should be in a good place, and you should be brimming with confidence and a positive attitude. If that's not the case, then, as they say, your results may vary. At least you'll have some areas to improve as you ramp up your productivity.

Prepare to Write Quickly

I'm always amused by the way movies and television portray writer's block. While I'm sure it's accurate for a small minority of writers, few professional writers ever sit and stare blankly at the page with no idea at all about what to write. We're too busy surfing, or taking our kids to the hospital, or working at our day jobs. That's why we're not writing.

What happens instead is that we sit for a couple minutes at a time while our brains switch from active prose-creation mode to mind-wandering mode. Allowing our brains to push bubbles through our subconscious is a vital part of writing, but it's slow as hell. On the plus side, our creative juices often flow best when we're not worried about sentence structure and grammar and whether we already had our hero stand up or whether he's still sitting down.

In simple terms, we're organizing, plotting, building characterization, setting our scene, and generally doing our best to work on dozens of levels at the same time. We've already seen that the human brain isn't good at multitasking. If you want to speed up your writing, this is the first lesson to learn.

Give your brain less to do.

The most reliable way to do this is to know what you're going to write.

Ah, but you're one of the writers who can't do that? Fine. Your job is to write "The Novel Sketch" I covered in "Writing Quickly While Writing Well." This means you're writing your novel (so you can find out what your novel is about), but you're writing a version of your novel that no one will ever be permitted to read. This means you gag your internal editor and lock them in a back closet of your mind. Nothing matters except getting the ideas on the page.

Once you have a good idea about what you're going to write, it's time to make your final preparations:

- Do everything electronic that you need to do, meaning check text messages, email, voice mail, Facebook, Twitter, Pinterest—whatever is likely to distract you—and then shut it all down.
- Go to the bathroom, get a drink of water, and otherwise get bodily comfortable.
- Shut down your internal editor

Keep these preparations as short as you can. When I say to check your electronic communications, I'm not talking about searching for new recipes on Pinterest. I mean take care of anything that must be taken care of in the next hour, so that you're not distracted by any vital bits of communication that you left hanging out there.

Many people find it helpful to record how long they write. If you want to do this, you're going to need a start time, a stop time, and how many words you wrote. From there, you can track your daily progress on paper, spreadsheet, or via tattoos on your flying monkeys—whatever works best for you.

Go!

Generally the most effective and productive writing anyone can do comes in blocks. For all writers, the lengths of these blocks vary in time from day to day. In a perfect world—and the world enjoyed by many professional writers even today—your writing time each day will vary as your productivity during these blocks varies. What this means is that you write in frenzied blocks until your energy is gone or your daily goal has been met. Then you figure out what you're going to write the next day. Then you stop.

Most of the professional writers I know can only keep up this pace, at most, for 4-6 hours/day. Their exact stop time varies from day to day by an hour or two, but their start times are usually consistent.

If you don't have that kind of writing time, then your productive block of time has an artificial end. Your objective is to break up your writing time into manageable distraction-free blocks where you can be as productive as possible. As we've seen from our examination of the human brain, you want to give yourself a chance to get into a flow state. Once you're in that flow state, I don't recommend interrupting it according to some arbitrary schedule. Unfortunately, sometimes there's no choice.

For example, if you're working a day job and you're doing your writing in the mornings before work (an excellent thing to do if you can get away with it), you have a set ending time. Set an alarm for five minutes before that time and write like mad until the timer goes off. Then figure out what you're going to start writing the next day. It doesn't hurt to end mid-sentence, for example. If you're recording your writing time and words written, save those numbers now.

While you're actually writing, let nothing and no one distract you, not even yourself. Keep those fingers going. If you find yourself staring at your computer screen or a blank piece of paper, start writing. What you write at that moment doesn't really matter. If you can't write the scene, start writing what's going to happen in the scene.

> Joey walks into the bar. As he gets a martini, stirred, not shaken, he notices an eye looking at him through a decoration in the mirror behind the bar. Drawing his weapon, he fires into the mirror, shattering it and revealing a portal to another world, or perhaps just to Cleveland.

It doesn't really matter what quality you produce at this point. The idea is to get your thoughts, ideas, and creative notions down before they escape or before your time is gone.

Never, under any circumstances, should you be trying to produce finished copy from nothing. If it's not finished copy, then it doesn't matter how good it is. Have faith that you will fix any problems you create.

If you write for an hour, even writing legible longhand at 10 words/minute, you'd still finish 500 words/hour if you spent most of your time writing instead of editing as you went. (It would be 600 words/hour if you never stopped, but most people need to pause regularly to order a thought or stretch their hand or whatever.) For most writers, that speed (as a top speed) is much too slow. If it's the only thing that works for you, use it, but you'd be better off typing on a keyboard. If you're not worried about typos and you've tied up your internal editor and locked him in the trunk, most people can truck along at 50 words/minute or more. Again, allowing for stretching and a bit of thinking, that's easily 2,500 words an hour! If you really want to become amazing, dictate your fiction. With voice recognition software fully trained and at your command, you can sustain speeds in short bursts up to 100 words/minute. Giving ourselves the same allowances as before, that's 5,000 words/hour.

To hit any of the speeds given in the above paragraph will take practice. You must practice writing fast in order to write fast. Simply saying you can't write fast and giving up does not count as practice.

Of the methods above, use what works best for you. However, if you decide that writing longhand is the only method that works, I'd recommend you take the time to learn shorthand. Restricting your brain to progressing at a mere 10 words/minute is painfully slow.

For most writers I know, the ability to sustain the three forms of writing given above vary greatly. That's why you work in blocks. Have a break or two built in to your writing time, or more if you're doing the 4-6 hour sessions favored by many professional writers. These breaks should be short: a stretch, a bathroom break, a refill of your coffee or water, and a quick check of the most vital forms of communication with the outside world (if necessary).

Do What Works

This is all great and wonderful advice, but if you have other methods that work, use them. I'm describing what has worked for most of the successful writers throughout history, what works for most writers living today, and what neuroscience says will work best. If you've found some other method that allows you to crank out 5,000 words/hour, that's great. But if you struggle to get 100 words/hour written, you need to do something different if you're going to increase your productivity.

Many writers I know would rather cut off their own leg than change the way they write. They believe it's some sort of mystical process that allows their muse to perch on their shoulder and lead them joyfully along. Phooey! You say you can't write without correcting what you've written as you go along? How many hours have you spent trying to do just that?

I didn't say any of this would be easy, but we're professionals, remember? All good professionals work at their craft, with the key word being "work."

There is too much. Let me sum up

The older you get, the easier it is to see how little time we really have on this world of ours. To have any reasonable chance to be a successful writer, it's imperative that you learn how to be as productive as you possibly can. Some of us only have one great novel in us, but no one ever said that was the first novel. What a tragedy it would be to write for thirty years and be one novel short of writing the novel that would change your life (and the lives of millions of others).

- Confidence is one of the best tools in any writer's toolbox. Fortunately self-confidence can be improved through practice.
- Writing comes first.
- Procrastination is a great evil all writers must fight and conquer every day.
- Eating right and exercising improves long-term productivity.
- Writing anything at all is better than writing nothing. Never judge yourself if it keeps you from writing.
- When we multitask, our brains tells us we're getting more done, but instead we're accomplishing less, ruining our memory, and wearing ourselves out.
- The brain's flow state allows you to write better and ignore normal distractions, but it takes skill and practice to reach it.
- If you want others to respect your writing time, you must respect it first.
- Having a space you use only for writing helps your creativity every time you enter that space.
- Make sure your spouse understands what it's like to be a writer.
- Eighty percent of the effect prose has a novel comes from only twenty percent of the prose. Concentrate your greatest prose efforts on your beginning, your end, and the emotional moments of your novel.
- When it comes to writing prose, you should—at the very least—be competent.
- When writing a novel, concentrate on improving story and characters. Save elevation of prose until the final draft.

- Writing groups can be beneficial, but only if you don't allow them to hurt you.
- Free yourself of distractions before you begin to write.
- Use whatever methods work for you to establish, keep, and increase momentum when you're writing.

Appendix A

Common Proofreading Marks

Considering the age we live in, it may seem a bit archaic to learn basic proofreading marks. Isn't everything electronic these days? Not quite. Paper's still the quickest method for critiquing and commenting on a manuscript, provided we're all using marks we can understand for our changes.

The list below is far from complete, but rather than overwhelm you with a complete list, I've supplied the most common proofreading marks you're likely to see from a copy editor or need for your own editing.

Text/Formatting Changes	Examples
ℓ — Delete	Delete this extra ~~word~~ word.
◠ — Remove Space	Remove Ex tra Space
¶ — New Paragraph	First paragraph. Second starts.
No ¶ — Join Paragraphs; No New Paragraph	First paragraph. No ¶ Second paragraph.
(stet) — Leave As Is; Ignore Changes	Don't delete--no ~~extra~~ word.
] — Indent Right	Indent this paragraph.
[— Move Left	No paragraph. Don't indent.
# — Insert Space	Insert a space right here.
∽ — Transpose; Switch What's in the Left Loop with What's in the Right Loop	Transpose can be (for used) both transpositions. (horizontal and vertical)
≡ — Capitalize	capitalize first word of sentence.
ℓc — Lower Case	Help Uncle Jack Off his horse.
___ — Italicize	You just said what about Jack?
∿ — Bold-face	Chapter Title
⊙ — Change to period	End each sentence with a period.

Index

C

S

www.ingramcontent.com/pod-product-compliance
Lightning Source LLC
Chambersburg PA
CBHW031457270326
41930CB00006B/127